The Making of a Modern Salesman

Cyril L. Hudson

Crosby Lockwood London

Granada Publishing Limited
First published in Great Britain 1973 by Crosby Lockwood
Park Street St Albans
and
3 Upper James Street London W1R 4BP

Copyright © 1973 by Cyril L Hudson

ISBN 0 258 96874 5

Printed in Great Britain by
Willmer Brothers Limited Birkenhead

Foreword

Cyril Hudson is a friend of mine. Not only do I have the pleasure of knowing him—and his charming wife, to whom this book is dedicated —personally, not only have I worked with him and listened to his lectures at Ashridge Management College, where I was Deputy Principal, and elsewhere, but I know him also as a most helpful author, to whom I can turn when in need of a sensible answer to a vexing question.

We both came to management teaching after years of practical executive experience in different companies, here and overseas. Some years ago I returned to industry, whilst Cyril Hudson did something much more useful: he picked up his pen and committed his extremely wide knowledge of marketing and selling to paper, in a number of books from which everyone can profit who reads them attentively and takes the advice they contain.

Now he has done it again: he has written a manual for all those connected with the difficult art of selling—for all those whose task it is to select, create, train, supervise and assess the effectiveness of a sales force and each member of it.

In spite of this country's long and distinguished history in international trade and commerce, few people have analysed the process of selling, and all activities connected with it, so thoroughly and well as the author of this book.

The salesman is the vital link between the producer and the consumer. He has to recognise a need and satisfy it by selling the most suitable product. More than that: the good salesman will be observant enough to recognise the changing needs and, by reporting these changes back to headquarters, will influence improvements in product design or even initiate the creation of a new product. The good salesman, well used, is not only the customer's best friend, but also the company's most effective sensorial part.

Cyril Hudson is a good example of a good salesman : he sensed the need for a book like this, and he has satisfied this need by writing it, most admirably.

Stephen K. Manstead, Ph.D.
Director
Grundy (Teddington) Limited

Teddington, Middlesex
January, 1973

Contents

Part Two

The Company Headquarters' Role in the Making of a Modern Salesman

Part Three

The Field Sales Manager's Overall Role in the Making of a Modern Salesman

For my wife Barbara

Preface

Much thought and cash have been devoted in British board rooms during the last few years to fostering developments in production and processing technologies; and to creating more effective costing and management accounting techniques. In short, a campaign has been mounted to secure a much closer and tighter control of cost in a search for greater profitability and growth throughout British industry and commerce.

In the same period, a small degree of attention has been paid to the practice of marketing, particularly in the area of marketing research. But little if any thought has been given to the sharp cutting-edge of marketing, namely selling and salesmanship. This comparative neglect has been most marked within industrial and technical marketing organisations.

At last there seems to be a belated realisation that unless a company can sell its production at a satisfactory rate of profit, and can ensure its continued growth, it may well be heading for Carey Street. And the highly competitive threat implicit in the entry of this country into the Common Market is beginning to be realised. So, many more companies are now expressing an interest in their forgotten men, the members of their sales forces, for so long unhonoured and unsung. Interest is one thing. The dynamic thinking, planning, and organising essential to creating a competitive sales force is quite another.

A company Sales Force is composed of working members of a geographically disposed linkage-system, the communications network that bridges the gap between the company and its markets—its customers and users. They form also a highly skilled interpreting and negotiating body, a central core of a contactual network that creates an essential two-way feedback system between factory and field. Selling is thus a creative, imaginative, entrepreneurial activity. It persuades people to buy a company's products and services in preference to those of competitive houses. It can and does create changes in people's purchasing attitudes and actions. Selling, despite its professional nature and its commercial importance, is largely an unsupervised activity. It needs a wide portfolio of personal skills, of the persuasive arts, and a wide spectrum of technical knowledge. Salesmen must possess outward-looking empathetic minds. They have to like actively doing business with a wide range of different types of person, and be enthusiastic and competent handlers of problem areas, problem people, and problem propositions. Salesmen need to possess a gregarious attitude, a servicing bias, a willingness to help people to find satisfactions and benefits from their mutual relationship. They need to become merchants of ideas and benefits, and creators of goodwill.

Selling demands both diagnostic and prognostic skills, similar to those used by a medical practitioner. Salesmen need to be respected for their skills, and liked for their personal attributes. Many orders are placed with salesmen because they are liked, and their competitors who are offering similar propositions are disliked. It is as simple as that. First class salesmen have always been in short supply. Even the above average men take a long time to 'make' and to nurture towards their peak performance. It is indeed a costly activity to grow one's own salesmen. But there would seem to be no visible practical alternative available.

This book offers a blueprint to the thinking, planning, organisation that are necessary to create, make, and to grow competent sales forces. It sees this job as a human, rational manpower development process, continuous and endless. It involves many human, methodological and educational arts and skills. It implies a decentralisation of management into the actual contactual field of selling operation. In this way, the preliminary induction training offered each new man at company headquarters is carried on smoothly, in an integrated fashion on the actual selling job by carefully selected and highly trained field sales managers.

The pages that follow deal in considerable detail with the active creation of a working climate in which men become motivated to give of their best, the methodological creation of working conditions in which ambitious men will flourish, the bed-rock problems of what has to be done to find men who can and will excel, and, with the pursuit of excellence, the will to win. It discusses the counselling, guiding, tutoring, educating, and training roles of the field sales manager. It considers in some depth the matter of man appraisal, and the very real problem of triggering-off the latent potential in each salesman. It studies and discusses the human need of men to achieve job satisfactions, and to aspire to the realisation of career ambitions on their road to full attainment as both salesmen and members of the community.

This book is devised to help all those members of company management who are involved in better selling and in their companies making better salesmen. Members of company board rooms may gather what will have to be done to ensure that sales forces adequately support and meet the challenges flung at them in the achievement of company objectives. Particularly it will help all members of company sales management both at headquarters and in the field to take a broad view of what needs to be done to achieve selling excellence to optimise market shares and defeat competitive threats and innovations. Finally, it is directed at every salesman and field sales manager who has a burning desire to raise his sights to higher levels of practical achievement.

Written in a straightforward style in practical prose, the work offers a large number of illustrative diagrams and recommended reading for further and deeper study of items of specialised interest. It covers the basic reading material vital to study for the projected syllabus for British National Diploma in Salesmanship and its examinations.

The author finds it difficult to thank adequately his host of friends who have been so generous with their time, constructive criticism, and advice upon the format, content, slant and style. An author must take complete responsibility for his script, his views, and his beliefs. I do this gladly, and hope that readers will gain as much pleasure and benefit from its study as the author did in its creation.

Storrington, Sussex.

PART ONE

The Introduction of New Salesmen into a company

CHAPTER ONE

Sales have a Dynamic Role in Modern Business

INTRODUCTION

We are now in a commercial era where buyers seem to hold a tactical advantage over salesmen who call upon them to secure business. It is not a loaded pistol held at a salesman's head, but a ruthless value analysis of every product, service, and proposition offered. Value analysis assumes that there will be one product, service, or proposition that will show a competitive, comparative differential in overall value and buying benefits. This will be the best buy obtainable.

There are two other pressures upon the potential buyer besides that of getting the best value for money invested. The first is to establish the utter reliability and dependability of those suppliers from whom the buyer is considering making a purchase. This is a vital matter in a professional buyer's search for peace of mind. The second is the growing complexity of technical products and services that are being offered to buyers who are but laymen in a number of the newer technologies: who nevertheless are expected to make preliminary value analyses of available offers, then submit the most competitive for the scrutiny and approval of their technical brethren.

Buyers can in such circumstances consult the literature provided by suppliers who seek the buyers' business. But letters and literature, however well designed and however factual, can only do an initial introductory job. This is to make buyers aware of what is available on the open market. Normally, the convenient way of getting detailed information is to request a visit from a supplier's salesman. What a buyer seeks is proof of the supplier's reliability and dependability on all counts—product specification and performance; freedom from trouble; length of active effective life; certainty of delivery to time; certainty of price level reliability; quick service on enquiries, suggestions, and complaints. After this opening skirmish a buyer wants to get down to a detailed factual discussion of value analyses offered. Finally, a buyer needs to get sufficient knowledge from all competitive sources to reach a decision on the best all round buy for suitability and for benefits.

This is a far cry from the picture of a traditional hard-hitting salesman or a friendly, glad-handing representative in search of orders. A modern buyer wants nothing to do with either. A buyer's company is also operating in a fiercely competitive market. He needs to get the very best buy, and he needs technical and commercial help in doing so. He seeks a salesman who is utterly honest; and who is able to act as an 'interpreter' of the technical and commercial values contained in his offer of products, services, propositions, and buying benefits.

This may look at first glance to be an easy role to play needing merely to be word-perfect upon products, services, and propositions, and give the buyer the information that he needs. In reality, it is a difficult role to play competently and dynamically. It is a combination of giving advice and dynamic selling. The qualities that are ideal to the successful carrying out of each role are different and sometimes diametrically opposed.

There is a further demand made upon the modern salesman. He must be able to handle, competently, company executives of all kinds and at all levels, by understanding what they demand of their company purchasing officers in both commercial and technical terms. This is particularly evident where and when a salesman has to deal with a buying committee. He will have to satisfy each member completely before the latter will add his support of the seller's proposition and the placing of the order.

Here is the crunch in the selling situation. Where are we to find these selling prodigies? How can we detect their flair in a short interview? What will it cost us to recruit and select such people? How long will it take? Again, how much will it cost to convert the raw human selling material into competent salesmen through intensive and continuous training, education, motivation, and control? In contrast, what would be the cost to the company's marketing and sales future if such salesmen are not sought, employed and trained to create peak sales in competitive markets? A company's research and development, production techniques, industrial engineering skills, financial resources, market research, product design and value may be excellent. However, what will happen if the company has not a dynamic sales force to obtain its major objectives of return upon investment and capital and market growth?

Marketing and sales force operation are two major company cost centres. They are crucial to company success. In the case of salesmen a company takes a shot-in-the-dark in making an investment in manpower, but through training and motivation it hopes to convert the investment into a company asset. The salesmen selected are looking for adequate and progressive job satisfaction and career expectations. Ideally, these two lines will converge at an early date. If they do not, there is a heavy price to pay for poor selection, inadequate training, and ineffective development and control. The cost of a wrong selection of a salesman will rarely be much less than £5,000 per annum until he either is discharged or leaves.

What we are seeking to do is to make a salesman who is an expert planner of his own activities; a profitable revenue producer for his company; an optimiser of available business; a defeater of competitive activity; an exploiter of opportunities; a poser and solver of customer problem areas; a customer and user satisfier; a builder of business. This cannot be done on the cheap. It is a continuous process throughout a salesman's lifetime.

THE DESIGN FOR A DYNAMIC SALES ORGANISATION

A passive sales managerial outlook is one that is happy if it obtains regular annual increases in revenue and profits. On the face of it an uncritical observer might say that the company's outlook is set fair. But is it? It may well be that although the company concerned has increased its turnover and profits over the year it has slipped behind the actual percentage rise of business available in the overall market, upon which its competitors have gladly optimised. Thus, such sales managers are set upon a course that can lead ultimately to company failure unless the dangers are foreseen and rectified.

A dynamic sales managerial attitude, on the other hand, is concerned with making an adequate return on investment coupled with an increase in market share and capital value. To do this regularly and successfully is the hallmark of a professional approach to business building. What is involved and how is it done?

Everything starts in the company board room where dynamic policies and plans are made. Here every company department is harnessed to the support of the sales function in its efforts to optimise upon sales targets and budgets. This is much more than a marketing-oriented concept. It is a customer-satisfying and good-will-creating approach to business building over the long term. It is in fact an integrated approach to the buying–selling situation. The board of the selling company regards its customers and users as the external extension in the market of its own marketing and selling Organisation. This is the beginning of a marriage between seller and buyer, an identification of mutuality of benefit, and a mutual loyalty that speaks well for long-term satisfactions. In return, the buying organisation, once satisfied, sees the seller as its extension in the supplies field, the guarantor of reliability and continuity of material, specification and delivery, so long as they are required.

The point to be stressed is that two different functions in two separate companies are seeking a mutuality of satisfactions. Each to quite an appreciable degree will be dependent upon the help, goodwill, and expertise of the other in a mutually interactive, interlocking, interpersonal, interdependent relationship.

Such a close relationship between buyer and seller can come to judgement in the personal relationship created by the salesman upon whomever he calls. It will be nourished by the value of the services which he renders. Thus a successful dynamic sales organisation will be built upon the quality of each salesman in a company sales force, and his dynamic, positive, creative, persuasive, business-winning capacity in his selling role.

CHARACTERISTICS OF A DYNAMIC SUCCESSFUL SALESMAN

Personal salesmanship of this quality is not easy to describe. It calls for effective interpretation and negotiation at a variety of different commercial and technical levels. It calls for a combination of analysis and synthesis skills similar to those of a general medical practitioner, whose job it is to solve problems by relating causes to effects against known syndromes. In a similar way analytical selling skills have to be deployed in the solution of buying problems.

Selling at these levels also demands a knowledge of synthesis skills that can enable a salesman to see new applications of existing products or processes to solve buyers' problems in a simple and satisfactory fashion. In fact, it is this visualising and inventive skill that separates the dynamic salesman from the also-rans. Obviously one invaluable asset for such salesmen is an encyclopaedic knowledge of products and services, both inside and outside their own particular expertise and business practice.

A modern salesman needs to assume a new role of honest brokerage, to interpret ideas about buying benefits and advantages. He should be merchant of ideas that identify mutual interests where profitability, the best comparative buy in values, benefits, and advantages, will lie.

Personal salesmanship must therefore assume a new dynamic emphasis and dignity in full accord with its importance. It must create a new impetus and respect, a new prestige in full accord with its ambassadorial, consultancy, advisory status. To achieve this, it must know precisely what to add, adapt, adopt and discard.

For example it should avoid even the relics of a visible hard selling technique—any hypocritical approach to gain interviews by guile and flannel ('I'm not here to sell you anything. Actually, I'm doing a survey. It would be so much more private and pleasant if we could chat about it inside your home or office').

It should drop the canned presentation—the peripatetic parrot reproducing a boring spiel of his sales manager's devising—the one-way needle-stuck-in-the-groove effort that convinces none but the biased already committed in the product's favour, or the nestling new to the buying role. Mere telling will never be selling, however articulate a practitioner may be.

It should question the current value of the old-hat formula approach A.I.D.A. to the buying inteview that purports to create Attention, Interest, Desire and Action by the planned canny use of sequential stimuli. Psychologically this is a gross over-simplification. How can one predict in such a generalised way that buyers will react at all times in such a predetermined fashion to such stimuli? Highly skilled professional negotiators would agree that to succeed in such simple formulae selling would need a more than average percipience, flexibility of mind, empathy, plus more than a modicum of good luck.

It should also question the value of the so-called stimulus-response school sales approach. It is merely a more sophisticated-sounding variant of A.I.D.A. and suspect for similar reasons. A social psychologist would surely beware of stating that a particular flick of a specific semantic whip would create an identical buying response in all purchasing situations.

It should look much more closely at the need/want–satisfactions/goodwill selling approach. It is in this area of the creation of buying satisfactions that the future developments in selling techniques would seem to offer the best dividends.

THE DEVELOPING DYNAMIC ROLE OF THE SALESMAN

The more complex and sophisticated products become, the greater will be the pressures upon the professional salesman for information, interpretation, advice and services. Whether the purist marketing man will like this development is beside the point. The professional salesman is increasingly becoming involved in market and marketing research, product development, usage expansion, the pricing syndrome. He is tending to become the operational spearhead of his company's marketing targets. Neither his management nor he can shrug off these developments. Thus, a dynamic change is taking place in both the coverage and the slant of professional selling activity.

Salesmen will need to be trained by their companies in the arts of selective information collection and circulation, and in the accurate grading of both sources and contents of such information in such reporting.

Attitude changes will be needed of salesmen to overall responsibility for customer finding, creation, servicing and development. These are major contributors to the cost centres created by the sales force. Therefore calls will have to be graded, in number and in the time involved, strictly according to the differential values of each potential or actual customer and the anticipation of business to be gained in both the long and the short term. This will appeal to the sales engineer as the simple application of work and job studies to the selling task.

Salesmen will become responsible for the engineering of agreement between supplier and buyers, for lubricating good relationships by the creation of buying satisfactions, and for cementing future goodwill in the final bonding created by an identity of outlook and mutuality of benefits.

Salesmen must be more than mere exploiters of opportunities. They should become managers of change that takes place daily in the fluctuating market environment. There is a trend towards systems selling and buying, and towards package dealing. Salesmen in this context are projectors in the market of their companies' total product and ancillary services range. There has been much talk by many academics of theories about the benefits of offering an added value concept, or augmented values, as some pundits call it. In selling practice, what is emerging is a buying view of the need to get a comparative, competitive totality of product and service value that will indicate giving preference to one supplier rather than to a competitor.

Increasingly salesmen will play much more creative roles. As sales engineers technical and speciality salesmen tending to create extra and new uses for their products and services. They may do it by applying a product to a new use, adapting plant to take an existing product or modifying a process to incorporate a product or service that they are offering. Acting strictly within a value analysis concept they are trying to create more effective operations than those currently employed by their customers.

A salesman will become much more involved in company sales teamwork. He will be concerned with the analysis of problems that have to be overcome by the sale of a product or service which may bring him in very close liaison with his head office in the preparation of proposals and quotations. When ready he will, more frequently than now, deliver these personally to the customer, enabling him to iron out problems of interpretation on the spot and to progress the proposition towards the order-signing situation. In large companies it may well involve him in close and regular discussion with specialist engineers, accountants and technical people within his own headquarters.

We can sum up the sales situation as a dynamic in the following terms:

A buying situation occurs immediately a buyer can be convinced that he has an unsolved problem on his hands, or an unmet need or want that has so far not been satisfied. A selling situation occurs when a salesman realises the buying unsatisfaction and harnesses all his skills, knowledge, products and services to redress the adverse condition. Once he can offer an apparent totality of buying benefits the order situation is at hand and a customer creating situation has been faced and won.

THE CHANGING DYNAMIC OF THE SALES MANAGERIAL SITUATION

We have already visualised the company as a customer-satisfying oriented business system. At one time the sales manager not only ran the sales force. He was responsible for the majority of marketing activities now operated by the marketing manager or director, who has in so many instances absorbed the sales department within his operations. This book is not concerned with status of either sales or marketing management in the company business system, but with the increasingly important role that sales management and selling will play in the total structure.

Because the company is customer-satisfying oriented, it is the sales departmental functions that are contactually most closely involved with the customer. The sales manager is becoming in fact the key operational linkage between supplier and market, between seller and buyer. Thus, he is being loaded with many responsibilities that marketing management had recently absorbed. In some instances the responsibilities are limited and shared with marketing, under the company marketing and sales director. In others they are either solely a sales responsibility in practice, or drifting towards that position.

Sales can be seen as a sub-system within the company marketing system, itself a sub-system of the total company as a business system. This is in no sense derogatory; quite the reverse. Sales managerial responsibilities are increasing upon a wide and diverse front.

The modern sales manager is responsible for creating the company sales forecast and budget. When accepted by the Board these become masters for the creation of other departmental forecasts and budgets.

He in turn divides the forecasts and budgets by individual market segment, county, sales territories, individual key outlets, products, industries and usage. In this way he puts a quota system into force. Each salesman is given a shared accountability and responsibility for his activities in pursuit of the targets laid down.

Market and marketing research as providers of vital information for the company information bank, upon which marketing and sales policy-making decisions and plans are made, are now beginning to come within a joint operational responsibility of marketing and sales. Not only are they the raw materials of selling; the sales force has a feed-back responsibility to the information bank to provide new and confirmatory information from actual customers and users about market opportunities and competitive threats. Input–output analysis procedures are particularly relevant as market indicators which can be converted by a sales force into new business and new customers.

Market research has a responsibility with product designers to strengthen the whole product mix and line by the creating of new products. It runs parallel with new product ideas that spring from the research and development departmental staff, or at times from board members themselves. The acid test should be, of course: can the sales force sell such new products, and do so consistently over a long life cycle at an acceptable profit, increasing the company's market share in the process? Alas, many such new ideas are stillborn non-starters in the sales managerial handbook. Here sales management and the sales force should not only have powers of rejection if they can prove their contentions of non-saleability, but themselves be acceptable as suggesters of new products based upon their own knowledge of the existing and future market demand and needs.

Often an acceptable product with a potentially long and profitable life cycle does not get off the ground, or fails to hold its progress, due to a non-competitive or not-acceptable selling price. Pricing has been for too long a perquisite of marketing management. The alchemy for price-setting talents has sometimes seemed mysterious to salesmen with a wholly pragmatic outlook of 'the price is right or wrong, too low or too high'. With their regular contacts in the Market Place salesmen should know the score in pricing strategies and tactical ploys. They should have a say in the initial pricing strategies and in any tactical situation where a price alteration would obviously be beneficial.

Physical transportation is a very heavy cost centre. Especially where and when a company operates a number of branch offices and warehouses. There has been a tendency either for the factory to be responsible for goods flow to customers, or for a transport manager to do the job under a headquarters director. When a sales manager is given this responsibility, it is a logistics matter for him in consultation with his sales force to predict with considerable accuracy the various stocks needed by customers within a stated time period. Here is a simple control mechanism with which to reduce a heavy cost centre to a minimum consistent with stock maintenance.

There has been a recent tendency to regard some marketing managers as people with an in-built flair for innovative selling strategies. In such cases the Sales Manager has been treated as a person of lesser intellectual stature. His *métier* has been confined to the tactical disposition of his sales force implementing the marketing manager's magic wand waved with a fairy like flair. The sales managerial role must be centred around the most profitable deployment of his sales force and their optimum revenue-producing capacity. Because of the sales function's regular contact with the market, it seems stupid to imagine that salespeople have no innovative skills or imaginative and creative flair to contribute to the marketing pool.

It is in the leadership role that a sales manager should come to the full flowering of his skills and ambitions. It is his job to provide a climate of enthusiasm and optimism based upon the realities of the opportunity situation. This will enable the field sales management to grow salespeople to their optimum professional potential. The motivational process can be vital in sales expansion. It has so far been little researched, but the work of the American psychologists Maslow and Herzberg[1] throws much light upon the opportunities that can be exploited in job enrichment and rewards (not merely of a financial kind) in building a company sales force as the spearhead to achieve total company aims.

The sales manager and his sales force, where they are seen as an integral part of a company business system, are *per se* involved in modern methodologies to back up the sales forces's sharp cutting-edge in the competitive market places of the world.

The sales manager should no longer be a passive factor carrying out the behests of a marketing director but become a very much valued senior colleague in the day-to-day interpretation of actual and potential market demand and characteristics. He should be the voice and eyes of the company's customers and users in the company board room, a practical analyst, a detector, a commentator of the passing market show whose personal knowledge cuts theories down to size and gives a realistic look to competitive threat and market opportunity. In a way, the Sales Manager is comparable to a bespoke tailor, cutting the product and service suit to the actual measure of each key outlet and each opportunity to optimise upon opportunity and customer and user satisfactions and goodwill. In a similar fashion he should be the board room interpreter to the sales force and their customers and users of beneficent company marketing policies and plans; in short the projector of the company corporate image to the buying world.

Diagrams 1 to 4 show the major elements and characteristics of the modern sales manager and salesman, and illustrate their dynamic roles in modern business building.

Diagrams 5 and 6 show the dynamic impact of the sales system within the marketing and company systems. It stresses the factors in the battle for the order in a highly competitive market. The

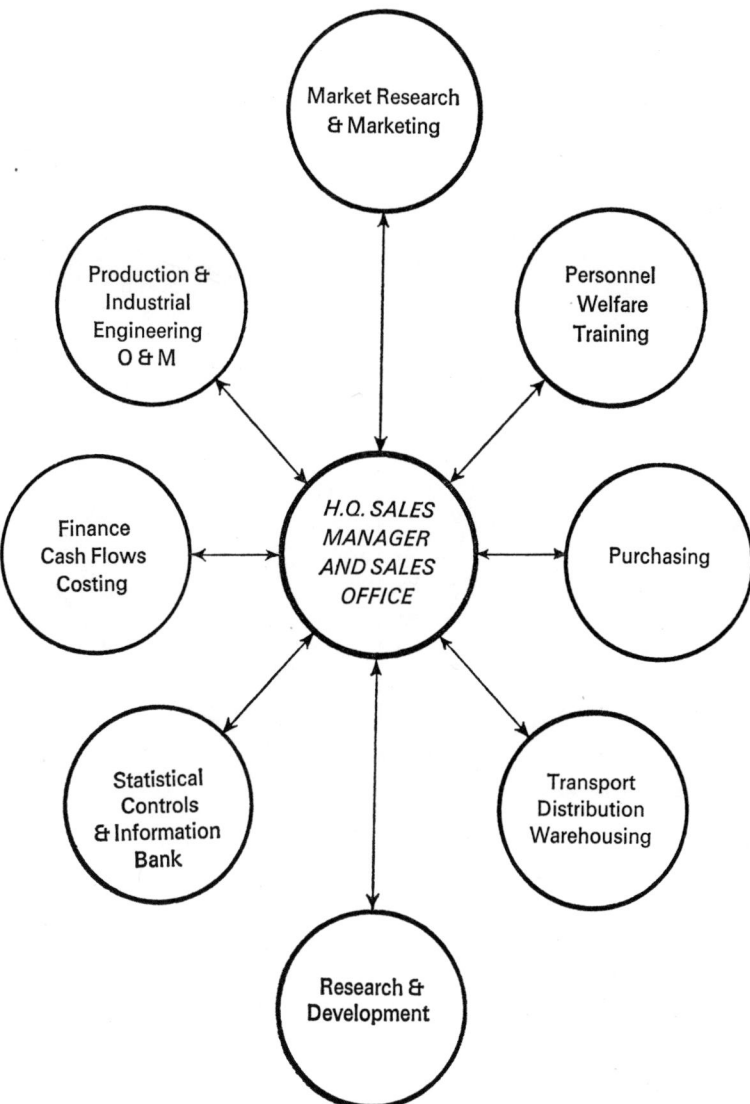

Diagram 1   Sales management interface activities with company departments

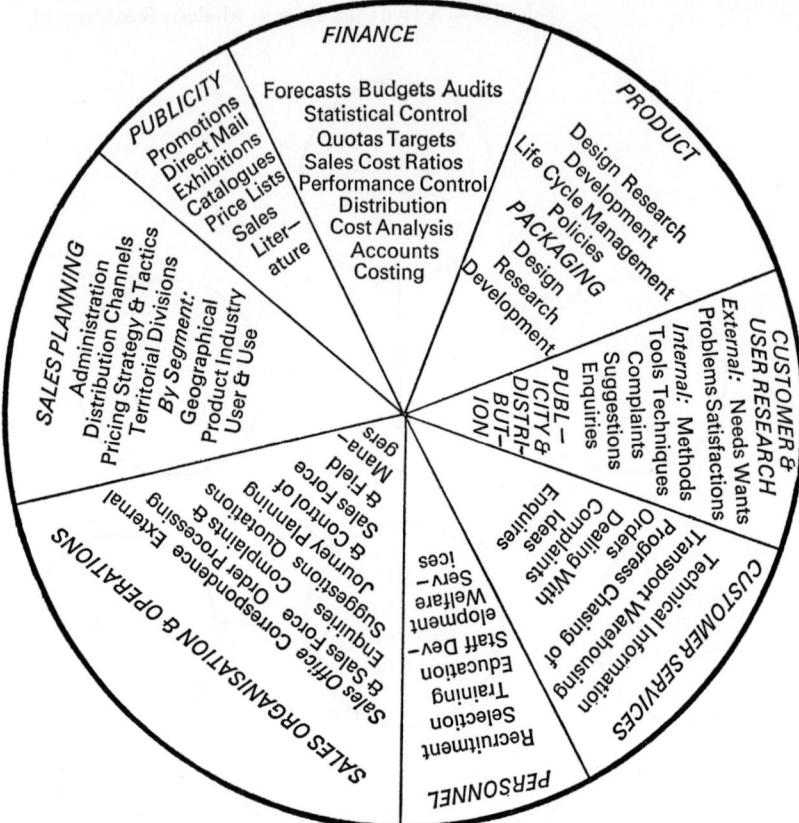

Diagram 2 Sales management activity analysis

quadrilateral of forces employed is of great importance to the salesman and his sales manager.

The Importance of Dynamic Sales Roles

This is not a book on Economic Theory. However it must recognise the existence of specific economic forces in the creation of successful business trading. Income should exceed expenditure and yield a satisfactory profit in the process. We should not get bogged down in theories about economic absolutes such as demand and supply for in daily practice an absolute demand is usually a generic one. For example, we must have food, raw materials and a source of power and light, but some need necessarily be specific.

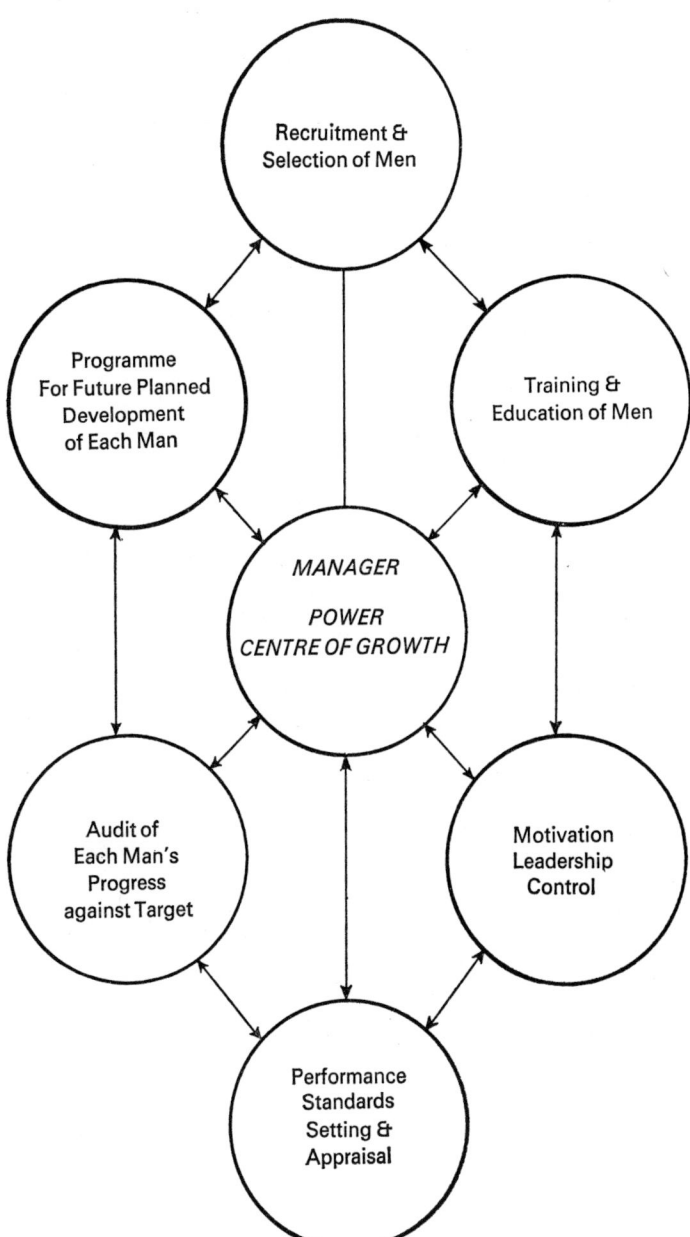

Diagram 3   Sales management's role in manpower development

THE COMPANY MARKETING ORGANIZATION

The Board of Directors
Policy
Managing Director
Marketing Director

Financial Control · Technical Services · Training · Advertising · Sales Promotion · Market Research

SALES OFFICE
Field Branch
Control

THE SALESMAN'S OPERATION

PLAN		PLAN		PLAN		PLAN		PLAN	
O	Divide Territory/Routeing	EACH	Name and Titles Potential Buyers.	P	Complete knowledge of products, features and benefits.	O	Link buying motivation, features and benefits.	F	Establish selling norms per customer.
V	Call frequency. Existing work load per section.	C	Seek appointments. Cold calling if necessary.	R	Trade/Industries. Individual customers. Individual buyers.	P	Eliminate objections.	U	Targets by products and use.
E		A		E		E	Create desire.	T	
R	Potential of each sector.	L	Extra time face-to-face.	S		R	Get buying action.	U	New customers.
A	Potential each customer.	L	To get attention. Create interest.	E	Competitive { Strength Weakness Acceptance Potential	A	Clinch order.	R	Records.
L			Identify & allocate balance time with customer.	N		T	Get point of re-entry for next call.	E	Reports.
L	Potential each product.		Potential buying power.	T	Use variant of presentation most likely to sell	I		D	
WORK	Maximum use of time.			A	Best time, place & people within company to whom to present, merchandise or demonstrate.	O	Create satisfaction and goodwill.	E	
E	Best £/Hour Ratio.			T		N		V	Get maximum information.
F				I				E	
F				O				L	
O				N				O	
R								P	
T								M	
								E	
								N	
								T	

Diagram 4   The salesman's duties and responsibilities in the selling operation

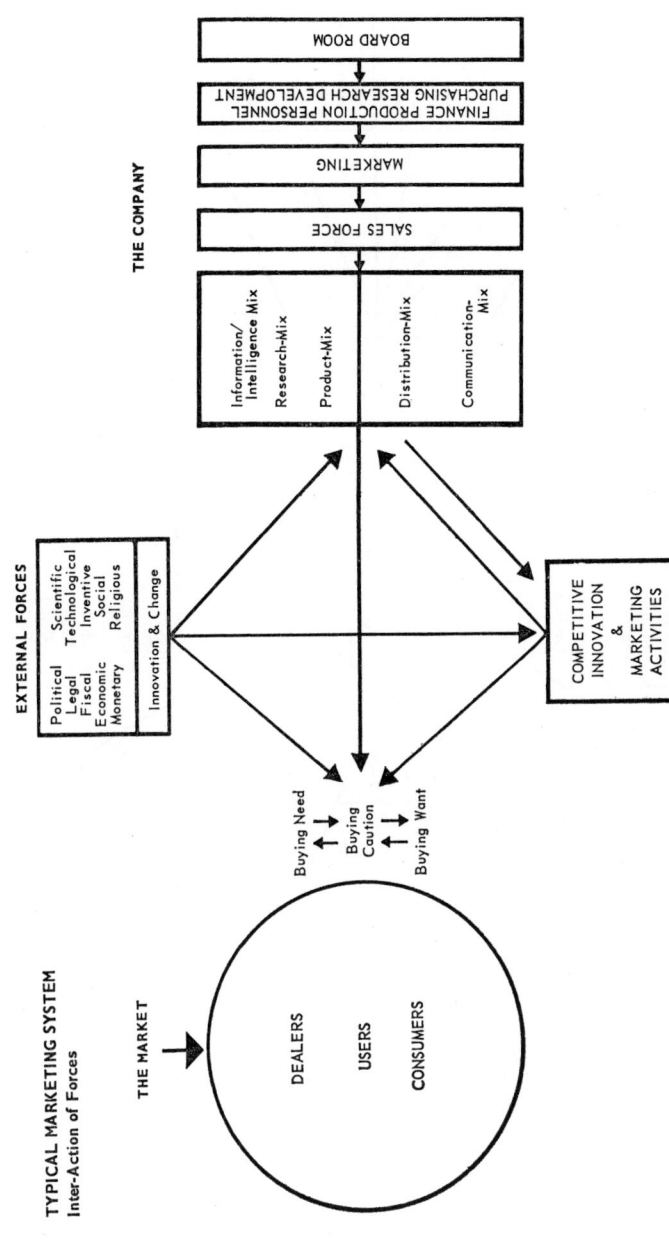

B

Diagram 5   Typical marketing systems: inter-action of force

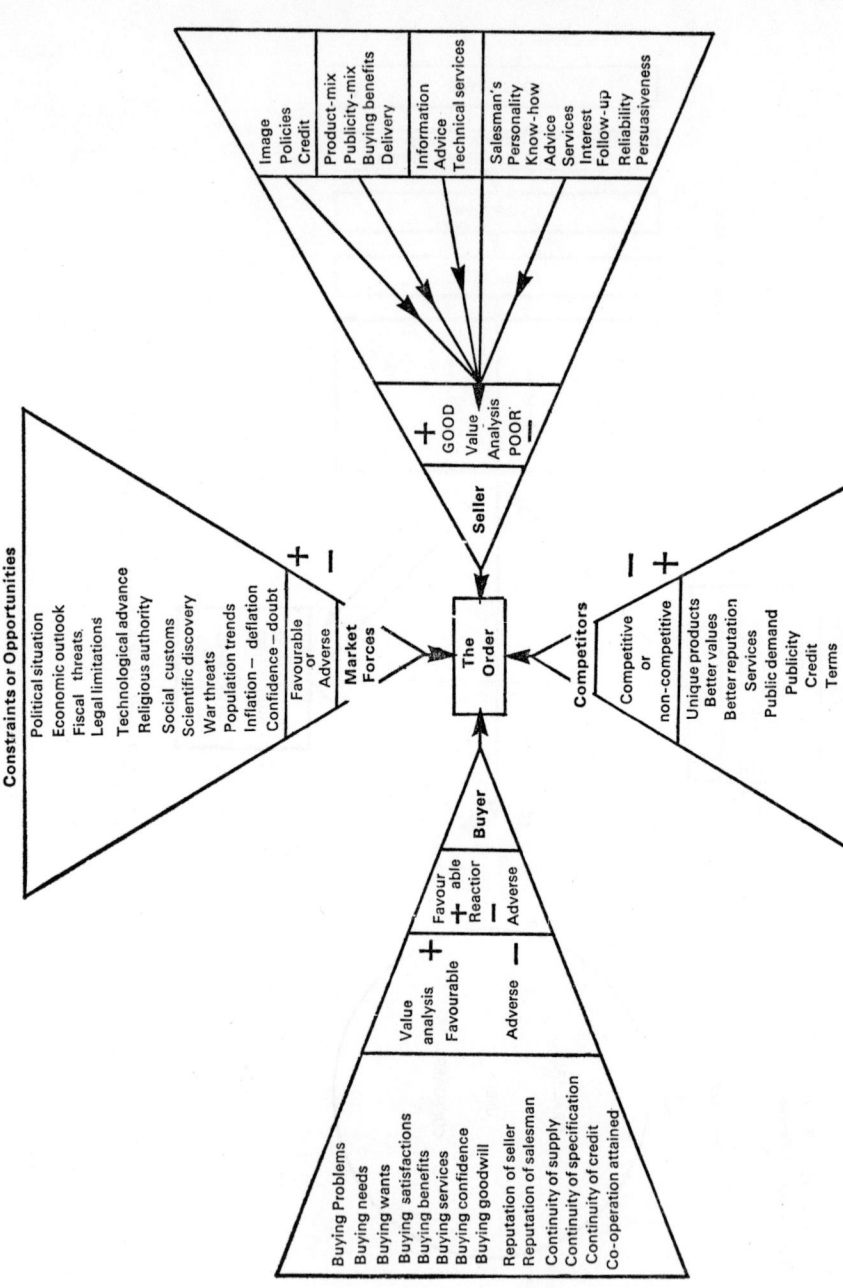

Diagram 6   Activity analysis of order procurement: quadrilateral of forces affecting order placement

Here we come to the crux of this particular discussion: the demand for a specific product or service has to be deliberately created. People have to be made aware of a specific item, be told of its advantages, and sold upon its preferential benefits, before they can be persuaded to try it. This persuasive, publicising selling role may work via the national press, technical journals or direct mail and by the direct contactual visit of a salesman. Some companies use all these media. Smaller companies may well concentrate the bulk of their sales expenditure upon planned sales calls.

The nub of this activity is the Sales Process; however much of it is based upon prior marketing planning, research, and effort. Of what use is a fine organisation, financially sound, productively strong, possessing impeccable research establishments, if their products and services cannot be sold in continuity, in optimum quantities and at the right prices to show the right profits, with a right measure of increase in market share and capital growth?

The selling process and roles are becoming progressively vital to the success of our national economy and to our society. Successful selling is a direct creator of company employment, profits, progress and wealth. These creations are of similar importance to the community, the customers, the consumers and the country at large. There are still some weird ideologists who decry selling as a dirty word and a non-intellectual employment, largely because they are directly associated with the production of profits and wealth. Fortunately the majority of our population now sees selling in its true light and at its true value: an instrument of the greatest worth to our economic strength and to our society.

Being profit and wealth oriented, the selling process and roles are invaluable ingredients in the community's living standards, professional prestige and overall social benefit. They create demand, increase production, and raise wage and income levels. These in turn create a higher level of demand and with it further production, income, profits and wealth. Optimum production plus optimum sales should yield an optimum of employment at the highest income that the entire economic process can stand. Perhaps one of the greatest contributions yielded from optimum profitable selling effort is the money available for ploughing back into the company in the shape of new machinery, plant and methods of processing.

In the personal visitation of customers and users by suppliers' salesmen the selling process and roles can help to increase a customer's efficiency and his rate of profit through the supply of new ideas and information, by problem-solving, by value analysis and cost/design engineering techniques, and by innovatory ideas and proposals. This is an output selling dynamic from the sales force.

There is a reverse process of equal importance to dynamic selling roles. This is the input from customers and users to the supplier. It is of two kinds: innovatory and confirmatory. Innovatory information is that which offers new ideas about areas of non-satisfaction in the guise of suggestions about new products or services, the use of new materials, the substitution of one material by another, or of competitive activity. Confirmatory information is that which proves the suppliers' contentions about performance criteria, etc.

This feed-back from customers can trigger off a spate of new thinking in experimentation and research. It keeps a supplier upon his toes, triggering off a spate of new ideas through this constant scanning of customer and user thinking and need.

SUMMATION

How should the ideas about dynamic selling affect both sales manager and salesman in the general selling context?

The sales manager has a key role to play. Like an expert strategist and tactician he must read three games that are being played simultaneously, and do so with expertise and flair. They are:

1 *The Headquarters' Company Game.* He must achieve his set objectives within the hierarchy of objectives set by the board for the company as a whole. He has to read the effect of inter-departmental manoeuvres upon his own targets, and find ways and means of getting their supportive activity in all circumstances, typically where his own forecasts go astray, and he has to make demands upon other departments.

2 *The Competitive Company Game.* He must find reliable ways of interpreting and monitoring competitive activities and potential threats, so as to anticipate their manoeuvring and counter with appropriate strategies and tactics of his own to keep his initiative in the market.

3 *The Market Segment Games.* He must keep an informational

grip via salesmen and other sources on the market segments in which he moves or plans to enter. In this way he can deploy his sales force to optimum effect. The usage of input-output analysis tables is a good example. (*Vide* detailed account in Chapter 5.) The making of each salesman and field sales executive is a crucial factor in the H.Q. sales manager's strategic and tactical control of the company game. For in the last analysis, it is these 'troops' that will establish his company's market share and success in the field.

H.Q. sales managerial leadership and management expertise are obviously determining factors in sales force dynamism and success and in the achieving of company aims.

WHAT OF THE DYNAMIC SALESMAN AND HIS ROLE FOR THE 1970s?

It may seem to be a far cry from the traditional tallyman, the glad-handing commercial traveller, to the salesman, the engineer and technician carrying ambassadorial and advisory status to world buyers. What of his current professional standing within the social and commercial communities of which he is an essential part?

Clearly, he is a link man, a professional linkage mechanism of great consequence to the commercial community, and to the national economy. It is he who is the communications centre between supply and demand, between seller and buyer, with a professional and honest brokerage job to do.

Upon the modern professional salesman's shoulders lies the responsibility for the creation of effective two-way empathetic understanding between supplier and buyer. This is the only sound basis for the use of his all round and specialised knowledge.

There is another spin-off to this ambassadorial, consultancy and advisory service. It is the influence upon the buying company's effectiveness in its own markets. This a competent salesman wields by the quality and vision of the services that he gives.

In his own company, the competent salesman is a positive influence in the creation of customer and consumer demand; of the resultant revenue and profits; of the employment that is created to produce and service the goods and the customers that buy them; of the ensuing wealth that is created by the successful growth in capital value and market share.

However, this is no claim in support of the vocal non-intellectual minority who insist that until a company sells something nothing happens. This is sheer nonsense. Nothing is sold in a real sense until the goods are made and delivered, regardless of statements of intent or the prior exchange of money against order placed. Nor is it contended that the sales manager is the most important company manager. What is implicit in this discussion is a belief that the sales manager and the salesmen are executants, not architects, of company selling. They are the tacticians, not the strategists. Architecture and strategy in this sense are the prerogative of the board, delegated where advisable to the marketing and sales director in the board's behalf.

Nevertheless, however good the planning at H.Q. and the attractiveness of company policies, the salesman comes to judgement in behalf of the company board when he confronts each potential buyer and user, in pursuit of optimum business. When he fails, the company usually fails too, so far as that buyer or user is concerned. Where the salesman succeeds, the company also automatically succeeds, unless they countermand the order, or fail to deliver it satisfactorily against time and specification and price. Thus the professional salesman is the *deus ex machina* in the ultimate extension of the marketing dimension where and when the actual revenue is gained and company profit is made. It is in this finalising of transactions between seller and buyer that the salesman rules supreme.

He has a treble role: a pre-transactional role, the finalising role, and the post-transactional role of progressing the order safely through to its ultimate delivery on time, exact in every detail.

Even then he has not finished. He has an extra role, a combination of servicing the customer and user, keeping him happy with his purchase and, by advice and planning, preparing the next transaction ahead.

Alert, ambitious, competent sales managers and salesmen can exert more influence upon the flow of economically viable and profitable business within a community, industry and nation than almost any other combination of departmental manager and employee. This is the justification for their dynamic roles and an evaluation of their vital importance in the current and future business economy.

NOTES

1. Herzberg F., *Work and The Nature of Man*, Staples Press, London, 1968. Maslow A. H., *Motivation and Personality*, Harper, New York, 1954.

CHAPTER TWO

The Continuous Search for Salesmen with Potential Growth

This chapter examines in great detail those methods that a sales manager needs to use in the successful search for suitable salespeople with an adequate growth potential.

In effect this search pivots upon two programmes, each of which contains ten principal points, and a three-point interviewing approach. They are:

A Ten-point Recruitment and Selection Programme

Announcement of vacancy
Application form
Screening for short list for interview
Interviewing
Evaluating

Comparing
Selecting best three
Special testing
Final decision
References

A Ten-point Patterned Interviewing Programme

Appearance of candidates
Attitudes
Aptitudes
Personal qualities
Education

Experience
Skills
Suitability
Potential
Ego drive

A Three-point Interviewing Approach

What each candidate can actually do
What each candidate could do if suitably trained and motivated
What each candidate will do when trained, motivated, led and
controlled.

These three programmes, the product of considerable research,
have been tested and proved to be successful in a number of
companies selling both to commerce and to industry. The author
has no wish to be dogmatic. Each sales manager will have his
own ideas and methods which he will test, audit, and confirm in
the light of his own experience. The three programmes are offered
as a proven guide to those who have not found a wholly reliable
method. Those who have might try out their skills in comparison
with the three programmes outlined and see whether they cannot work out a still more productive combination. The more
stringent selection requirements become, the greater will be the
demand upon sales managers to choose infallibly the very best
men.

Good salesmen have always been in short supply. First class
salesmen are in still shorter supply. Salesmen with real growth
potential and managerial capacity are very rare birds indeed.
This does not mean that there is a dearth in potential numbers.
It is rather a condemnation of current sales managers and directors that they have not taken enough trouble to search for potential raw material in a systematic, thorough and painstaking
fashion. Nor, it should be said, have they given enough thought to
the necessity for training and educating such raw material in
order to convert it into first class operational salesmen and
managers designate. In far too many cases sales managers and
directors have accepted the shortage as an Act of God, over
which they have neither control nor influence. Others, more pragmatic but still cynical, have handed this hot chestnut to one of
the many specialist employment agencies.

Even among those sales managers and directors who have
followed a more systematic pattern of recruitment and selection,
results are rarely outstanding. There are thus two main areas of
disquiet: knowing exactly what one is looking for; and the effectiveness of the recruitment and selection procedures and techniques themselves. The aptness of these two observations is confirmed by those rare exceptions, where research into recruitment
and selection of potential salesmen against a carefully tailored

job specification and man profile of the people sought is meeting with more success. Although it must be said that even where and when the right men have been found, it is still possible to get bad results through a failure to train, educate, motivate, lead and control them with optimum results.

A JOB SPECIFICATION FOR A FIRST CLASS SALESMAN

Unless a company is seeking men for generalised company sales training who can be found suitable openings after graduation, salesmen are sought for the purpose of filling a specific job in a specific area. A job specification contains a number of general requirements and usually a number of special ones. Thus in some companies where a general requirement is more important than a few special items, a pattern of general job specification can be published. In such cases, salesmen can be switched easily from one selling job within the company to another. There is the opposite extreme where the thought of switching a man from his initial job to another is quite out of court.

This study of a job specification is of a typical kind, because it includes all the factors common to the needs of a majority of sales managers and directors.

1 *The salesman must know exactly what the company requires of him in what he has to do, where, when, with whom, at what budget of cost and with what frequency*

This requires a precise job study of the sales territory in question by the field sales manager or H.Q. sales manager, and will include:

(*a*) The current work load in number of customers, their sizes, locations and regular differential frequency of call rate.

(*b*) The number of different types of call by industry, by trade, by products bought and by usage.

(*c*) The amount of free time that new salesman will have for developmental selling and for cold-canvassing for new outlets for new business.

(*d*) The intention of the company to require further market segments to be opened up by the newcomer and the availability of time for this work.

(*e*) The intention of the company to innovate further or to diversify into new product ranges, requiring new distribution channels to be opened up, new selling methods to be acquired, with new specialist knowledge to deal with new levels of buying expertise. (f) The known and anticipated future switches of population or of factory development that could expand or restrict the selling role and scope.

(g) The ideal location of the salesman's home.

(h) Whether such possibilities should pre-empt territorial boundary revision at this stage, in order to avoid under-coverage or over-coverage of potential market outlets.

(i) The current productivity and profitability of the operation. An analysis of what the newcomer may be needed to do to redress an unfavourable situation, or to optimise upon favourable indications.

2 *The education, special training, and skills essential for the effective carrying out of the selling role*

(a) There are minimal standards of education and training essential to the proper carrying out of any job. These are merely the tip of the iceberg. The development of the job may make it essential for further educational standards and training skills to be acquired. These must be stated and the newcomer must either possess these higher standards or be capable of acquiring them easily. Here we have a rough guide. The required standards are likely to be imposed externally by the customer levels upon whom the newcomer will have to call for business: social and cultural, as well as commercial and technical. The newcomer's face will have to fit those of the men whom he will have to service in the continuous search for an increased share of company markets.

(b) Technological development will not stand still. Salesmen must learn to match the new levels of customer needs and expertise by greater fluency in the interpreting role and in the problem-solving areas. Company training will have to be continuous in the field, on the job, from the field sales manager, and at the company H.Q. for refresher training, developmental education, the assimilation of new product and usage knowledge and use of new techniques. Such requirements must be written into the job specification.

3 *The overall conditions of work, travel mobility, night or weekend working, period of absence from home*

(a) This is no routine requirement for a stated working day in hours, although minimal hours per week could with advantage be stated. The newcomer should be told in the specification his duties as a car driver, or owner; the required mobility, and the frequency and duration of absences from home; and what expenses are allowable for the purpose. It should include all items for which expenses may be drawn and in the way they should be handled. (b) Demonstration and exhibition duties should be included. Will there be a duty to collect cash, or to be involved in credit fixing, or bad debts recovery? Will the man have to be bonded, by whom, for how much, at whose cost? Home duties and telephone stand by needs?

4 *A salesman must be told and must know his precise status within his company and externally*
(a) Status is much more than a professional symbol. It is a public expression of the company's regard for the man and his role, in terms of comparable value with other company employees. It is equally a value assessment that the company places upon the individual customers whom the salesman is directly employed to service. It has also a profound public relations image. The man is a measurement of the company's standing and prestige.
(b) Status is also apparent to the buying world in the degree of authority a salesman is given to negotiate price or terms, or to get special services rendered by the supplier at little or no cost.
(c) Status is also correlated to professional rewards and titles. The world tends to judge a salesman's status by his salary and perquisites; by the authority that he wields over other company employees; by his direct line to higher authority where and when a speedy top level decision has to be made.
   All these vital human engineering matters must be clearly stated in the job specification with crystal clear lines of reporting to and through. This is a most sensitive area of human relationships within a sales force. Failure to grasp the nettle can create bad blood and inefficiency. Successful handling can pay immediate, lasting and invaluable dividends.

5 *Remuneration, rewards and expenditure must be clearly stated*
   Here we have the father and the mother of all possibilities for friction, invented for the disillusionment of salesmen and their managements. These data must be clarified beyond any real possibility of doubt of fact or interpretation. What the salary is, when it should be paid, in what form and where. Details of commissions and bonuses must be stated in complete clarity. Expenditure which is refundable must be clearly shown and that which is permitted only after reference should be clearly defined in all its possible variances and permutations. Further, it should

be laid down when such refunds are to be made and when bonuses and commissions become due for payment and in what form. Split commissions must also be firmly dealt with in clear wording. The timing and duration of paid holidays should be stated, plus qualifications and legal entitlements to them.

6 *A Salesman's Job Hazards*

Trite warnings about the dangers of drinking spirits to excess, gambling, smoking, drug taking and loose women are surely by now old hat. We should not employ men whom we think that we might have to warn or to watch in terms of undesirable social habits or conduct. The true pitfalls which management needs to watch are much more subtle, more difficult to diagnose and much more dangerous in action. Each is dangerous enough to create a functional failure. Here are some of them.

(*a*) Failure to possess a continuous enthusiastic job attitude of creating customer goodwill and satisfactions.

(*b*) Failure to maintain company and product enthusiasm.

(*c*) Failure to keep in the peak of physical and mental condition.

(*d*) Failure to follow a continuous discipline of job improvement and self-development.

(*e*) Failure to plan continuously the optimum usage of productive time in pursuit of profit.

(*f*) Failure to follow through every task to its successful conclusion.

(*g*) Failure to seek ever-higher standards of job performance.

(*h*) Failure to plan the optimum development of business with each actual and potential outlet.

(*i*) Failure to secure an ever-increasing share of the markets in which he works.

(*j*) Failure to fulfil himself to the optimum as a man and a salesman.

7 *Entitlement to Company Services*

Company services, particularly in the shape of fringe benefits, are very important to a salesman's well-being, adding a warm glow of security and confidence to the visible rewards which the salesman and his family regard as their minimum entitlement. Company services are seen by the staff as a direct expression of the company interest in their welfare. Welfare is in fact the operative word, for such company services include health schemes, sickness benefits, accident payments, hospital benefits, life assurance, superannuation, social services, further education, usage of company car and house, profits sharing, share purchase on special terms and housing mortgages and loans. All should be clearly stated in the job specification.

8 *Entertainment Expenditure and Home Services*
(a) A salesman must know exactly how far he is expected to go in the provision of entertainment for his actual and potential customers in hotels, restaurants and in his own home, and what company services his wife is expected to render in support of the hospitality offered by her husband.
(b) Is he expected to provide an office in his home complete with telephone? Is the wife expected to attend to the telephone in his absence, and do typing and clerical work?
(c) Is he expected to provide a garage in which to house the company car and company samples etc.?
(d) Is he expected to provide a workshop or service bench in his home for company work?
(e) Who is to bear the costs of the above services? If split, in what proportions?

9 *Legal Agreement*
No job specification would be adequate without details of the terms governing the salesman's employment: the terms of notice for disengagement for both company and salesman, etc.

10 *Work Loads, Targets, Quotas, Budgets*
This is an extension of Clause No. 1. It specifies in exact detail the work load for the territory; the precise sales revenue targets for the given year ahead; the particular sub-targets in the shape of product quotas to be sold; the exact budgets of accompanying costs.

Note There are legal purists who would object to the inclusion of Clause 10. They are on a bad wicket. The essence of any job specification is its annual review. To leave out targets and budgets is to provide only a sterile document.

DIFFERENT TYPES OF SELLING ACTIVITY

We have now reached the point where we should try to identify the major divisions of selling activity, of which there are two :

selling to commerce (including the wholesale trade, retail trades, and the home) and selling to industry.

Each of these major divisions should be sub-divided into different types of activity.

There are four clearly defined kinds of *Commercial Selling*:

1 The General Order Collecting Activity

Typical examples are:	The commercial traveller, the consumer goods representative, the durables and semi-durables representative.
2 The Merchandiser	This is broadly point-of-sale selling in which the supplier's representative helps the trader to sell out more effectively and speedily by professional display and promotion of products to the public. This is linked to helping the trader to buy to best discount terms based upon maximum speed of stockturn.
3 Speciality Selling	The speciality salesman is the lineal descendant of the hard selling tallyman who got his business by knocking upon closed doors and persuading housewives to buy there and then. Typical examples are the selling of equipment such as trade scales, cash registers, office machinery and typewriters, equipment for the home, encyclopaedias, brushes, cosmetics, etc. Selling advertising space is still a typical hard sell.
4 Services Selling	This is a fast-growth sector of selling activity to commerce, traders and the home. Typical examples would include insurance, power (especially central heating and ventilation), office catering and cleansing, office supplies, factoring, maintenance of central heating boilers, television sets and gardens on an annual contract basis and various forms of consultancy.

There are five clearly defined kinds of *Industrial Selling*:

1 Sales Engineering	An engineer who can sell ideas, products and propositions to buyers who have to purchase items where a knowledge of

	engineering is essential if the right deal is to be made.
2 Technical Selling	A technically qualified salesman who has specific knowledge of the scientific or technical problems that beset the buyer of particular products and processing equipment or systems.
3 Speciality Selling	There is much common ground here between selling to commerce and selling to industry, except that equipment and problems tend to be more complex and sophisticated.
4 Services Selling	There is much that is common between services selling to both commerce and to industry. The latter tends to be more complex in its nature, and more far-ranging in application and scope.
5 Commercial Selling	This bears a close resemblance to the general order collecting activity described under selling to commerce. Men of similar calibre can do both jobs successfully. Under this category come fast-selling industrial items such as nuts, bolts, screws, wire, packing materials and the like.

We are trying to create a simple pattern of reference against which we can measure the differing requirements of men to do differing selling jobs well. We can try to do this by finding out what each selling job demands in the way of work, plus the description of an ideal man to do each job well. This means the matching of the twin profiles of work and man.

DIFFERENT KINDS OF BUYING PRACTICE

It would be foolish to ignore the important role of the buyers upon whom our selected salesman will have to call. We shall not solve this problem by talking about buyers in general terms such as purchasing directors, office managers, commercial managers, head buyers, branch managers, wholesalers, retailers, the housewife, etc. Titles can be most misleading, and roles differ in every company. There are for instance five different kinds of commercial buying and seven different types of industrial buying practice.

Commercial and Trade Buying

1 Consumable Items	Wrapping materials, packing, string, sellotape, office supplies, cleaning materials, etc.
2 Equipment	Office machines, cash registers, typewriters, showcases, display materials, fire extinguishers, inter-communication systems, etc.
3 Products for Re-Sale	
4 Technical Services	Computering, insurance, consultancy, factoring, etc.
5 General Services	Laundry, telephone, cleansing, equipment maintenance, etc.

Industrial Buying

1 Raw Materials	Coal, wool, cotton, steel, salt, cocoa, sugar, etc.
2 Components	Nuts, bolts, screws, washers, springs, rivets, etc.
3 Consumable Items	Acids, alkalis, solvents, lubricants, mordants, paints, etc.
4 Packaging and Wrapping	Paper, card, plywood, plastic, cans, foils, tapes, wire, etc.
5 Plant and Equipment	Machinery, plant, cranes, machine tools, scales, etc.
6 Technical Services	Drawing office, communications, insurance, finance, etc.
7 General Services	Janitorial, catering, telephone, laundry, maintenance, etc.

One simple conclusion that emerges from even a casual glance at the differing categories of selling and buying activities is that there is a selling hierarchy. Some jobs can be done well by men of average intelligence and intellectual development without specific technical, engineering, or accounting skills. Other jobs demand greater knowledge and sophistication and an ability to mix well at managerial levels.

Table 1
COMMERCIAL SALESMEN'S JOB PROFILES

ITEM	General	Speciality	Merchandising	Services
Example :	*Food* *Cigarettes*	*Cash Registers* *Scales*	*Food*	*Insurance*
1 Title	Sales representative Field executive	Speciality man Area manager	Merchandiser H.Q. sales manager	Agent, inspector Branch manager
2 Responsible to	Call to Pattern.	Cold-canvass.	Call to plan.	Cold canvass.
3 Principal targets and aims **Responsibilities and Duties**	Sell whole mix. Show new items. Get displays. Leave showcards. Collect cash. Report to H.Q. Keep records. Try to get all quotas and budgets. Plan for growth.	Sell at call. List prospects. Get surveys. Give 'dems'. Report each day. Get 3rd party. introductions. Get interviews by telephone. Keep records. Plan for growth. Get quotas and budgets.	See top men. Sell package deals and promotions. Arrange co-operative advertising. Get planned displays in window, gondolas, aisles. Help to sell-out. Keep tabs on shop stocks.	Call to rote. List prospects. Get interviews. Get surveys. Make proposals. Arrange portfolios. Use 3rd party recommendations. Get appointments by phone. Keep records. Report each day. Get quotas.
4 Areas of knowledge	Food outlets and usage. Window and counter display arrangements. Credit control. Trade trends. Getting best out of different kinds of outlet —the independent, symbol groups, the chain.	All trade outlets and customs Book-keeping and accounting practice. Avoidance of waste. Inwards and outwards controls. Data processing. Art of Demonstration, quick closing of the order, and the signature on order form. How to sell benefits.	Food outlets and promotional work. Display and advertising. Modern stock and inventory control. Housewives' needs and likes. Salient spots in each store for promotions. Profit planning. Regular audits of viability of selling methods used.	Much as in Services Selling to Industry (vide Table 2).
5 Level of contact	Owner or manager.	Owner or manager.	Top management and all staff.	Owner or manager.

Table 2
INDUSTRIAL SALESMEN'S JOB PROFILES

ITEM	(a) Sales Engineering (b) Technical Sales	(c) Speciality Sales	(d) Service Sales	(e) Commercial Sales
Example:	(a) Machine tools (b) Solvents	Weighing eqpt.	Insurance	Screws etc.
1 Title	(a) Sales engineer (b) Technical salesman	Speciality man	Consultant or representative	Salesman
2 **Responsible to**	Field sales manager	Sales manager	Sales manager	Sales manager
3 **Principal targets and Aims. Responsibilities and duties**	Get quotas/budgets. Plan best use of time, effort, and territory. Get surveys, interviews, demonstrations. Make regular reports. Get optimum development of each customer. Sell entire product mix. Cold canvass regularly. Keep impeccable records.	Cold canvass. Sell at first call. List prospects. Get surveys. Get 'dems.' Report each day. Use 3rd party introductions. Sell on 'phone. Get interviews by 'phone. Keep regular records. Get quotas/budgets.	Cold canvass. Get interviews. List prospects. Get surveys. Make proposals. Use 3rd party introductions. Get appointments by 'phone. Keep records. Report each day. Get quotas/budgets.	Much as under (a) and (b).
4 **Areas of knowledge**	All manufacturing and process industries.	All manufacture, processing/control.	Insurance of plant and goods.	Much as (a) and (b)

Table 2—*continued*
INDUSTRIAL SALESMEN'S JOB PROFILES—*continued*

ITEM	(a) Sales Engineering / (b) Technical Sales	(c) Speciality Sales	(d) Service Sales	(e) Commercial Sales
Example:	(a) Machine tools (b) Solvents (a) Engineering standards and usage. Statistical control. Computering and data processing. Production engineering and industrial engineering. (b) Chemical engineering, metallurgy, recovery engineering.	Weighing eqpt. Engineering and accounting practice. Elimination of waste, and interdepartmental shrinkage of material. Despatch and inward inventory control.	Insurance. Assurance of life. Pension needs. Investment appraisal. Transport. Group assurance.	Screws, etc.
5 Level of customer contacts	Buyers, production heads, cost accountants, O. and M. folk, project and design engineers and technical people, architects. Contractors. Maintenance engineers.	Production heads. Office heads. Accountants. Buyers. Designers. Architects. Contractors.	Financial executives. Buyers. General managers. Transport managers.	Buyers. Factory managers.

6 Minor jobs Observe company call instructions and paperwork requirements.
7 Information Act as procurers of market and competitive activity as needed.
Company car samples Observe company instruction and paperwork requirements.
8 Literature Use as professional promoters should to optimum effect.

Table 3
A TRIPARTITE PROFILE OF A FIRST CLASS SALESMAN

What a Salesman Should Be	What a Salesman Should Know	What a Salesman Should Do
Pleasing in appearance	His company policies and plans	Plan the best use of time/effort
Pleasing in attitude	His company products and services	Plan work-load and call frequency
Socially acceptable	Competitive products and values	Plan best routeing
Professionally acceptable	The markets he serves	Plan progressive development of each product, service, customer and user—in overall time plan
Technically acceptable	The industries he serves	
An excellent listener	The companies he serves	
A skilled questioner	The company officials who influence buying	Plan each call for best results
A pleasing persuasive speaker	The company policies and plans of such clients	Plan each presentation
A highly skilled problem-buster	The markets which he does not serve, but could do	Plan each proposition
A master of presentation skills	Individual buying company problems he must solve	Plan each demonstration
A master of demonstration skills	The strength and acceptability of competitors	Plan to overcome every type of objection
A skilled negotiator	Selling psychology related to buying activity	
A skilled interpreter	Why people buy, and how to exploit the reasons	Plan to get buying decisions by shortest route and time
A highly skilled communicator	Buying policies, strategies and tactics	Plan services for each call
A sincere, honest, man of utmost integrity	Value analysis, cost and design engineering	Plan satisfactions and goodwill
Enthusiastic and vital	The sales potential of the territory	Plan to acquire extra know-how and skills as required
Energetic and healthy	How to work-study the territory for optimum effect	
A thorough planner	Differential calling frequency planning	Plan on self-audits of results, and take remedial action
An excellent reporter	How to optimise on routeing	
A competent objection overcomer	How to keep form-at-a-glance records on map grids	Hold inquest on every failure
A skilled closer and clincher of sales	How to optimise upon each customer's order yield	Plan self-development by each yearly period to be ready for the next promotion that lies ahead.
A creator of satisfactions	How to make the utmost value of productive time	
A builder of goodwill	How to forecast and budget effort and get quotas	
A merchant of ideas and benefits	How to strike the balance between maintenance and developmental selling	Plan for management job by regular study and appraisal.
Resourceful, resilient, persistent, optimistic		
A Serviceman, a co-operative personality	Appointments and cold-canvass	
An exemplary value analyst.	How to get co-operation of commissionaires receptionists and secretaries.	

Table 4
A COMMON BLUEPRINT FOR A FIRST CLASS SALESMAN

Common Job Description

1. To make effective contact at all buying company levels.
2. To create a favourable impact upon all contacts.
3. To create effective two-way communication between company, customers and self.

4. To identify buying and using problems, establish buying and using needs and wants, and to create a mutual climate of confidence and trust.

5. To make effective individual presentations and demonstrations at all levels.

6. To eliminate buying objections, to convert needs into wants by directly relating buying motivations to product and service benefits, and using techniques of value analysis to prove the comparative competitive superiority of the total offering of products and services of every kind.

7. The foregoing implies the buyer making the best buy and the salesman taking the right order. Here emerges for the first time a climate of mutual identity of interest.

8. To create customer and user satisfactions with their purchase, seen as a buying investment effected by the buyer's percipience and the salesman's advisory help.

9. To build a basis of personal goodwill with customer and user, to get a point of re-entry for the next call, to get away gracefully without loss of time or of friendly feeling. This is empathy at its best.

Common Qualities and Skills

Positive, creative, friendly empathetic attitude. Likeable appearance, friendly helpful manner. Empathetic approach to people, expert listening and questioning skills, plus reliable feedback.

Analytical approach, curiosity, awareness, alertness, flexibility, ingenuity, resource, judgement, integrity.

Artistic flair, linguistic skills, empathy, alertness logical analysis and synthesis, imagination.

Awareness, analytical skills, persuasiveness, merchandising of ideas, courage, self-confidence creative imagination, willingness to give very personal service.

Empathetic understanding, interest in buying welfare, sincerity, tact.

Linguistic skills, interpreting skills, persuasiveness, integrity, empathy.

Consideration, good manners, initiative, and time sense coupled with empathy.

Table 4—*continued*
A COMMON BLUEPRINT FOR A FIRST CLASS SALESMAN—*continued*

Common Job Description

10. To keep effective records for future planning and servicing. The idea is to create information as a basis for planning the optimum yield of business from each individual outlet, actual or seen, as a potential prospect.

11. The Planning of optimum territorial development infers an attack upon outlets that are not yet customers, and upon entirely new market segments within the territory. This assumes the striking of a balance between the development of existing accounts and the search for new ones. Here records need to be reinforced by the systematic procuring of information about the market from every suitable source. In this respect, salesmanship has a marketing research and information acquiring dimension. Input-output analysis is a fair example. This is strategical planning.

12. Tactical planning is equally important. The best use of productive time is a priority. Upon its yield all profitable growth and revenue will depend. Best daily routeing of work. Best distribution of work load in terms of differential calling frequency. Planning how to get factory and plant surveys and inquiries for quotations. Planning a satisfactory conversion rate of quotations into orders. Immediate information about market changes and competitive activities can spark off effective counter measures to circumvent threats to business and to optimise upon unforeseen opportunities. All this is summed up in a daily inquest upon the attainment of quotas and budgets, through impeccable tactical planning.

Common Qualities and Skills

Methodical manner, planning skills, self-organising skills, self-discipline, selectivity of choice, analytical and synthesis skills.

Planning competence and flair, knowledge and sympathy for systematic analysis. Dedication and regular auditing skill. Selectivity and judgement in grading of information truth and reliability of information sources. Telescopic thinking.

Planning ability and microscopic thinking in the daily analysis of apparent trivia, which in the aggregate can be a definitive factor in profitable operation. Capacity to relate time measurement to operational activities in terms of target quotas and budget achievement, thus establishing true priorities within the daily stint. Seeing the selling job in the round in a managerial and cost-conscious manner. Seeing the true worth of threats to profitable activity and the doors that open to opportunism are hallmarks for the judging of a professional salesman's potential for future managerial promotion.

Table 5
JOB AND MAN PROFILES FOR SELLING WEIGHING EQUIPMENT TO
INDUSTRIAL OUTLETS

Task	Qualities and Skills
1 Find prospects	Planned cold-canvass/curiosity
2 Get to see prospects	Determination/courtesy/resource
3 Get on to shop floor	Ingenuity/resource/persuasion
4 Survey equipment in use	Knowledge industrial processing
5 Assess its efficiency	Judgement and costing ability
6 Identify unsolved problem areas	Imagination/percipience/resource
7 Propose practical/profitable cures	Creativeness/ constructiveness
8 Overcome objections to proposals	Logic/analysis/resilience
9 Demonstrate proof of viability	Engineering/persuasion skills
10 Sell the proposition	Persuasiveness/negotiating skills
11 Get right order	Value analysis/utter suitability
12 Sell satisfactions with choice and get point of re-entry for next visit	Empathy/helpfulness/integrity

The basic need is for an engineer who can sell at all technical, accounting and general managerial levels. His costing capacity must be above average. He will often have to choose between a negotiating and a speciality selling role.

Table 6
JOB AND MAN PROFILES FOR SELLING WEIGHING EQUIPMENT
TO WHOLESALE AND RETAIL TRADES

Task	Qualities and Skills
1 Find prospects	Planned cold-canvass/curiosity
2 Get to see prospects	Determination/courtesy
3 See equipment in use	Normal eyesight
4 Assess its efficiency	Knowledge/Costing ability
5 Introduce equipment that will do a better job	Factual accounting competence
6 Demonstrate superiority by value analysis	Logic and dexterity
7 Overcome objections to instant purchase	Resource/resilience/knowledge
8 Get right order there and then	Persuasiveness/negotiating skills
9 Sell satisfactions with purchase	Empathy/friendliness
10 Get introductions to likely purchasers	Integrity/helpfulness/sincerity

We need an excellent speciality salesman. Engineering knowledge minimal. Accounting, costing and commercial knowledge should be comprehensive and competent.

Here we have in Tables 5 and 6 one company recruiting two quite different types and levels of manpower for two quite distinctive jobs, although many of the actual tasks and qualities and skills demanded for their competent execution are similar. The vital difference lies in the markets contacted, the technical knowledge required and the types and levels of buyers. These simple and clear profiles have proved over a number of years to have reduced the fatality rate in bad selection, and much more valuable, they resulted in a type of man being chosen who was more successful and who showed greater ultimate managerial potential.

In short, there is a racing analogy. A professional punter does not bet blindly upon horseflesh in a race, however distinguished its pedigree. He selects the horse for the course which it has to run and the race which it has to win, if he is to make a profit upon his day's outing. He looks at the previous racing record of each horse and the horses of pedigree that it has beaten on similar courses, under similar conditions. He looks at recent and current form, the weight the horse has to carry, the experience and record of the jockey, the going, and at the competition to be feared from the other horses, weights carried and jockeys in the current race. Upon this broad spectrum of comparison the professional punter makes his final decision and invests his money hoping for a worthwhile return upon investment.

Here we have a framework upon which we can try to create job and man profiles upon which we can recruit and select the salesmen we need to do specific jobs well. At the same time we can try to identify those qualities that will ensure the growth of the men selected (given adequate motivation and training) into long term company assets. By this means we can hope not only to make first class salesmen, but also Field and H.Q. sales managers of the future.

At this stage we should try to erect a series of job and man profiles, so that we can see at a glance the main features we should look out for in prospective recruits to a company selling a specific type of product or service, either to Commerce or to Industry.

Some General Comments upon the Differences in Jobs and Men Needed for Them

Some selling jobs can be carried out quite well by men of average intelligence without a technical background. General commercial selling of foods, cigarettes, cosmetics, hardware, garden equipment, electrical goods, clothing, confectionery are typical examples. Here the emphasis is upon the creation of good buying relationships that can be steadily improved upon each monthly call, yielding in turn an improved business turnover picture, and it is hoped an increase in the company's market share.

However there are certain cases where the type of usage of equipment will pre-empt a quite differently educated and trained kind of salesman. A typical example is shown in Table 5. Weighing equipment sold to industrial rather than to commercial outlets demands a quite different kind of knowledge, coupled with an ability to negotiate at a series of higher managerial and technical levels within industrial buying offices, compared with those in a simpler commercial buying organisation.

We have a similar comparison between an insurance agent calling on a door-to-door basis for housewives' weekly contributions, and a man selling group life assurance and superannuation schemes to industrial companies at board level. The latter activity needs a much more sophisticated man, with a deep knowledge of board room thinking about motivating staff morale through social and monetary benefits of this nature. He will need also to have a deep knowledge of the many different kinds of policy, the relevance of income tax law, and the value of competitive offers. Above all, he will need the social capacity to negotiate at top management levels with ease, enthusiasm and real enjoyment.

In commercial selling there is a similar comparison to make between a man calling on behalf of a leading food firm upon independent retailers and small self-service shops and a merchandiser calling upon the larger supermarket operators capable of buying food to a tune of £1 million per week. The latter activity demands a man who can talk to purchasing directors on a parity level of esteem and make a package deal within the limits laid down by his sales director without having to refer back to his H.Q. He should be expert in arranging local co-operative advertising, in discussing promotions within stores, in arranging store displays, and special terms for bulk buying and drop shipments to branch supermarket stores. Above all, a man who can talk profitability of operation in terms of speed of stock turn and make unique suggestions for new kinds of promotions.

INDUSTRIAL SELLING — TECHNICAL MAN OR SALESMAN?

This is the 64,000 dollar question that haunts leaders of seminars throughout Great Britain. It is astonishing that a sales manager should think that it is a simple matter of opposite polarity. In his private life he would not accept that there were no intermediate shades of grey between dead black and glossy white. There is a simple answer to this hoary query. It depends upon the job the salesman has to do, the product and service he has to sell and the kinds and levels of buyer involved.

In the three examples given, we can see quite clearly that all salesmen have a key responsibility to sell. However, in the more routine selling tasks indicated, technical knowledge is of a simple and minimal kind. But in the sophisticated levels of selling products and services of a technical kind to top management levels, considerable knowledge of both a general and special nature are vital to success. In addition, there is a social need—an ability to negotiate well at executive levels through a capacity to create a parity of personal esteem.

So, we have a simple answer. A sales manager should recruit, select and use technically qualified salesmen where this is necessary or advisable, provided that they can sell well, or can easily and quickly be trained to sell well. The second leg of this answer refers to the simpler selling tasks. It is that a sales manager should recruit, select and use men who sell well and who are capable of hoisting in a simple technical brief when necessary to meet the growing expertise of the professional buyer or buying committee.

Tables 1 to 6 give the sales manager a backcloth, a framework, against which he can measure a precise job specification for a sales territorial vacancy and assess the manning description to match the work load involved.

The first difficulty to overcome will be to create a norm for the job. This will be fixed between the ideal applicant who never presents himself and the minimal applicant whom he is not prepared to engage. This is the old compromise met with in services' planning committees between the best case and the worst case to be made out for the predictive success of any plan considered.

Ideally, a sales manager will opt for the shortest list of qualities and skills that will fit an applicant for the job under consideration. Tables 5 and 6 illustrate this point. Taken from an actual consultancy case book, they proved to be simple but successful models upon which to base selective success. Over a period of five years in the company concerned their use raised the quality of the men engaged, improved the sales force's profitability and reduced the cost of failure (that *bête noire* of all sales managers).

The Recruitment, Interviewing, and Selection Process

There are still many companies where their sales managers are not yet involved until the last lap of active selection. The preliminaries are conducted by company personnel departments, which present their sales managers with a final short list from which they are expected to make their choice. *This is a questionable practice upon which to make the choice where failure can run at a cost of £5,000 per man per annum. Salesmen are notoriously hard to judge well upon a single interview. Even after a series of, say, three interviews, experienced sales managers often find difficulty in making a final choice between the best six men. In the author's experience it is always best for those sales executives who have to carry the responsibility for a newcomer's training and development to be given a definitive say in the choice of the men whom they will have to 'grow'.*

How should a sales manager tackle this crucial task? To do so on a hit or miss basis would clearly be quite remiss. To deal with vacancies on a unilateral basis is equally lacking in responsibility. The only rational approach would seem to be the process as a search for the right men to represent the company in each territory. Here rightness is a meld of customer satisfactions and growth with the supplying company's profit and growth in pursuit of its planned objectives. Here is a case for a systematic approach to a creation of sales teams, carefully chosen, to present a desirable company corporate image to the buying world. Within this framework of common qualities and skills there can be an infinite variation in special attributes, each man being chosen with the exact mix to match the needs of the buyers upon whom he will call, in terms of experience, technical expertise, education, social skills and managerial demands. It would be unwise to ignore the important and definitive role of the buyer in allocating business to salesmen with whom he feels a professional and personal affinity and with whom he feels in full accord.

Thus, a wise sales manager will draw up his own needs in terms of the vacancy he wishes to fill, whilst remembering that they should please the buying world too.

It is imperative for the recruitment, interviewing, and selection activities to be seen as a carefully co-ordinated, integrated and continuous process. It is unwise to split up the activities, as many sales managers do. Under the mantle of a heavy work load, they hive off such matters as recruitment to their satellites in the sales office, mouthing such nonsenses as 'put in the same advertisement as last time, it seemed to pull in some likely candidates'.

Recruitment is a highly specialised activity, and is not to be mishandled as a friendly gesture by amateurs in the sales office. For instance, if you do not know what and whom you are looking for, and where they are most likely to be found, or you do not know the best means of arousing their interest in your proposition, then the whole process is abortive and sterile. And, more important still, the whole process of interviewing and selection is negated before it can even begin.

VARIOUS SOURCES OF RECRUITMENT

Where and how are we going to find the paragons we seek? Are they available in embryo in our own organisations awaiting discovery? If they are, how do we find a reliable means of knowing them? If they are not, where else and how should we seek them? Shall we ask our own sales force to recommend men whose sales capacity they know and respect, even fear? Or shall we seek to entice men away from our competitors? Again, shall we seek men who, whilst not in direct competition with us, know our particular industry well and could sell our products and propositions? Shall we ask buyers whose judgement we respect to recommend men who are calling upon them and whom they think would be suitable for us? Shall we advertise either in technical journals, professional magazines or The *Daily Telegraph* and other similar papers. Or shall we abdicate our responsibilities completely and put our problem in the hands of an experienced employment consultant? Let us look at each possibility in turn, analyse it and see it for what it really is.

Recruitment within our own Company

In a small company, a budding salesman is felt, seen and heard. It is impossible to overlook either the man or his potential. He may be on the factory floor, a service man, or in the sales office itself, even in the purchasing department. This can be an ideal solution. We know the man, we have worked with him, we are aware of his strengths and weaknesses. There is no mystery about him, other than his untried potential in the sales field itself. He can be gradually broken in. His training can be carefully arranged between factory, office and field with a minimum of cost and disruption of other efforts. But should he fail it is unlikely that his self-esteem or professional pride will permit him to go back inside as a walking monument to personal failure and thwarted ambitions.

The author was involved in an interesting case of recruitment from within a firm, a leader in the welding field. They are nationally operative, and well respected for their technical flair and competence. However, they were running short of recruits for their sales force who could demonstrate effectively as well as sell. Many were extremely effective salesmen but in terms of demonstration left a lot to be desired, in many cases needing the services of expert welders from the headquarters factory. The salesmen were mostly middle-aged. Youth had not been allowed a fling and seemed to be suspect for this reason alone.

The sales manager was all for experimentation. The author knew of two of their staff who had recently won a coveted technical college award in engineering practice with welding as a special commendation. It seemed logical to see whether or not these two youngsters could be trained to become as competent in their human relations tolerances as they were in their engineering ones. They were enthusiastic to be trained as sales assistants. After a short and intensive course in human relations and communications techniques, supplemented by the arts of presentation and demonstration, plus the skill of persuading buyers to buy, they were launched on an unsuspecting industrial buying world. That they were successful surprised only the traditionalists within the sales force. It has opened the door in that company to the desirability of recruiting engineering trainees who can be taught both to weld and sell to high standards of demonstrable proficiency, thus creating a pattern of recruitment for the factory with a watching brief for eventual transfer to the sales staff.

Here is an example of input, throughput and output as a planning whole, not a unilateral, disconnected activity. Young men in this context can be recruited to a preconceived plan to qualify as company sales trainees.

Whilst there are no grounds for claiming that this could be a major source of company recruitment, its attractiveness and potential should not be despised.

Recruitment from Competitors

Apart from any ethical considerations of poaching, this seems attractive on the surface to many a small company breaking new ground in a new industry, or industrial applications. The illusion is that this device can secure ready-made salesmen who not only know the particular industry but have active personal buying connections within it. A further illusion consists in believing that ready-made success results from this process of buying-in. It works well on occasion, especially with an expert who has no built-in loyalties. He can of course leave your service with as little compunction for your convenience as he showed to his previous employers.

There is an important psychological implication here. It is concerned with behavioural patterning of mind, and shows in outlook, attitude and working habits. Once a salesman has become convinced that his product or service is the best or the most suitable for a particular purpose, he has effectively conditioned his brain to this conviction—the equivalent for practical purposes of self-brain-washing. At the same time he has projected this belief to the buyers upon whom he calls. So a working relationship founded upon this belief has been established. Imagine the effects upon such a salesman and his friendly buyers, when in the course of one month the salesman has received a revelation from Providence that his new company and product have at a stroke superseded the old.

This is switch selling. We do not in the main in this country like people who switch horses overnight. The buying-selling relationship is based upon mutual trust. We are slow to trust, and slow to switch loyalties, if at all.

The author carried out a considerable piece of research in this field. In the main, the findings were adverse to its desirability and any degree of success achieved. Good salesmen do not lightly switch to competitors. Employers do not lightly let good salesmen leave. It is easy to be deceived into recruiting competitive flotsam and jetsam at a cost of £5,000 per man per annum as they fail. The exceptions were those men who for some very good reason were really unhappy with their company and genuinely sought new fields to conquer. Even here, the psychological patterning took a considerable time to wear off. Similarly, friendly buyers took their time to switch, even where they eventually did so. *In the general view, recruitment from competitors' sales forces is fraught with considerable risk and should be carried out with due caution.*

Recruitment via own Sales Force Recommendation

This is a major source of recruitment with many small companies. There are many obvious snags to guard against. For instance, one's own salesmen tend to judge another salesman who is a friendly, co-operative chap, well regarded by buyers, as a potential recruit—provided only that he poses no promotion threat to themselves. It is the author's experience that only very rarely indeed can one depend upon one's sales force for a recommendation for a strong salesman, adequately skilled technically. Even where a recommendation is prima facie a worthwhile one, caution should be the watchword only because the normal salesman is not qualified by experience to define the make-up of a selling type that his sales manager is looking for to fill a vacancy. In short, a salesman will tend to appraise another in terms of the reflection of his own image. He pleases the salesman in those facets of personality and skill which he considers to be paramount in importance—and which the sales manager might not agree with at all.

This does not mean that this approach to recruitment should be overlooked, but that its inherent snags should be appraised and assessed with care.

Recruitment through Buyers' Recommendation

This method can in rare cases be useful and profitable. However, a sales manager must know the buyer well, and be able to judge the buyer's standards of appraising the merits of salespeople. A buyer tends not to like an aggressive selling type; neither will he like the man who fawns upon him. However, he will tend to like those who really help him, perhaps overmuch. Here again there is a tendency to like people who are at least partly a reflection of their own views, outlook, attitudes and image. There is another snag. Once a buyer has been asked for a recommendation, and gives one, and the sales manager does not act upon it, there is often a feeling of being snubbed. Snubbing one's fellows is rarely good business. To solicit help and advice, and then to reject it—in the case of a buyer from whom one hopes to receive increasing business—is at best a highly undesirable risk, and at worst pure folly.

Recruitment through Professional Associations

Where and when the requirements of a candidate are for very high technical expertise, a professional body can help, but purely in terms of expertise and qualification. Here again, a sales manager should ask himself the basic question 'Why should a really good candidate for a post use a professional body rather than watch the Press?'.

Recruitment through Specialist Employment Consultants and Agencies

This is a foster child of the last two decades. It sprang from the inability of many sales managers to find time and staff to do the job effectively. This led to the rise of specialist consultancies and agencies to provide an essential service.

For a smaller company without the necessary facilities the specialist is a sound bet. Such a man will visit the sales manager, take his instructions about the vacancy and the man needed to fill it well, go through all the motions of finding an adequate number of applicants from whom to create a short list, which he will submit to the sales manager for his ultimate choice. It is not a cheap operation, but it does cut all the preliminary worries and operations.

For a larger company which decides to expand its national sales force in a hurry a specialist has his place. Here again the detailed pressures are taken off the sales manager, who can leave the national search for applicants to people who are used to doing such a job every day. Once again the sales manager will come into the picture at the final stage and make his own selection. The cost will be commensurate with an extensive operation.

In the long run is such an activity really desirable?

There is no rational answer to this question. Sales managers will always be ready to pay for the administrative convenience of relief from a major chore. Alas, this is still a prevalent attitude. On principle, no self-respecting sales manager should ever permit other people to choose his staff for him. By permitting a specialist to provide short lists a sales manager is deliberately limiting his choice. He will not know whether desirable applicants have been turned away, nor whether the short list is really the best available. He has abdicated his responsibility and professional judgement in transferring a choice to other people. The real snag is one of communication and language. In good faith the sales manager will have told the specialist exactly what the job profile and man profile are in words that are definite to the sales manager.

How sure can he be that these mean exactly the same thing to the specialist as to himself?

The author is a consultant. He has also been a practising sales director actively charged with the recruitment and growth of National sales forces. He has thus a foot in both camps. Where does the recruiter stand on this thorny problem? It depends upon the individual sales manager. If he is a sound selector of men, he will wish to do the job himself with the services of his own trained staff. If he is not, he will tend to delegate these heavy responsibilities to an outside specialist.

Recruitment through The National Press

Here is the main vehicle of recruitment. The national press is the salesman's market place for seeking vacancies. It is also a company's shop window upon the world, particularly when advertising for staff. This is a public relations exercise with successful deployment and acceptance of very real importance to the company image. The company is selling a product—itself—to the fortunate people to be chosen.

What we need is the right advertisement in the right place, in the right medium, on the right day, in the right edition, telling the right story to the right candidates. Further, the framework of this advertisement will be based upon the blueprint of the job and man covering the individual vacancy. This is such a vital ingredient of success that we should study the subject closely.

SELECTING THE PRESS MEDIUM AND CHOOSING THE ADVERTISEMENT

Choice of medium is not difficult. The *Daily Telegraph* is outstanding by any standards. In the provinces and in Scotland, various papers have their keen following. In London, the *Evening News* and *Evening Standard* also have a following for the less technical jobs in the selling arena.

The choice of the advertisement format is, on the other hand, a very difficult one to make. It is fair to say that the more important the job, the higher the qualifications demanded, the more sophisticated the advertisement will need to be. There are two distinct types of reader candidate : the man out of a job who has the time and the need to be extremely careful in assessing a prospective job. The second type is a man already in a job and

c

reasonably happy with it. But, in order to reassure himself upon his comparative market value, he will from time to time look carefully at the jobs being advertised within his income bracket. Such men will neither waste their time on unsuitable job applications nor risk their reputations by applying for jobs where specifications are not fairly fully stated. Nor, be it said, do they relish applying for a blind date through a box number.

This leads us to an important decision. Should we write our advertisement in sufficient detail to satisfy these two types of applicant? If so, precisely how much vital detail should we be ready to reveal? This is another way of saying that it should be more important to address our advertisement to the fairly few people whom we would like to apply than to receive a host of burdensome replies from wholly unsuited people. There are still some sales managers who value the pull of their advertisement by quantity rather than by the quality of the applicants. To do this is merely to provide a whip for one's own flagellation, a time-consuming, costly, unrewarding occupation.

What then should we say? How large should the advertisement be? Should it be in a solus position?

The Advertisement

Because putting a job vacancy advertisement in a national newspaper is one aspect of projecting a company's public relations image, size and solus position should be judged by this criterion as well as that of presenting a comprehensive case to the candidate. It is also a supremely difficult selling job. We are approaching an unseen, unknown audience. We do not know who will read it, or when, or if they will be sufficiently impressed to be persuaded to write in for a company proposal form. Neither do we know whether the people who apply represent a fair cross-section of the men who would either like the job if they had read about it or are available at that time. So we must give at least as much time, care and thought to preparing a job advertisement as we would normally give a company product that needed a lot of hard selling. Getting the right man is a very hard sell indeed. If it were not so we should not see the wealth of regular advertising for selling paragons, nor should we be aware of the large number of failures at £5,000 per man per annum.

Just how should we set about preparing a suitable advertisement that will pull in the men we want to apply?

First by being frank and forthcoming about the job specification and the man we are looking for to fill it. Second, by being ready to talk about the potential of the job and the potential of promotion within the company for the right man.

What are the essential ingredients, apart from clear, brief, succinct English, in which to clothe the selling communication? Well-worded advertisements are rarer than they should be. Many are tatty, unclear, and couched in jargon that would not deceive a prurient child.

The first requirement is to give the vacancy a title and a brief description. It should say where the job is located and the principal duties and responsibilities and what qualities and skills are essential. It should stress the required levels of education and experience and mention important items like holidays, superannuation, and fringe benefits such as company car etc. It should give an idea of the salary range and promotion prospects, along with the degree of mobility required and the base of operations. The company's name, its address and the name and rank of the person to whom candidates should send their applications should be included, along with a positive guarantee of confidentiality.

Some advertisers seem to be so short of good applicants that they are now ready to talk on the telephone to prospective candidates and fix subsequent appointments with those whose voices and oratorial skills have impressed them. Doubtless these methods must seem appropriate to their users, or they would not continue with them. Yet there are doubts in the majority of sales managerial minds whether this is the real method of choice. For instance, would you as a person and a reader speak about your personal aspirations and skills to someone whom you have not met, and whose capacity to read you by remote control on the telephone is suspect and unknown? How can you be sure of confidentiality? How can you be sure that you have had a fair chance to put your case? The protagonists of this method take a view that a salesman should be able to sell himself on the telephone to an unknown listener and that his success in this operation would be a clear indication of his success in the normal sales field.

This is questionable dogma. It is ethically suspect. Any man worthy of his salt regards the job of selling himself and creating his career as priorities in the art of self-projection. He wants a stage. He wants enough time. He wants to see just how he is affecting his audience. He wants to see whether he likes the folk who desire his services and to know whether he would be happy with them. In a very real sense he sees applying for a job as a supreme test of his negotiating worth. A challenge to his arts of diplomacy in self-presentation.

Chart 1

RARE OPPORTUNITY FOR SENIOR SALES ENGINEER

Job Specification	
Appointment	Weighing equipment sales specialist.
Responsibility	Direct to H.Q. sales manager.
Location	Home counties
Functions	To develop sales via existing outlets.
	To create new sales by cold canvass.
	To attain sales quotas.
	To work within sales budgets.
	To plan optimum work load/records.
	To operate differential call frequency.
Experience	Experience selling to wide range of
Qualifications	industrial outlets and processing.
	C. Eng. qualification is minimum accepted.
Rewards	Salary by negotiation. Above average.
	Will interest men now earning £3,500 +
	Annual bonus tied to turnover profitability.
	Non-contributory pension/sickness scheme.
	Company car – Rover 3500.
Potential	Management within 5 year period.
Write in confidence for	
Application Form to	John Jones, MA(Tech). C.Eng.
	Sales Director, The — Company,
	Loughborough, Leics.

Chart 2

EXPANSION CREATES CAREER OPPORTUNITY IN SPECIALITY SALES

Job Specification	
Appointment	Speciality salesman – trade scales.
Responsibility	Direct to regional sales manager.
Location	City of Nottingham.

Functions	To call on all wholesale/retail outlets To create new sales by daily cold canvass, and dynamic demonstration ability. To get as many orders as possible at first call. To get sales quotas and work within budget. To plan optimum productive calls each day. To use records for optimum planning. To exploit multiple outlets by regular calling.
Experience Qualifications	Experience cold-canvass selling to all types trade. Articulate – Literate – Numerate. Competent demonstrator. Competent order clincher.
Rewards	Salary by negotiation (not less than £1,500 p.a.). Large bonus on every sale *over* weekly quota (present staff average £1,500 p.a.). Non-contributory pension/sickness scheme. Company car – Ford Cortina.
Potential	Special sales posts and supervisory jobs within 5 year period (total earnings £5,000 +).

Write in confidence for
Application Form to   Arthur Smith, H.Q. Sales Manager,
The — Company, Loughborough, Leics.

Charts 1 and 2 show specimen advertisements drawn up to meet the criteria already discussed. Compare them with the very good, and the very bad specimens current in any one day's issue of *The Daily Telegraph*.

Look carefully at the advertisements' objectives:

(a) To attract precisely those salesmen whom the sales manager wants to interview.

(b) To deter the compulsive applicant without the necessary qualifications and skills.

(c) To persuade the likely candidates to apply for an application form.

Two interesting factors should be considered in this connection :
1 Many vacancies advertised are brought to likely candidates' notice by their ambitious womenfolk who want to know the score

and are far less trusting than their menfolk. This is why the language used must be crystal clear and convincing.

2 Why ask the interested men to apply for an application form instead of sending their *curricula vitae* with their initial applications?

The answer is simple. We are comparing men. Men are unique and their qualities and experience are disparate. Letters of application are equally diverse, even perverse, in their differences. So, to get candidates to fill in a company application form that has been specially designed to debunk semantic misstatements and to clarify any risks of obfuscation represents a bonus to the tired sales managerial eye making its first foray through the applications. Again, the application form is designed to provide only the basic criteria that the sales manager needs. First to decide whether a man is worth an interview, and second, that it provides a vital lead-in to the actual interviewing process of comparing applicants' responses paragraph by paragraph on vital criteria. There is a third bonus which wise sales managers have discovered. This is to include at least two sections of the application form devoted to asking the candidate to give the sales manager in his own words such important information as why he thinks he can make a successful career with the company in question and what the salesman's career ambitions really are.

Why is this so important?

A careful series of answers to stated questions, some of them loaded, reveal only precisely what the man wants us to know. What we want to find out before the interview are the dimensions of the man's character, personality and temperament—the very matters that men tend instinctively to keep to themselves. Yet no salesman can be judged professionally except in terms of personality, qualifications, skills, education and experience to determine his overall suitability for a specific job. Give the candidate a piece of blank paper to fill in about himself among the morass of trick-cyclist questions, and it looks like an oasis in the desert that he cannot resist. These impromptu assays in self-expression tend to be essays in self-revelation to the experienced reader. They are useful data lines against which to formulate very penetrating personal questions at the interview. They either check the validity of the reader's assessment or lead to further revelations that in turn help the interviewer to get a proper picture of the applicant,

Chart 3

HIGHLY CONFIDENTIAL

FOR JOHN JONES ESQ
ARTHUR SMITH ESQ

*APPLICATION FOR SALES POSITION
WITH
THE* COMPANY, LOUGHBOROUGH

Name and Address of Applicant
Telephone Number
Date

For Short List   ?
Date of Interview   ?
Final Decision   ?
Letter sent   ?
Filing Instructions   ?

Surname:	*Nationality:*
Forenames:	*Single:*
Address:	*Married Status:*
	Separated:
	Widowed:
	Divorced:

Date of Birth:

If Married Status: Is your accommodation:

A House   Maisonette   Flat

Is it: *Your own*   *Rented*   *Parents*

Number of: *Children*   *Boys*   *Girls*

Education

Date left School: *Name of last School:*

Date left University/Polytechnic. *Name of University/Polytechnic*

Educational Qualifications:

Professional Qualifications:

Membership of Professional Bodies:

Leisure Interests:

Previous
Employment: (Last Three Posts held)   (Dates of Employment)

Name/Address Employer:

Products Sold:

Reason for Leaving:

Transport: If you own a Car state date, make, and model :

Current Driving Licence State whether clean or endorsed :

Car Insurance Position State whether normal premium or loaded :

Personal Liabilities: Mortgage (Amt.)   Life Assurance (Amt.) etc.

Medical History: Serious Illness during last seven years ?

                  Any Personal Disability ? e.g. hernia etc.

Ambitions ?

*Reasons why you feel and think that you could create a successful
Career with this Company –*

Signature:

_____

Chart 3 illustrates an actual company application form that
has proved to be extremely useful in practice.

It is interesting to note that there have been mild criticisms of
two approaches on this form. The first concerns a candidate's
personal liabilities. The second, a candidate's state of health and
bodily freedom from weakness such as a hernia. These amount to
a feeling that they are personal matters which do not concern the
sales manager or his company. Are these strictures valid? They
are not. The reasons for their inclusion on the form are that a
candidate may have liabilities too high for the salary scale the
company intends to offer. Therefore an interview would be an
unnecessary embarrassment and a waste of time, effort and
money. Secondly, if the particular product demands demonstration, the lifting of awkward or heavy weights, then clearly a
weakness such as a hernia would invalidate a particular applicant. So why go to the unnecessary expense of seeing him?

SCREENING APPLICATIONS

In accordance with the principle and guarantee of confidentiality, the sales director or manager will personally screen the
application forms as they come in. He will by patient sifting
produce a short list that he considers to be the best cross section
for interviewing, and make arrangements for the most suitable
place for this purpose.

Where and what are the best places for the interviewing and
selection process? There are three main schools of thought:
1 At the factory or H.Q. where the candidates can see the hub
of the company activity in full operation.

2 At branch offices (where these are available) and are nearer the candidates' homes.
3 At five star hotels to impress the candidate with the company image.

Each has its points. The first is pragmatic, but not always convenient. The second is a concession to the fact that applicants may still be on another company's payroll, and time taken away from a job is a form of poaching. The third has its adherents in the shape of making a candidate feel more independent and on neutral ground. He will therefore be disposed to show his true colours to a degree unlikely if interviewed on company premises.

Clearly each sales manager will use the method that seems to be best for him. The author is in favour of initial interviews taking place on neutral ground in suitable hotels near to the applicants' homes, then transposing the final interview of the few chosen men to the company's head office or factory, where the true impact of the company's image and strength may be felt and used effectively. It is only just that a man on the final short list of three people should see the company at its base before he is asked to make a final decision. Not to do so is to make a blind date with fate that neither the company nor the man should be expected to do. There are instances of salesmen being taken on the staff without making a visit to company H.Q. who are appalled when they make their first acquaintance with the factory and subsequently leave. Another instance of losing £5,000 per man per annum through crass neglect of first principles in human engineering and man management.

On the matter of interview timing, there is much to be said for meeting candidates during the evening or on a Saturday. The sales manager is not then demanding that a candidate should have to visit him during his employer's time, or if on commission terms, the man is not asked to lose his livelihood for a day in order to attend an interview.

Before getting involved in a close study of the interviewing process, we should clear up the application processing in the sales management office. Here a private secretary will propose appointments with prospective candidates for the most convenient days and times for each interview. It is quite a wrong approach as well as a discourteous one to expect a candidate to appear at short notice to suit an interviewing sales manager, particularly when the candidate is still in an another company's employment. Thus the sales manager's secretary can offer alternative dates and times to suit every candidate.

One very important public relations chore remains: write tactfully to each candidate who has failed to get on the short list. The letter should tell him how appreciative the sales manager is that he applied, and regret that on this occasion it was impossible to include him on the short list, due entirely to the fact that others with wider experience had applied. At the same time, the secretary would wish him every success in his search for more ambitious employment elsewhere. Unsuccessful applicants may feel unhappy at the outcome but a pleasant well-typed letter of regret and thanks does wonders for the company's image once the first disappointment has disappeared.

Interviewing Procedures

Each sales manager has his own personal ideas about the conduct of interviews. There are still some who rely mainly upon hunch and horse sense. They feel that candidate A is the most suitable for them out of a large number they have interviewed. They like what they see and feel, despite the risk of choosing men in their own image, with all their inherent faults and frailties and regardless of the specific differences that exist between territories and types and levels of buyer to be encountered and sold. This is a relic of the days when the sales director had an infallible eye for a likely lad for the sales force. And who would be bold enough to dispute this particular version of infallibility if he valued his own security of tenure?

What then are we to put in its place?

Patterned Interviewing

The inherent fault in the 'I prefer Joe' method is that it lacks all semblance of method based upon investigation, comparison and knowledgeable selection of the most suitable candidate.

The essence of a patterned interview is that it is based upon a framework of the basic knowledge of the specific job to be done, and the kind of man with the type of skills who can do the job with the best chance of success.

The whole ten-point recruitment and selection programme is centred upon this search for the Mr Right.

Patterned interviewing is thus the culminating sector of a carefully designed recruitment and selection process. It seeks, by a simple system of getting as much reliable and relevant knowledge of each candidate prior to the interview, to be able by talk and test during the interview, to get a full dossier of each man.

Here the three-point interviewing approach is of the greatest importance. There are so many men who confuse wishbone with backbone and aspiration with perspiration, instead of seeing that each is necessary to the other in successful selling of both oneself and a company's products and services. Hence the need for a sales manager to spot those men who can and will, compared with those who merely hope through hit and miss methods to win the accolade. However this is, in the author's experience of salesmen selection, a far too generalised approach.

A better way is to make the interview a simulation exercise, in which the candidate unknowingly is portraying the selling role that he would carry out if selected. The sales manager on the other hand, very knowingly indeed, is simulating the role of a key buyer upon whom the candidate would have to call if he were given the job. The ten-point patterned interviewing programme is aimed to give the sales manager the precise information that is relevant to the best choice. He can in this way test each candidate against himself in the role of customer and buyer. So, let us get inside the particular sales manager conducting an interview, see the candidates through his eyes, listen through his ears, evaluate the total make-up of each candidate, compare them all, and choose the best man present. If there is no suitable candidate, then do not choose the best of the failures. Start the whole routine over again, and go on doing so until Mr Right is found and appointed. To choose a second best is merely to create another failure.

The Candidate's Appearance

The door opens. We have a vision of a profile and a posture as the candidate enters the room. We have a glimpse of his social flair as he utters a greeting, and awaits our pleasure, either to shake hands or to sit down. We can appraise unerringly how this entrance upon our stage would affect our main customers, either to our benefit in having such an appealing ambassador, or to our detriment if the image created is a poor one. This personal impact that the candidate's personality, aptitude and attitude expresses in clothes, stance, gesture and language is projected to us with the speed of light. It is our first impression that will subconsciously or consciously dominate the interview in the early stages, if not right through to the end. This is also what the man will do to our customers should we employ him.

Each sales manager will know exactly what he would like his chosen man to project through his appearance to customers and the world at large. Broadly, he would wish his man to look the part that he has to play as a professional man calling upon professional buyers. The particular job will produce variations upon this theme, but they will still conform to what the sales manager deems suitable. For instance, let us take a medical detailer employed by an ethical pharmaceutical house to call upon the medical profession and hospital consultants. Should this be in a country area, a carefully and conservatively cut lounge suit even in pastel country tweeds would be acceptable to both company and clientele. However, should the detailer be calling upon Harley Street consultants, town suitings, not country tweeds and brogues, would be appropriate. In this context, ties, shirts and hats are expected to be in general harmony with the ensemble. And, of course personal cleanliness and neatness should be consonant with a profession where the chief characteristic is hygiene.

What of his stance and posture, his gait? A man's positive approach to life and people can be seen immediately in the spring of his step and the balanced integration of every limb. He is ready to listen, to question, to talk, to demonstrate a point or product. Compare this with a sleazy slouch, an unco-ordinated stance, an ungainly step.

What of his social competence? Does he wear a friendly smile, exhibit a clear well-modulated, pleasant voice and await your invitation either to talk or to shake hands or to sit down? Compare such normal courtesy with an appraising stare, a face-splitting grin, a rough coarse voice, a grab at your hand, or at the nearest chair. The offering of a cigarette to a non-smoker can be an unwarranted solecism, showing social insensitivity.

Attitudes

The conversation is now going ahead. We have asked a leading question or two that we felt certain he could answer easily. It should have put him in complete control of his nerves and feel-

ings, whilst girding his mental loins to sell himself to us as potential and desired employers.

We are not going to try to sell the company and the job to
him as our forefathers were apt to do. We want to get the most
suitable man to fill our vacancy and enrich our staff and customer
relations in the process. He is an investment in manpower once
we employ him. We want to see the potential: that combination
of can and will which we can convert quickly and surely into a
company asset.

What of the captive audience's attitudes? He should be looking
for job satisfactions that are being denied him at present. He
should be looking for career ambitions that he cannot see now.
Are we the employers to offer him the millennium? He is an actor
in search of a stage and a part. We are producers in search of
the right actor for our stage and our part. So we have not put
our candidate with his face to the light. We are not deluging
him with a spate of verbosity about the rareness of such a
vacancy and the importance of the company. We have put
him at his ease (we hope). We are trying to exchange faces and
ideas within an extremely limited time spell—to ensure that he is
Mr Right. Psychologically, he will tend to run to extremes,
either be too reticent, especially about the twilight areas we wish
to identify, or too wordy about matters that enhance his prowess
and potential.

We want mentally to rub noses. We want to find out the real
man who if employed would be servicing our customers to our
benefit or detriment. We shall try to enter this hinterland by the
most pleasant questioning. We shall avoid the clumsy nonsense
of the traditional interviewer who asks all the questions to which
he has the answers on the application form, duly filled in by the
interviewee.

We want to know what his basic drives really are. What con-
stitutes his sense of values. What his ambitions are. Why for
example he wants to join our staff. What he sees as a viable role
for himself within our company. Is he mainly concerned with the
accumulation of cash? Or, is he primarily a long-term career
man? Or is he nicely balanced between the two extremes?

This matter of extremes is an important one and to be avoided
like the plague when interviewing. For instance, Mayer and
Greenberg in their article entitled 'What Makes a Good Salesman' in the *Harvard Business Review* in July/August 1964
appeared to stake their all upon empathy and ego-drive as the

dominant factors, whatever others might be present. Of course these are two vital factors in effective salesmanship. But it is the blend of all the desirable factors in a specific salesman's make-up that will determine his degree of success in specific buying situations. To have an extreme amount of empathy and ego-drive present in one salesman could cancel each other out and leave a sales manager with a very disturbed man indeed.

It is a blend in a salesman that will provide a man for all occasions and situations that we seek. Above all we look for a man who sees his job as primarily a servicing and selling one. A man who seeks to provide a maximum of buyer satisfactions and goodwill, whilst optimising his own profitability and growth in operation in terms of his company's market share.

Aptitudes

What do we really seek here? The flair for making friends of the most difficult buyers as well as those who are friendly themselves? The creative capacity to produce a never-ending flow of imaginative ideas? Is it as basic a matter of being an optimist and realist who sees opportunities even in difficult situations? Is it a matter of having potential managerial ability? Or is it the more obvious one of being a careful listener, an apt questioner, and a stimulating and convincing conversationalist? In short, an effective selling personality. Are we looking for a business builder *per se*? Are we looking for a planner?

Fortunately, the information that we need about both attitudes and aptitudes can be gained readily enough from the interviewee by a slow, friendly process of subtle and oblique questioning, in which you ask him for his reactions to a series of carefully loaded propositions.

Personal Qualities

Here we come to the core of the problem, the crunch of the enquiry and research. Just what personal qualities does each specific job need for its exemplary execution? We can of course list a hundred or more desirable qualities. Just how few of them are really vital to proper effective selling?

For instance, we can start with one basic quality around which every other rotates : Integrity. Without it, there is neither hope of continuity nor expectation of success. But what is integrity? It is really difficult to define. It is not just being honest as so many people think, although of course absolute honesty is a dominant characteristic of integrated persons. Integrated persons are the clue. This speaks of wholeness, of roundedness, of sincerity, of soundness, of utter dependability. You always know where you stand with them. There is a comforting sense of continuity. You feel, even after an absence of many years, that the conversation and the relationship would be taken up at the point where they had left off, just as though nothing had happened to stop them. This is why buyers both like and respect integrity in a salesman. They know precisely where they are. They do not need to read the small print on the back of the quotation form. They know that the particular salesman is worthy of their complete and utter trust. They know that their confidence will be fully respected at all times.

Loyalty

This is another term that we tend to use loosely. To many people it means that a man will support them through thick and thin, through good times and bad. In a much wider context loyalty refers to the faithful adherence of a man to a cause, to other people. It means that their allegiance can be taken for granted, that they will honour their promises and keep faith. People can be utterly dependent upon their word and intent. This is why sales managers like and respect salesmen who are loyal, men who can be trusted to carry out any delegated activity to the best of their abilities. Buyers like it too. It is important to them that their intermediary with the supplier, the salesman, can be trusted to be loyal to their interests.

Empathy

This is a word popularised in the U.S.A. in social science circles. It has begun to take a regular place in this country when interpersonal relationships are being discussed. It is not sympathy, although this is a dominant characteristic of empathy. Empathy goes deeper and wider. It has a three-dimensional application. It means in effect getting so close to others in terms of how they feel, think, and act that it is possible to predict with considerable accuracy how they will react to any given stimulus or happening. In a very real sense it means an ability to get under the skin of another person; to know his ethical responses; to appreciate what are his principal motivations; to understand his sensitive areas; to feel for his aspirations; to try to understand his problems; in short to be able to see the outside world and yourself through another person's eyes, and to exercise his qualities and standards of judgement upon any proposition or project you are putting forward for his consideration. This is why buyers respond with a warm glow of surprise and friendliness to a salesman who projects empathetic qualities and characteristics. This pre-empts that any selling ploy will be made with the buyer's interests in the forefront, and that mutual benefit will be the ultimate aim of the sales negotiations. Empathy seeks to create a mutual identity of interests between buyer and salesman.

Likeability

The writer has not found this word in pocket dictionaries. But each of us is a mélange of likes and dislikes that seem fundamental to our personal way of living. We tend to join circles of people whom we like. We interpret this feeling, when challenged, by a statement such as 'I like John because he likes the things that I like, and he seems to like me'. We may take the explanation further by saying 'We like doing the same things together. They's why we joined this club'. We refer to some people as 'likeable'. Again we mean that in general terms we are sympathetic to a common way of life or share similar values and views. So buyers find it much easier to direct business towards people whom they like (other things being equal). That means directing business towards the salesmen whom they like, and avoiding spending time with salesmen whom they do not like (provided that their business interests are not put in jeopardy). This involuntary projection of personal likeability is therefore a valuable asset in a candidate for a selling post. Further, it will sway the interview in such a man's favour (provided other things are equal). For, the sales manager (interviewing by the simulated patterned interview technique) will, in his role of buyer of the candidate's services, respond favourably to the idea of such a likeable character joining his sales force.

Stickability

Again it is unlikely that this word will be found in a typical pocket dictionary. We know what a man is like whom we refer to as a sticker. We cannot get rid of him without taking positive action. We know what getting stuck in means in terms of a game of football. Many sales managers confuse this word with perseverance. But stickability means much more than this. The nearest example readily familiar to most men is a football club manager's exhortation to a wing half to stick like glue to the danger man in a visiting team. This again is not the essence of stickability. Stickability has a limpet-like quality applied to propositions, to the overcoming of difficult situations, to the landing of really difficult orders. In a very real way it implies another quality: moral courage. However favourable, or however adverse a buying climate, Mr Stickable will be on the job, doing everything possible to land the business. Perhaps the ultimate accolade is given by one man to another when he says 'I would rather have John with me on a sticky wicket than anyone else in the firm.'

Stability and Reliability

Sales managers, when faced with the perennial problem of time allocation in field supervisory duties, automatically divide their men between Mr Reliability and Mr Unreliability between stability and instability. 'John doesn't need more than a casual visit from me to exchange views, to deal with odd problems, and to furnish additional information. He's foolproof,' says the sales manager. Joe, on the other hand, is a very different kettle of fish. Joe is a creature of whims and moods. He's quickly up or down, wildly enthusiastic or the very opposite. John is a realistic and opportunistic entrepreneur. Give him the smell of a chance and he's on his way. Joe will sometimes be like John. But you cannot depend upon his not being unrealistically pessimistic or cynical of his chances of success in a changing condition of competitive activity. The candidate who is a Mr Foolproof must always appeal to an interviewing sales manager. Here is a man who glories in the challenge and mastery of change. Here is a perennial asset, due to his mental and emotional stability. Buyers, too like these qualities in salesmen.

Courage and Resourcefulness

Most of us were brought up on a literary diet of heroic deeds. Few of us have to prove our latent physical courage in daily action. Most of us are however faced with making daily decisions that require moral courage for their right orientation. Usually these happenings refer to our respect for personal popularity and our determination to avoid failure or defeat in business seeking situations. For instance, if a valued buyer takes a stand about a matter in which you and your company are involved, and does so to your detriment, you have three main lines of verbal response : to agree (coward-like, often glossed over by the word tactics); to remain silent (coward-like hope that silence will give assent without openly avowing the customer's cause against one's company); to disagree pleasantly, firmly, rationally. This takes moral courage, but it also demands resourcefulness of dialogue and empathetic understanding.

No buyer respects a salesman who assumes the passive role. Neither does he respect a yes-man. He wants to prove himself to be right. You on the other hand cannot allow a major complaint that is unjustified to go by default. Somewhere, somehow, a salesman of courage and resourcefulness will find a middle way, where both the buyer and the salesman can find the true cause and put it right. This demands the personal ability to take the heat out of the situation. It is what is wrong, not who is the culprit that matters. With tact and goodwill, plus courage and resourcefulness, a salesman can first aim towards a compromise position. Then, realising that compromise is anathema to all entrepreneurs, whether they buy or sell, he will try to create a new solution to the difficulty. He will make himself responsible for finding an impeccable method for future dealings that will avoid any repetition of the complaint. Thus in an interview, you as a wise sales manager will ask loaded questions that will enable the candidate to display his courage and resource in weaning you from your entrenched position to a new one that pleases you both, and one that does not savour of compromise that satisfies nobody. He will handle your buyers this way too if you give him the chance. He will not easily brook failure or defeat.

Resilience

So far we have dealt with the firmer types of quality. Yet there is room for both a lighter treatment and some laughter in the conduct of the world's business affairs. There is room for ingenuity as well as firmness, for the rapier as well as the broadsword. This is because people are more important than propositions, and man greater than method and the computer. Whether we like it or not, inter-company communications and interpretation are becoming more and more the province of the salesman. He is our verbal projection in the marketplace. He may be telling the identical tale to a dozen different people in one day, but never in the identical words. The same objections to purchase may arise in each interview, but rarely in the same order or with similar emphasis. Your salesman is dealing with far more unknowns in each buying equation than the known qualities of your proposition. He cannot, with the best will in the world or with the most careful planning and knowledge of each buyer, foresee the exact progress of each interview. He must be prepared and able to pirouette upon a verbal pinhead with grace, dexterity and conviction. This does not mean that he lacks courage or resource. It does mean that he knows that to gain business in unforeseen situations, dealing with formidable objections and technical experts, he must be able to use his mental and verbal rapier superbly to win his duel with a friendly buyer, who yet needs overwhelming conviction to justify investing his company's money in the shape of an immediate order. This quality is linked with the following quality of creative imagination, and each can be used to stimulate the other.

Creative Imagination

There is a lot of nonsense talked about creativity in general. Many people associate creativity exclusively with artists, sculptors, writers, architects, and especially designers, as though it were a mystique for a chosen few. This confusion has arisen, one suspects, because people have associated creativity with originality. And the originators throughout the centuries have indeed been limited to a handful of people whose discoveries have amounted to genius—the wheel, the lever, gunpowder, printing, the abacus, electricity are typical examples. Creativity in the selling sense is an open-mindedness, an ability to see analogies, a capacity to improve performance through the use of ideas that have been adopted or adapted from other disciplines, a willingness to experiment with new tools and new techniques. Creativity does imply the possession of imagination that can perceive or conceive precisely how an adaptation could benefit a prosaic selling or industrial process. For instance, value analysis is a sophisticated buying tool that most professional purchasing officers now use *ad nauseum*. Selling techniques have been founded upon a capacity for extolling the excellence of one's products and services. Buyers on the contrary are concerned with suitability and value. Thus a bright, imaginative, creative salesman would automatically experiment with using value analysis techniques in the construction of his sales presentations to potential purchasers. How many of our professional salespeople are as yet practising this simple adaptive technique? Far too few!

Creativity can and should be applied even to the presentation of a selling personality. Let us look at this suggestion within an interviewing-for-a-job situation. Sales managers, like buyers, get fed up with a dreary procession of unimaginative candidates for jobs and orders respectively. It is the same unenlivened tune, even if the individual faces and voices produce a slight variation.

Suddenly the door opens, and out of the blue a personality arrives whose appearance, whilst not in any way extreme, is out of the general run. There is a force about him and in him that shines out. He radiates pleasure at seeing you, the sales manager, although you as the interviewer hold powers of acceptance or rejection of his candidacy. He oozes self-confidence too, in a quiet, subtle way. His stance and conversational tone and content are absolutely right for the occasion and your position as the host. He has obviously prepared himself in his ability to answer your questions frankly and well. He has bothered to find out as much as he possibly could about the company, its products and services and the job on offer. He shows, when asked, imaginative ideas about the development of the job. You feel about him a creative pulse, a controlled energy, a willingness to try every kind of method to uplift the job potential, should you appoint him to the staff. Creative salespeople are restless folk with a sense of urgency about their actions, plus a refusal to be satisfied with anything less than perfect peak performance and achievement. Along with mental and emotional maturity this is a quality that sales managers hope to find and so rarely do. Its presence denotes a lively unsatisfied approach to every job, and is a harbinger of professional performance. Its absence is a guarantee that only prosaic performance may be expected from the man in that territory.

Maturity

Many sales managers tend to overlook this vital quality in the ideal selling mix. They would tell you that they look for the man with the right experience. That is fair enough, so far as it goes. He can have the right experience but, because he is still immature as a person, is unable to use his experience to its fullest potential. So what precisely do we mean by the term maturity? This term is used in this context as a description of certain qualities that are necessary to the viability of the mix.

Briefly we want to be certain that the the candidate is capable and willing to stand firmly on his own two feet and his judgement culled from experience. We want a man who is capable and willing to investigate facts and situations, identify problem areas, evaluate their importance and decide what action should be taken, subject to any overriding managerial veto.

We want a man who will be balanced enough to take the rough with the smooth in a daily stint, without bellyaching. On the contrary, we expect him to exploit the rough (where it has potential) and convert it into the smooth sweet sound of customer cash rattling in the company's till.

This calls for a man who is self-disciplining and self-managing. He must be able to see exactly what chain of actions and reactions any decision or action of his will create either for his company or for his customers.

We want wholeness and balance, yet we are talking about his rugged individuality as a prerequisite for his own territorial planning and action. Is there any likelihood of friction from this apparent dichotomy? On the contrary, in this technological era we need individualism, directed as an essential part of team effort. And it is in team activities that the very best swim unerringly to the top of the selling pool. They do so regardless of their managerial potential, although this is usually well apparent. Here we see what suitability of a man for a job really can mean in a team context.

The acid test of such a man having star quality in team work is his keenness to be visibly accountable for his actions: to be willing to have his rewards made in strict accordance with his effort and skill; to be continually seeking further job responsibility. Here you should find a maturity of attitude to others. There would be no signs of arrogance or exhibitionism. You would find also a wish to help and to serve his fellow man whether a member of the public, a customer, or a staff colleague.

Ego Drive and Competitiveness

Obviously a man's self-confidence and desire to succeed in his job will condition the strength and direction of his ego drive. So will his attitude towards those who compete with him for business both in the market and in his own company. The former can condition his success in actual selling achievements. The latter will condition his speed of promotion and the plaudits of his peer group. Competitions are fair game for a sales manager wanting always to keep his sales staff on their toes. Yet, they can be a source of team sourness, even where and when they are conducted with apparent fairness. There are only two legitimate forms of competitiveness in this writer's book: the enemy outside the company, and one's own ability to improve one's score.

An ego-centred salesman is never satisfied with his score. He sees every sales quota as a personal challenge that must be beaten, if he is to keep faith with himself. Beating quotas, particularly if they are tied to bonus rewards, enhances his ego by additional income. These are often invisible to his peer group, and an ego-centred salesman likes others to admire, even envy, his virtuosity. Thus, to beat sales cost ratios that will advance a salesman's place on the team list can be heady wine to the ego-centred, for attention is drawn to his higher standards of performance, and both his peer group and top sales management are made forcibly aware of his prowess.

Traditionally minded and prosaic salesmen will often refer to the more strongly ego-centred brethren as mere materialistic go-getters. This is a quite unfair. Moreover it is untrue. Ego drive is not a mere moronic pursuit. It knows the score. It realises that to get to the top of the heap and to stay there will require more than good luck and hard work. Ego-driven salesfolk know that they must follow a carefully patterned system of self-education with which to buttress their experience and maturate their judgements.

A salient characteristic of ego drive is a real concern with timed career goals. Such a salesman knows precisely where he planned to be at the beginning of a given year. He holds an audit of progress and takes remedial treatment where it is necessary to get back on course. This is a vital area for the interviewing sales manager. He should be looking very carefully indeed for evidence of planned career objectives. It may need specific loaded questioning to bring the facts to light. Few of us have ever been fully stretched careerwise. Only ego drive will secure this happening. It is vital therefore for a sales manager to know just how far the manpower material that he is about to hire can be stretched in both his and the company's behalf.

When the sales manager has made his final comparisons of the worthiness of the candidates he has to make a final vital decision to choose the best. He knows the cost of failure. He cannot predict accurately the value of success. So, in the last analysis he poses a question about each candidate on the final short list. It will be in terms of Can he? Could he if trained? Will he? This will be an overall evaluation of the qualities, attitudes, aptitudes, skills, education and experience offered. But it will depend upon the right amount of ego drive to be applied to this portfolio before it is put into effective action. Too much ego drive can be a personal liability. Too little can be a disadvantage. It is the right amount that is needed, and is not easy to assess. For it has to function equally well in adverse conditions as in favourable climates.

Education

We can start with a general observation that all candidates must be articulate, literate and numerate. 'Naturally', your typical sales manager would reply. However, we mean much more by this observation than an ability to talk, read, write and count, although we should tremble at the thought that an uncomfortable percentage of our school-leaving output each year cannot even do these simple things with any degree of accuracy or expertise.

Salesmen must be able to converse knowledgeably, skilfully, and wisely at a number of different managerial and technical levels when they visit customers' premises in pursuit of business. Conversely, they are expected to be able to understand readily what such customers' executives say and ask. This two-way feedback is not so expert at the present time as sales managers might either think or wish.

For a similar reason salesmen must be able to read and understand both the printed and the written word. For these are the tools of language they will have to exploit. A salesman needs a large general and technical vocabulary to get by even modestly in highly competitive conditions.

There is a special application of literacy in the sales manager's book. This refers to the art of reporting! Reporting back to H.Q. in clear, simple, succinct, exact language is an art that must be developed. Field information or intelligence is often of vital import to the sales manager, provided only that it is immediate and accurate. This essential accuracy can be easily lost by a salesman whose literacy is suspect. Inaccurate information can involve a company H.Q. in considerable loss, entirely due to a salesman's inability to write exact Queen's English.

Numeracy is another imperative acquisition. A salesman must understand how to read and analyse statistical information, to interpret performance criteria and data accurately, and be expert in the use of percentages, the decimal system and ratios. He should be able to read a balance sheet knowledgeably, and to understand the basics of forecasting and budgeting mathematics. What of the scope and thoroughness of candidates' education?

This depends primarily upon the type of job being filled. On the other hand, a candidate should be judged also by his potential value to the company. This means that ideally his educational expertise should exceed the level of job for which he is currently being interviewed. Education can be a very limiting factor in promotion to more sophisticated company posts. Hence its significance in the interview appraisal.

Taking on a man with a defective education in the hope that you can remedy it is to take an inordinate risk with your company's cash. Equally a man whose education level is far higher than that needed for the job that he will fill for the next five years is also a risk—although it can be a calculated one. The risk to be underwritten here is one of boredom, or loss of face and self-esteem. It can easily lead to another case of £5,000 loss per man per annum until the agreement is cancelled.

Experience

The experience needed for a vacancy will vary enormously. For example, a sales manager may prefer to recruit men without selling experience, or at least without experience of the specific operational field. This would imply the existence of a sound experienced company training operation that would convert the recruit by easy audited steps to professional competence. We are always hearing that there is no substitute for experience. We might at the same moment stop to think that wisdom cannot be taught. So the recruit must learn to sell against a backcloth of company experience distilled from the cut and thrust of years of operations, some successful, others comparative failures, but each yielding its lessons for those who come with their eyes and ears fully open and willing to learn.

In fact there is a meld of education and experience that springs from a man's eagerness to learn, rather than from the company's willingness to teach. Salesmen should not be fed with education as though they were broiler house chickens on a conveyor belt. This applies as much to the regular sales managerial homilies culled from experience that come through salesmen's letter boxes each week-end.

Skills

Human relations skills, communication skills, social skills, interpreting and negotiation skills, presentation and demonstration skills, reporting skills, persuasive skills—all of these, a blend of heredity and acquisition, play together a key role in the way a salesman successfully deploys his whole armoury of blandishments upon a prospective purchaser.

There are many points of similarity between a successful salesman in full cry and a barrister pleading his case to a cynical jury and a critical judge. Each has to sell himself, his company or client, his product or case and the justice and attractiveness of their claims so well that a decision is made in his favour.

There are many points of similarity between a successful salesman and a successful actor, artist, sculptor, or musician. Each lives successfully to that degree to which he can influence others to respect, admire and like what he does.

All of the professions compared share to a considerable degree a competence in the portfolio of skills listed above. They are vital to success. Therefore a sales manager must devise ways of testing out these skills in each candidate during interview, so that he may form a reliable view of each man's current strength as a potential company ambassador. Asking a candidate how he would tackle a specific problem, or questioning him on his methods of carrying out specific tasks, can give a sales manager much of the information that he needs in this important area.

Suitability

Here is a vital problem area in human relations and team work. Will your new man fit in? If so, how well? Will he quickly become one of us? Will he be easy to direct, train, motivate and control? Will he help to ginger up his new team mates, or will he upset their friendly equilibrium? In short, will his face fit?

Salesmen have in the past been equated with rugged individualism. Why should the emphasis be changed quite so dramatically? The answer is that the whole activity of selling is changing fast. Buyers are not enemies to be overcome in a battle of words, or outmanoeuvred in a tactical war of attrition. They are people who demand and need our co-operation. Further, in many cases of advanced technology selling there is a need for teams of experts from both supplier and prospective buyer to hammer out the framework of mutual co-operation.

Teamwork is a demanding master. Men from the same company must be able to work well together, to put over a common front of policy, plan, outlook, and service to a buyer. This is where a candidate's suitability is an overpowering factor in a sales manager's preference between two men of otherwise equal attainments. A sales manager should know the answer to this problem better than anyone else.

Potential

Here again we have an important area for a sales manager to assess. How does one candidate's potential appear to differ from that of another equally gifted in current skills and suitability?

Judging the potential of one candidate in terms of the job vacancy, and comparing his desirability with that of another, is no easy task. This is because judging potential is like making a forecast: it is a wholly predictive technique. It is made more difficult still because the judgement is in the nature of a paradox. For example, a man's potential for a job varies with the actual job offered and the person for whom he will have to work. Thus, a sales manager is not trying to measure John's actual potential as a salesman or as a person. He is assessing his potential value in the job he has to fill under supervision.

This brings us to the consideration of a snag common to all interviewing for selling posts. The candidate asks about his career potential with the company. The sales manager tries to give a truthful reply in very general terms. In short, he makes a long-term forecast of the company's likely position in x years and tries to relate the candidate's likely position with the company by that time. Alas, potential is tied to the market and to a time scale. Events rarely happen as they are predicted. Sales managers come and go. Thus the marriage of career with predicted potential may never be consummated. Then we have another candidate for a post elsewhere. Or, should he stay, there is the risk of a disgruntled member of staff who, like a rotten apple, may taint all others.

The moral: tell the candidate that there is an opportunity to be grasped. It will be largely up to him how he exploits it as a basis for a progressive career.

The Three-point Interviewing Approach

We are looking for a reliable decision-making process. This, alas, is not easy to discover, because the process is bedevilled by the personalities of the interviewer and of the candidates. It is the impact between personalities that can so easily create misjudgements and faulty selections. For instance, a sales manager and the candidates whom he is interviewing are rarely completely balanced personalities. They have their preferences, their likes and utter dislikes. In fact they have a built-in bias that baffles balanced judgement making. In terms of electric charges some have minus signs and others show plus signs. In psychological terms they are either fear-conditioned, or success-oriented.

Thus, a sales manager will tend unless corrected to choose men after his own heart, and in his own image. A sales manager who bears a minus sign will rarely be tempted to choose a man who would cause him trouble, or even threaten to be a competitor for his job. A sales manager with a plus sign would be looking for men with strong success orientations in their make-up.

To complicate the issue further, we have been bludgeoned by writings and exhortations from the U.S.A of the importance of men who are positive thinkers and doers. Of course a success-oriented man will be on balance a positive and creative thinker and a man of positive action. It is the balance that is the crucial factor in selling success and in successful interviewing and selection.

These writers touching the peripheral applications of psychology never mention that a positive thinker can be a crashing bore, a bigot and a boor. They forget to say that a man with a positive mental attitude can with his excessive ego-drive create enemies much more easily than he can friends. Further, that he will certainly influence people but against him rather than in his favour.

So, although it is vital to look for men who can and will do, it is equally vital to discover people who can and will achieve without upsetting people, other than competitors; in fact, people who will win friends and influence people favourably on a continuous and progressive basis, creating revenue and profitable growth in the process.

This brings us to a consideration of the three main types of interviewing:

1 *Individual Patterned Interviews* One man face to face with another in complete privacy and relaxed surroundings.

2 *Group Interviewing* One man interviewing a group of candidates, or a group of interviewers seeing one candidate.

3 *Stress Situation Interviews* Either individual or group, where candidates are submitted to stress situations that in the interviewers' view simulate selling conditions in the field where competition is rife.

An individual interview gives both candidate and interviewer a chance within the very short interviewing period to get to know each other's point of view and aspirations relating to career and job potentials, to get to grips with the real man behind the facial mask, to assess the strengths, weaknesses and potential value of the candidate to fill the job, and to progress with the company. Loaded questions can be posed and answered in good humour. The interviewer, as prospective buyer of the candidate's services, can judge his impact upon the company customers' buyers, if entrusted with the job. And, as most interviews between salesman and buyers, are tête-a-tête situations, we have a fair simulation upon which a logical and informed judgement can be made.

Group interviewing savours of buying committees where a company group is interviewing one candidate. It can be a most trying situation for a salesman who has not had great experience of dealing with groups to find who has the power to make the ultimate decision, and which people can influence this decision in its making.

This does not apply to a final interview in which the original sales manager interviewer brings in for the final assessment the field sales manager under whom the successful candidate will have to work. Here faces fitting well with each other is a vital matter. For a field sales manager who is encumbered with a choice which has been foisted upon him may not rebel openly. But the recruit is unlikely to have an easy or comfortable ride in training and may well be encouraged to fail by default and seek his fortunes elsewhere, at a failure cost of £5,000 per man per annum.

Many excellent candidates of fine potential are either disqualified by group interviewing or choose to disqualify themselves during the process. And such group interviewers should pose a question to themselves. It is : Will the successful candidate be wholly or mainly occupied in selling to buying committees? If so, there is a great deal to be said for a preliminary individual interview followed by a final group interview. In this way both the sales manager and the candidate could get the better of both worlds.

What of the single interviewer dealing with a group of candidates? You would expect the man with a superabundance of ego drive to scramble to the top of the heap. But are you interviewing to select a commando? The very combative belligerent qualities may outbalance those vital to successful selling. Customers may feel overpowered in their presence and prefer to deal with less buccaneering folk who possess more empathy in their make-up. This is presumably what Mayer and Greenberg[1] had in mind when pontifying upon the need for ego drive and empathy in successful salesmen.

Stress interviewing is allied to commando training mentioned above. Its protagonists insist that life is a stress situation and salesmen cannot opt out of it. So, how better to conduct a life-like interview than to put it under stress conditions? This is partly true, like many other specious theories, but life is not wholly a stress situation, unless certain individuals choose to make it so—and may Providence preserve us from the breed!

A wise interviewer introduces stress situations within reason. He does so by subtle questioning such as a salesman can expect a prospective buyer to pose. The applicant knows that the sale involves himself instead of a product; that success or failure can hang on the wisdom of his answers, words and illustrations. For example, the interviewer may pose a question of how the candidate would deal with a specific customer objection or complaint. Here the candidate is on trial in terms of his own attitudes to selling, buying, customer satisfaction, company goodwill and profitability. He is holding the balance between company and customer and telling his interviewer about his competence to hold down the job being offered.

COMPARING CANDIDATES, MEASURING THEIR COMPETENCE, COMING TO A DECISION

The sales manager needs to take vital notes, so that he can compare answers at successive interviews, and so judge continuity managerial response to candidate suitability for the post. Similarly, he needs to have a basis for comparing one candidate against all others. Interviews are a mixture of impressions, memories, queries, hunches. It is easy to confuse in retrospect one candidate with another. There must be a simple, factual, reliable method of recording, measuring and comparing so that a right choice may be made, or none, should no candidate measure up to criteria needed.

THE HUDSON TEN-POINT MAN MATRIX—FOR INTERVIEWING

1 **APPEARANCE**   Score 1 to 10 marks according to reactions

2 **ATTITUDES**   Socially acceptable
                       Empathetic
                       Communicative
                       Interesting
                       Problem Solving
                       Helpful
                       Decisive
                       Diagnostic
                       Prognostic
                       Enthusiastic   Maximum score 10 marks

3 **APTITUDES**	Friendliness	
	Resourcefulness	
	Resilient	
	Courageous	
	Creative	
	Positive	
	Enquiring	
	Self-Organising	
	Planning	
	Self-Managerial	Maximum score 10 marks
4 **PERSONALITY**	Extrovert	
	Sparkling	
	Mature	
	Strong	
	Forceful	
	Balanced	
	Sincere	
	Pleasing	
	Leadership Quality	
	Suitability	Maximum score 10 marks
5 **MOTIVATION**	Ego Drive	
	Empathy	
	Pride	
	Purse	
	Power	
	Status	
	Prestige	
	Security	
	Competition	
	Service	Maximum score 10 marks
6 **EDUCATION**	Secondary	
	Comprehensive	
	Grammar School	
	Public School	
	Polytechnic	
	University	
	Technical	
	Scientific	
	Arts	
	Commercial	Maximum score 10 marks
7 **EXPERIENCE**	Engineering	
	Design	
	Accounting	
	Costing	
	Planning	
	Control	
	Technical	
	Negotiating	
	Managerial	
	Sales	Maximum score 10 marks

8 **SKILLS**   Technical
                              Negotiating
                              Selling
                              Presentation
                              Demonstration
                              Planning
                              Closing Sales
                              Overcoming Objection
                              Managerial
                              Leadership   Maximum score 10 marks

9 **SUITABILITY**   Good Team Man
                              Works to Plan
                              Plans to Work
                              Accepts Delegated Authority
                              Accepts Accountability
                              Responsible
                              Mature, Balanced
                              Integrity
                              Thorough Thinker
                              Servicing Outlook   Maximum score 10 marks

10 **POTENTIAL**   Considerable
                              Managerial
                              Specialist
                              Consultant and Advisor
                              Ambassadorial
                              Teaching and Training
                              Overseas Marketing
                              Home Marketing
                              Marketing Research
                              Publicity   Maximum score 10 marks

NOTES   This is a barebones framework upon which a sales manager can build his own pet bodywork to create a viable interviewing model.

He can introduce more items or reduce their number.

He can weight or load those items which are crucial or significant for a particular vacancy, raising or lowering individual marks accordingly.

He can introduce test material in any sector of the interview to prove worth.

If he wishes to have psychological or graphological confirmation of any portion of the questionnaire, the answers given can help the specialist to frame his tests, and load them as thought wise.

The framework forms a useful three-dimensional model within which and against which to compare the scores of otherwise comparable manpower material.

The overall manpower picture built up within this framework gives a realistic basis not merely for selective purposes but also for the initial performance criteria profile against which a company sales trainer and field sales manager have to work. Instead of being presented with a new man to brief and to train, the company sales executive has a carefully designed assessment of the quality of the man whom it will be his responsibility to nurture and to grow.

In many ways this is the individual basis for the making of a salesman.

D

The Hudson Ten-point Man Matrix

Pages 79–81 illustrate a simple system of man measurement and evaluation devised by the author a decade or so ago, particularly for the help of sales managers in the salesman selection process. You can see how simple the criteria are. Under ten selected subject headings we cover all the essential matters concerned with the selling and representative job. Each subject heading carries a maximum of ten marks. The total possible score would therefore be 100. This creates a convenient back-cloth for showing each mark immediately as a percentage score of the potential whole.

What are the specific advantages of such a system compared with the traditional method of making notes as the interview goes along? Some of the more significant are:

1 Interview ratings are usually too subjective for rational comfort. What do excellent, very good, average, abysmal really mean when used on a comparison scale? A potential marking of 1 to 10 under a subject heading enables the interviewer to visualise the candidate's capacity in more concrete terms. There is considerable inbuilt flexibility.

2 A total score related to a maximum of 100 makes comparisons easy. There is no reason why the interviewer should not weight those special matters under a subject heading that are most important to the job vacancy, or, for that matter, why he should not weight headings for a similar reason, so long as the total remains at 100 maximum. There is no virtue in the figure 100 except that other totals will have to be reduced to 100 if a percentage is required for comparison purposes.

3 This man matrix throws up immediately variances that the interviewer notices under subject headings in the same candidate's score at different interviews. These variances may be seen objectively, subjectively, or as a mixture of both. This liability to variance is a justification, if one were needed, of having at least three interviews for candidates upon the final short list, so that a rational average may be struck.

4 The average scores of, say, the final three candidates on the short list can now be examined in statistical detail. You can see at a glance which candidate possesses the edge over the remainder.

5 This vital criterion plus the potential of the individuals concerned will give the sales manager a rational choice of the best candidate available. However, if he is not up to the minimum

standard required, it is wise not to appoint him, but to start the recruitment process all over again.

6 The trouble with the traditional interviewing pattern is the tendency to spend the major portion of the time available looking for quantitative assets such as proven skills and achieved performance. However, the qualitative factors are just as important, probably more so. But the individual is like an iceberg, he shows only the tip of his potential; the rest, submerged, has to be looked for and measured. This is where the man matrix keeps the interviewer's eye upon the need for locating and identifying the unseen factors in the personal equation.

Validation of Selection—Checks, Tests and References

Because it is so hard to judge people well within a short interview, we resort to checks as an acid test of interviewing reliability and skill.

For example, we used loaded questions to check the exactness of some statement on the application form, just to see whether the candidate has chanced his arm, or is weaving a fairy story about his origins, connections or qualifications. Or we set a candidate a written test which will clearly show (we hope) just how up-to-date his technical information is in terms of a degree taken a decade or so ago. Again, we may ask a series of questions about the method he would use to solve a hypothetical problem. We should also definitely ask questions that will reveal precisely how much the candidate has found out before he came to the interview about our operations, status and marketing and selling policies.

This is a vital question area. This candidate is trying to sell his personal services to the interviewer to advance his career aspirations. If he has not taken the trouble to be well informed upon the company he is hoping to join, how well will he inform himself upon customer problems and plans should he join your company?

Psychological and Graphological Tests

This is dangerous ground for the layman. It can be equally dangerous for a psychologist. General tests of competence—intelligence, personality inventories, technical and technological skills

—all have a place in confirming whether the sales manager's interviewing skills have furnished a generally reliable report upon the candidate's marked competence figure.

But, we are not concerned with generalities. We are vitally interested in finding a man who will carry out a specific job impeccably. Thus, any psychological or professional test is invalid in this context unless it is specifically geared to the man and job profiles of each vacancy.

If a sales manager wants a guide to form, or a check upon his selection prowess, let him get a psychologist to produce a series of special tests relevant to the job and the appropriate man. This could help if it questioned the managerial decision. Then there would have to be a re-run of the selection interview. Unless a sales manager has a very bad day, or is spoofed by a confidence trickster, he is unlikely to get other than a general blessing from his psychological tests, which will send him away for the week-end more than ever convinced of his interviewing excellence.

Both the Max Planck Institute of Psychiatry in Munich and The National Institute of Industrial Psychology in London are reported to have ceased intelligence testing as a major indicator for job selection and career potential.

Max Planck are further credited with a view that a man's past record in job achievement may well prove to be a reliable predictor of both the line and the shape of his future performance. This observation is in direct line with many sales directors' experience over the years in man recruitment and selection.

However, it would be unwise to neglect the uses of general tests of intelligence that try to place men in performance percentile groups within a total population. For instance, a man who falls within a middle group in his percentile score, and all other personality factors seeming to be favourable, would appear to be a better prospect than a scorer in the lower percentile ranges. On the other hand, a man who is rated intellectually to be within the top ten per cent of the population, and with all other personality factors seeming to be favourable, would appear to be of managerial potential.

Personality inventory tests (such as those developed by Eysenck) can be useful to supplement a percentile psychological score. They measure quite reliably a man's degrees of introversion and of extraversion. With a combination of both scores, it is easier to choose men who avoid either polarity of percentile measurement of intelligence and are not too introverted or too extraverted to pose social, professional, or disciplinary problems.

When we reflect that successful selling and successful management of the sales force both demand balanced and harmonious relationships being deliberately created between salesman and buyer, and salesman and manager, it is easy to see that tests which indicate a harmonious balance in a man between his ego drive and his empathy and between his treatment of his fellow-man and methods he uses, must command at least our respect. For a salesman and a manager are at all times involved in the active creation of excellence in their human relationships.

Graphological tests are an entirely different kettle of fish. Experts who claim to see variances in human nature clearly displayed in an individual's handwriting should be accorded prima facie respect for their views and their work. Whether its addicts can build up an accepted professional practice in this area remains to be seen. It should not be suspect merely because of its novel contribution to selection processes. Neither should it be a sole cause for selecting or rejecting one man rather than another.

References

Are general references worth the paper upon which they are typed? Would any self-respecting person give another as a referee who would damn his future prospects, even by faint praise?

Taking the opposite extreme, is a current employer who is unaware that his best salesman has applied for a job elsewhere likely to give the chap an excellent reference when he opens quite unsuspectingly a letter asking about his competence?

Human nature being fairly predictable in these respects, are such references worth the effort of taking them up? Does it matter whether we take up references or not?

There is a case for taking up references of a specific character over a very limited area, only if the candidate has given permission for this to be done. Even the closest of professional interviewing will rarely in retrospect reveal whether a candidate would prove to be better employed upon current account development or upon the cold-canvassing opening of new accounts. A previous employer, preferably once removed, will in most cases give an honest reply about the man's experience in this narrow field of activity. A further example would be a query whether the man had proved to be better at dealing with top executives rather than at lower levels, or with technical executives rather than commercial men. This is precisely the knowledge that a sales manager needs to have. And there would appear no other way of getting it that could be said to be reliable.

American companies in this country have in many cases advocated the policy of taking up references upon the telephone. They say that it works. Where is the validation of such a policy? On principle, a normal British employer would not want to talk about a man's future over the telephone with someone he has not met and does not know, unless he has the candidate's permission and he can give a good reference. Further, a normal British employer would prefer to have the query in the proper professional way in writing from one employer to another in confidence, so that he can see that it is a genuine query. If there is a breach of confidence with a written reference there is the chance of legal redress. Who can get redress from a telephone reference given by one voice to another?

The End or the Beginning?

Many sales managers still feel that their major contribution has been made to their companies once they have gone through the motions of recruiting good men for their sales forces. Good men, they appear to think, will build up business with the very minimum of jollying and supervision. Presumably having found enough men who conform in general qualities to their own images, they feel that their futures are secure in their markets. This is of course very superficial thinking indeed. This state of affairs was brought once again to the author's attention at a recent seminar for top ranking sales managers and directors by the sales manager (training) of a leading company in this country with several hundreds of salesmen passing regularly through his hands. He stated categorically that he recruited and selected staff with one thing primarily in mind. This was a quantitative capacity to get their sales targets without fumbling and without fail. On being questioned fairly ruggedly by some seminar members he said quite unashamedly that he was little interested in the character or qualities of salesmen, merely in the encouragement of skills which would guarantee the regular securing of sales quotas. When challenged that he would not seem to be interested in the growth of salesmen in his control, but merely in the automatic creation of higher sales figures per man, he reaffirmed his view that the only good salesman was the man who did his daily stint in terms of quotas set. In short, the growth of a salesman could be measured only by his quota achievement.

Is this a valid view? Will a company grow in stature upon this purely quantitative and materialistic basis? Will a company even keep for long the thinking salesmen whom we all seek, once they know that their competence can be measured only by their capacity to secure a series of arbitrarily fixed goals? Has professionalism no place in a company's set-up? Is there no room for developmental training for the next job ahead, other than to increase a capacity to secure larger and larger quotas? Is there no management development scheme other than a capacity to secure quotas? Is there no room for the deliberate planned making of men on the sales payroll, so that qualitative skills play a proper part in the development of quantitative goals?

This book is written to underline the desirability of seeing the recruitment and the selection of salesmen as but the first steps in the beginning of the creation and the development of professional salesfolk. Unless these first two steps are absolutely effective, the remainder of the building process will be bedevilled with hazards.

Regular training and education; regular motivation and incentives; regular personal contact between sales manager and man; regular leadership and control; regular fixing of performance criteria and their regular audit—all these management areas are vital to the growth of the salesman in both quantitative and qualitative excellence.

In contrast, the use of salesmen as mere mechanical collectors of quotas within a highly mechanised company does little in the long term for either company policy or image, and certainly little for their men, other than in a very short term, if then. This is man wholly subordinate to machines and methods and money. Of course, the regular securing of quotas is vital to company success. It is the deliberate downgrading of the individual that seems so illiberal. Yet if the man is recruited and selected to fit the job alone, without any allowance being made for his potential and planned growth in the company, we are back with the proposition that man was made for the Sabbath which is wholly unacceptable. What then is the simple solution?

A wise sales manager will initially pick the man to fit the job. He will lever the man into the job with a shoehorn. But this is but the primary stage to find the man who can and will do the job well. The second step is for the man slowly and rationally to mould the job to fit his developing character and skills in terms of the planned growth that carefully individual and directed training will create. We are in fact looking for a meld of trustee and entrepreneur. The man who will get quotas, but the man who will also build business through the maximum use of his personality and overt and latent skills. We are trying to create men who will become marketing and sales managers for their territories, not mere salesmen with heads to the ground grinding out a daily quota stint within their myopic vision.

NOTES

1. Mayer D. and Greenberg H. M. 'What Makes a Good Salesman', *Harvard Business Review*, July/August, 1964.

CHAPTER THREE

A Salesman's Initiation into a New Company

INTRODUCTION

We all remember the butterflies we experienced in our stomachs on our first day at school. Mixed with the fear of the unknown was a lurking excitement of new vistas ahead. Many of us feel precisely the same blend of anxiety and excitement when we make our way to our new firm's premises for our very first day on a new payroll. Wise teachers and managers are fully aware of the stresses and strains going on in a newcomer's mind as he strives to seem unperturbed in a strange world. It is a very human gesture to try to ease a newcomer into a new job in a new working climate. This friendly and kindly attitude pays enormous dividends. Getting off to a good start enlarges a man's horizons. It makes him feel happy to belong to the new team, and eager to show his professional paces as an effective and worthy performer. In a rather subtle way the excellence of the newcomer's initiation orientates the man's mind in favour of the company as a whole, and not merely that of the sales force. He creates his own idea of the company corporate image. It is this image that will motivate his actions and which he will project to his company's customers. Do enough sales managers realise the importance of a painless, pleasant, exciting induction operation or lay this activity on as a planned piece of promotion that will condition manpower development in the sales force to the optimum effect?

When we realise that it will cost the company up to £5,000 in

the newcomer's first year with the sales force before he is accli-
matised and fully effective, we are not playing for peanuts. The
recruitment and selection process should have ensured as the
first step that we have the best, most promising candidate for a
particular sales territory. The second step is to ensure that he
will start out fully aware of the company's potential for growth,
the potential on his territory to increase the company's market
share, the strength (and weakness if any) of his product mix, the
company's policies towards the customers and users, the buying
values of his product and the user benefits compared with competition, and the career opportunities open to him as a part of a
planned escalator of his development.

This can be effected only by a carefully planned course of training, preferably (in fact ideally) at headquarters, before taking up
field responsibilities, where continuous on-the-job training will be
carried out either by his sales manager or field sales manager. *This
concept of continuous training is absolutely mandatory for the
planned development of every salesman and field sales manager on
the payroll.* It is a meld of on-the-job training for the sales force
combined with regular visits to headquarters for specialised training
on new products or processes, and for developmental training in
customer handling and servicing and self-management of his job.
At a later date it may include supervisory training. In the case of
field sales managers, training in new ways of handling men, in new
methodologies, in career training for the next echelon of management ahead, are the norms of company education planning.

To cynics who still feel that training activities are expensive
gimmicks and unnecessary contributors to company cost centres,
we make the points that no company can afford to stand still.
Our competitors certainly will not, and who wants to play at
being a modern Canute?

The commercial race is not merely to the swift. It is won by the
thorough knowledge of what customers need and want, and by
first class modern salesmen who have been handpicked and
trained to see that their customers get what they need and want,
at prices they can afford to pay, when they want to buy the
requisite products and services. This is an era of advanced technologies in both the buying and selling fields. Salesmen cannot
hope to be successful unless they are trained completely and
continuously to meet every challenge of every purchasing situation and deal with it victoriously.

THE RECEPTION AT COMPANY HEADQUARTERS

Imagine the thoughts of the new boy as he mounts the steps of his new company's headquarters? What will happen? Will he make a good impression? Will he be able even to cope with the manuals of instruction and perhaps new technologies and their applications? Is he at the right door? Is he expected?

A salesman has major twin occupational fears. Fear of failure itself. And fear of not being accepted by his peer group, his customers, and his company management as the professional expert he believes himself to be. Puncture this precious, non-visible, vulnerable bubble of his self-respect and self-confidence and the blow will be traumatic and the recovery a protracted and painful process. He will not expect the red carpet treatment laid on for visiting V.I.Ps. But he will anticipate that the receptionist will be expecting him, know his name, and direct him to his new sales manager's office without delay or embarrassment. This is a vitally important psychological ploy. The newcomer will equate his reception with the importance the new company accords to him and to his company selling role. Here again the company corporate image is at stake, this time in heart and mind of a newcomer in whom the company has invested at least £5,000 in his first year of employment.

Yet it is simple enough for a sales manager to delegate his attractive personal secretary to be in the reception office at the expected time of arrival of the new boy, to greet him by name with a pleasant smile, to lay the firm foundation of goodwill between company and salesman, and to take him to the sales manager's office to meet his new boss. Here again there is a further potential danger to the vital initial impression that a newcomer should get. His new boss should have left himself absolutely clear of all calls to greet the new boy without delay, and to have a preliminary talk about the planned programme laid on for the new boy's delectation, then personally to take him along to the training centre or person allotted to the newcomer's first session of induction training, introduce him, and not leave until he seems to be happy and ready to settle down to his first morning's work.

These are indeed simple things. But they are vitally important to the birth and growth of an individual and his role. Neglect them as being beneath a sales manager's personal dignity, or as an unwarranted demand upon his valuable time, and the sales manager stands condemned as unsuitable to direct a manpower development programme. The newcomer then will have made a detrimental assessment of the sales manager. It will be current for a considerable time ahead and hard to eradicate. Exploit this opportunity, and a sales manager has an enthusiastic follower of his leadership. First impressions that a new salesman has of his new company are more important than even the first thoughts formed by a prospective customer. The new boy will project his own impressions of the company (willy nilly) to a host of prospective customers in a series of services rendered. They will be either enthusiastic or the reverse. The shrewd buyer will soon see the straws in the wind and act accordingly in his assessment of the firm.

ORGANISING A SALES TRAINING HEADQUARTERS' CENTRE

Ideally, a sales training centre should form an integral part of a company training centre. In this way it can get a proper income allocation with less argument at board level than if it stands in solitary isolation. This is because the company has been converted to a training-oriented policy for the whole of its employees instead of regarding sales training as a special case or even a luxury.

Essentials of a sales training centre at company headquarters include :

1 A progressively increasing budget for at least a decade ahead, otherwise it cannot align itself behind long term sales objectives. Also, it could otherwise become the plaything of management accountants looking for economy areas during a period of recession. It is at such a time that emphasis upon training needs to be increased; not reduced.

2 The marketing director and sales chief executive should be in charge of all planning and supervision of sales courses, as well as responsible for the course content and direction. In addition, they should be accountable for a continuous audit of return upon the investment, and the taking of remedial steps to correct deficiencies and to enhance values by the inclusion of new techniques and knowledge.

3 Clear, concise terms of reference for administration and operation should be obtained from the Board.

4 External moderation of course value and content should be regularly obtained to compare with internal assessment of values gained. This can be obtained by the regular attendance of a

senior sales executive at training seminars offered by various consultants and professional bodies.

5 There must be a regular link with the field sales managers who act continuously as the company on-the-job trainers of the sales force. They are in a position to appraise the working benefits shown by recent attendance by salesmen on headquarters courses, and to suggest those areas of training that would benefit most members of the sales force if sent for refresher courses at headquarters. Company training officers sometimes develop a myopic view of certain selling techniques whose effective deployment by salesmen are mandatory to selling success : they tend to leave them out of course material or to restrict the time devoted to them. Field sales managers have to act as prophets calling from the wilderness to be sure their men get what they really need. That is not always what company training officers think may be good for them.

A TYPICAL INDUCTION SALES TRAINING COURSE

We have a tripartite content to such induction courses: men, methods and management. Methods are of course vitally important in the contribution that they can make to selling efficiency. Managerial direction and control are equally vital to overseeing the effective work of the sales force. But in the last analysis it is the company newcomers we are concerned with as men, each with unique personality, temperament, and contribution to make, if only he is trained aright. To achieve this human goal we must beware of too much standardisation and uniformity in the selling operation. It can produce well educated and nicely spoken morons speaking a common company line, robot like efficiency, but lack selling effectiveness. How can we combine a tested method of training with a regard for the optimising of each individual's special skills, both human and commercial?

Men have specific personal ideas about the satisfactions they want from their jobs and the rewards they seek from their career development. They want status, prestige, esteem, rewards, promotion, and the self-realisation of having reached the pinnacle of their potential performance both as professional salesmen and as individuals. The company wants a proper return from its investment in manpower, and planned optimum growth through training and motivation. The induction training course has to try to get off on the right foot so that both salesmen and company get

what they desire. Each man if he is to realise these dual and interdependent specifications must learn how to accomplish three
separate things simultaneously. They are to know, to do, and
to be precisely what the company requires to carry out its specific
duties and responsibilities. Yet he has to realise his personal
ambitions and achievements in that process. Too few company
training managers seem as yet to be giving this duality of aim
the attention that it deserves.

The Basics of Initial Training

Where the new boy has had little previous selling experience,
then his initial training will be a fairly long proceeding in selling
techniques, buying behaviour and human communications and behaviour, quite apart from training in the product, company policies,
etc.

An experienced salesman will still need to be appraised in his
selling and promotional skills. As well as introduced to the company's policies, products, propositions, services, etc.

It is obvious that an induction course, whether held for two or
more men, will have a mixed content. There must be the expa-
tiation upon company policies and product knowledge, knowledge
of markets, trades in which the sales force operates, and competitive strengths, activities, and customer acceptability where there is
common ground for teaching and learning. There are usually however, large gulfs of understanding, competence, and required
levels of know-how between salesmen. These will accord with
their previous experience and the particular job specifications
which they have been hired to carry out. This calls for a great
deal of differential study, course material, and individual tutoring
by the trainer.

The trainer will therefore in most cases be well advised to take
the following steps :
1 Get to know each new boy in some depth, in particular his
attitudes and aptitudes, his skills and areas of weakness. He can
then tailor each recruit's learning course to his actual mental,
temperamental, and professional needs and levels. Each man should
be given a blank sales manual. He will build it up as the course
proceeds with hand-outs and his own notes.

The individual courses must be tailored to the speed of learning
which newcomers usually exhibit, and to the job specifications which
they are trained to fill. The courses will vary very much in

content, apart from the basics concerned with selling psychology and buying behaviour, and the particular needs for specialised communication skills, and presentation and demonstration arts.

For example, a newcomer to the food trades would have to specialise upon the patterns of wholesale and retail selling including supermarketing, self-service, and merchandising. In addition, he would need to learn the accountancy of speed of stockturn and the square footage of retail display space.

On the other hand, a newcomer to industrial selling would need to learn about the processing patterns he would meet among his customers; the arts of quotation, surveys, and contracts; the skills of economical ordering, quantity buying and value analysis techniques.

Each would need also to know the strength and weakness of competitive effort and potential threat, and their acceptability to his customers.

2 Arising out of the foregoing the newcomer must acquire a background of the nature of markets, industries and trades which together comprise the medium in which he will have to work and service successfully. Only in this way will he be able to see the true potential for all his products whether for use or consumption, and be able to create purchasing demand as well as to optimise upon previously unforeseen opportunities.

Similarly, the newcomer must also acquire a potted history of the relationships between the company and the customers whom he will be called upon to develop; to make broad plans before he leaves the H.Q. training school.

3 The newcomer must be given a full history of his new company, its policies and plans for forward development in which the newcomer will be expected to play an active role.

4 In this context product mix policies and pricing policies are extremely important. The newcomer must understand from the outset its policies on planned obsolescence, life cycles, break-even points, cash flows, credit, and promotion.

5 The newcomer must understand the importance of regular two-way communication between himself and the company, the nature and frequency of reporting and its speed and accuracy of relayed content, and his information seeking and information projecting roles.

6 The newcomer must be given a thorough product indoctrination. He must understand the features and the buying and using benefits of his own products and services, both in their absolute sense and in comparison with those of competitors. He must be given a

true indication of the innovation and diversification likely to be met with in the customers' operations with which he will have to cope. Thus he will create a selling policy to overcome competitive threats, market inertias, and be able to optimise upon the opportunities as they arise. In this way he can create his own short and longer term selling plans.

7 The newcomer must understand the techniques of his own company's production processes as they can affect the selling and buying roles. He must also see the selling role as it is affected by his customers' investment appraisal of buying benefits. He must understand his own relationship with each company department. He should be introduced to all those executives in all departments with whom he may have to correspond or to whom he may have to furnish reports via the sales office.

This shows the absolute need for senior executives of most company functions to participate in sales training and to forge a personal link with each newcomer. Thus both salesman and company departmental executive can understand the nature and importance of each other's roles.

8 The newcomer must receive a thorough grooming from his own sales office in the two-way communication vital to a day-to-day understanding of what each is required to do fully to support the other: selling methodologies, credit operation, order processing, report making, expense account operation, car care, ordering of stationery and samples for show and demonstration, etc. In addition he must obtain a clear understanding of correspondence procedures between himself and sales office and customers, and how the sales office deals directly with customers.

9 The newcomer must be given a clear picture of his direct relationships with the sales promotion department and publicity as furnished by the advertising department.

10 Each company has its own sales organisational picture, its customs, and its line and staff officers. Here the newcomer has to fit in painlessly, productively and happily. This will not just happen. It will have to be created during the induction training period. The selling style and methods, the role of the field sales manager as an elder brother and that of the sales manager as an elder statesman must be understood and respected.

A newcomer without selling experience will have to spend a considerable time within the H.Q. course learning his new craft. An experienced salesman from outside the company will need to be unobtrusively tested for style, knowledge and skills. Both a remedial and development course are usually needed for the expert from outside.

Caveat

The sales manager should at the selection interview have filled in a basic chart giving his preliminary yet considered appreciation of each successful candidate under qualitative headings. The manager of the sales training school must have copies of these so that he can report further to the sales manager on developmental

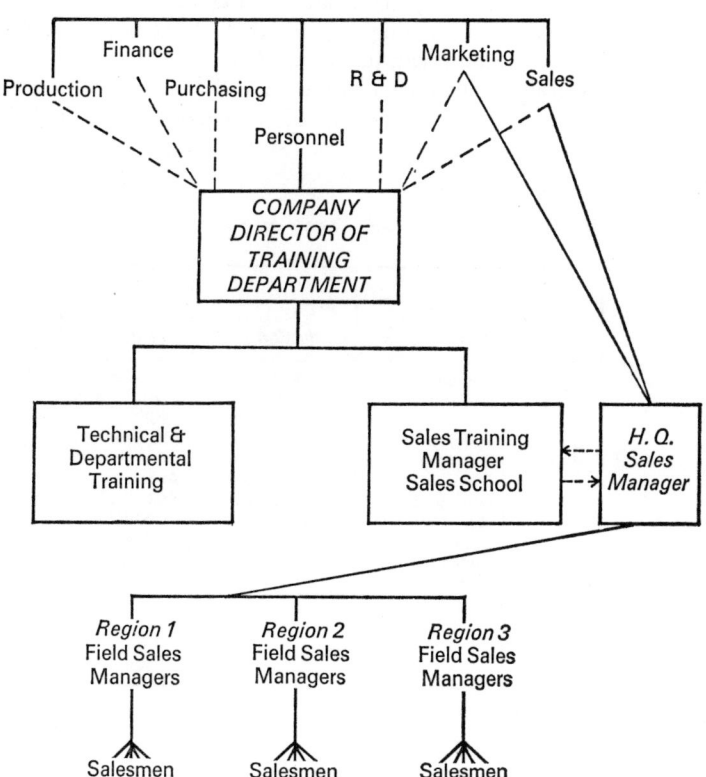

Diagram 7   Typical company HQ training organisation chart

responses. Together these two documents should create a basis for the performance specification criteria for regular reporting by the field sales manager.

There should be absolute continuity of policy, plan and purpose between each section of training as well as a smooth two-way information flow, graded and fashioned to the exact measurement of each man at the time it is given. Thus he can use it without delay in an operational activity in his daily round to the benefit of himself, his company and his customers.

As with all attempts to formulate a general rule there are exceptions. For instance there will always be information in circulation that is given as background knowledge against which to deploy action in the future or in unforeseen circumstances. In the main, training that cannot be tested by each recipient and proved viable in action will rarely have any lasting or beneficial result. This is why on-the-job training is so vital. It must really work. It must be so practical that it can justify itself on the spot.

Field sales training will be dealt with fully in a later chapter. Meanwhile the three illustrations of a headquarters' training

Diagram 8   Headquarters induction sales trainee programme

DATE	Function	Board	Production	Finance	Purchasing

NAME
 	
EXPERIENCE
 	
JOB
 	
TERRITORY
 	
FIELD SALES
MANAGER
	S
	U
	B
	J
	E
	C
	T
		Company
		  History
		Strategies
		Policies
		Communication
		Plans
		Information
		  Systems
		Control
		Audits
		Growth
			Processing
			  Methods
			Budget/Forecast
			  Link with Sales
			Quality Control
			Special Orders
			Stock Piling
			Product and
			Technical Manuals
				Budgets
				Credit Control
				Costing
				Management
				  Accounting
				Accounts
				Statistical
				  Control
				Cash Flows
					Budgets
					Forecasts
					  Link with Sale
					Buying Metho
					Value Analysis
					Economic
					  Order Quanti
					Reserve Stock

Dates of talks					
Speakers					
Times					

organisational structure offer a logical continuum of induction training of the newcomer to a business.

Diagram 7 is a typical company organisation chart showing how the board through its managing director is in charge of all training activities. He must direct training and validate its cost benefits to the board at intervals. There is a company training department under a director of training. Each department head channels his requirements through the director of training, who may be responsible for day-to-day conduct to the personnel director under the managing director. The director of training offers a technical and professional training course for all departmental personnel, other than the members of the sales department who are trained in a sales training school (subsidiary to the company training department). This will be under the day-to-day control of a sales training manager who answers in turn to the director of training. However there is a direct route by which the sales director can approach the sales training manager via the headquarters sales manager, who has a lateral and direct connection with the sales training school. This is wise because once the head-

| rsonnel | Research and Development | Marketing | SALES | | |
			Salesmanship	Sales Methods	Control
elfare	Short Term	Research	Psychology	Manuals	Targets
affing	Long Term	Desk & Field	Communication	Planning	Quotas
olicies	Product Testing	Product Mix	Talking	Presentation	Budgets
ucation	Material Testing	Policies	Questioning	Demonstration	Differential
motion	Innovation	Product Life Cycle	Listening	Overcoming	Call
reer Goals	Technologies	Pricing Policies	Persuading	Objections	Frequency
nsions	Competitor	New Product Policies	Satisfying	Using Value	Call Cycles
kness	Assessment	Systems Marketing	Goodwill	Analysis	Routeing
	Techniques	Publicity	Business Creating	Clinching Orders	Ratios
	Design	P.R. Press Advertising	Business Building	Promoting	Cost Analysis
			Reporting	Merchandising	Time &
				Research	Motion
					Study
					Audits

10-DAY EXAMPLE INDUCTION COURSE — INTENSIVE BASIS

TIME	DAY 1	DAY 2	DAY 3	DAY 4	DAY 5
0900	Welcome by Sales Director or Managing Director	Market & Sales Forecasting. Break Even Point Budget Creation by HQ Sales Manager	Sales Dept. Organisation and Working Procedures by Sales Office Manager	Selling as a Planned Career by Personnel Manager	Making the Presentation and Product Proposition by Sales Training Manager
0920	Vital Role of Sales by HQ Sales Manager				
1020	COFFEE	COFFEE	COFFEE	COFFEE	COFFEE
1030	Start to compile Sales Manual. Company History – Policies – Plans by Managing Director	Product Mix Policy New Product Strategy by Sales Director	Order Processing and Liaison with Production, Transport and Stores by Sales Office Manager	The Psychology of Persuasion and the Techniques of Communication in Personal Selling by Sales Trng. Manager	Dealing with Buying objections of every kind – true and false by Sales Training Manager
1130	BREAK	BREAK	BREAK	BREAK	BREAK
1140	Company Organisation & Communications by HQ Sales Manager	Pricing Policies – Product Life Cycles by HQ Sales Manager	Correspondence Handling Enquiries Handling Quotation Procedures by Sales Office Manager	Preparing to Sell by Sales Training Manager	
1245	LUNCH	LUNCH	LUNCH	LUNCH	LUNCH
1400	Company Markets – Market Shares – Plans for Growth by Sales Director	Distribution Channels and Sales Policy by HQ Sales Manager	Inspection of 'Key' Products. Technical Detailing by Production Director	Anatomy of a Planned Product Presentation Getting in to see Buyers Cold Canvass Calling	Role Playing by Course Members
1515	TEA	TEA	TEA	TEA	TEA
1530	Market Research by Marketing Research Manager	Planning a Territory Routeing – call cycles – differential call frequency. Time Management by Sales Training Manager	Features – Buying & User benefits by HQ Sales Mngr. Appraisal of Key competitive products comparative value analyses by HQ Sales Mngr.	Breaking the conversational ice by HQ Sales Manager	And a Regional Field Sales Manager
1700	BREAK FILM on Two-Way Communication e.g. More than Words	BREAK	BREAK	BREAK	BREAK
1715		FILM	DINNER	DINNER	DINNER
1800	BREAK	BREAK			
1900	DINNER	DINNER			
2030	Discussion on Communications Film seen at 1715 by HQ Sales Manager and Sales Training Manager	Discussion – What the Purchasing Dept. thinks a Salesman should know, do and be, by Purchasing Director and Sales Training Manager	Discussion on Planning Salesman's strategies and tactics on selling Product mix to various market segments by Sales Training Manager and a Regional Sales Field Manager	Role Playing to enact – Getting in and down to business with Buyers by Sales Training Manager and Course Members	Film – Dealing with Objections Discussion on how to anticipate buying objections and *deal with them* in the presentation by Sales Training Manager
2200					

10-DAY EXAMPLE INDUCTION COURSE — INTENSIVE BASIS (Continued)

TIME	DAY 6	DAY 7	DAY 8	DAY 9	DAY 10
0900	Clinching Orders – a positive process by Sales Training Manager	Reporting and Grading Information by Sales Training Manager	Creating Performance Standards by HQ Sales Manager	Study of History of Salesman's Territory with Sales Office Personnel (Individually)	Forum of Departmental Managers answers Course Members question
1020 1030	COFFEE Film: Getting the decision	COFFEE Dealing with customer suggestions, complaints and needs for special information services by Sales Office Manager	COFFEE Devising Quotas and Budgets for each territory	COFFEE Morning in Sales Office with Section Clerks illustrating procedures as above	COFFEE Each Course Member has Private Talks with Sales Director and HQ Sales Manager
1130	BREAK Role Playing in Order Clinching techniques	BREAK	BREAK Control by Sales Ratio by HQ Sales Manager		
1245 1400	LUNCH Creating Buyer Satisfactions with Order Placing by Personnel Director	LUNCH Creating a first class recording system by Sales Office Manager	LUNCH Performance Appraisal by Ratio and Qualitative Growth in skills by HQ Sales Manager	LUNCH Review Period of notes taken by Sales Training Manager	LUNCH COURSE DISPERSES Sales Training Manager makes up his detailed Reports on each Course Member for rendering to HQ Sales Manager
1515	TEA	TEA The Uses of Publicity by Salesmen	TEA – in Board Room with Managing Director	TEA	These will be compared with Interviewers' Selection Reports and Field Sales Managers are advised of revised situation for guidance.
1530	Film – Controlling the Interview		Tour of Company Departments and introduction to Departmental Heads by Sales Director	Issues of Sales Kit, Samples, Literature to each Course Member	
1700 1715	BREAK Discussion on creating points of re-entry for subsequent calls by HQ Sales Manager BREAK	BREAK PR Advertising Sales Promotion Merchandising	BREAK	BREAK	
1800	DINNER	BREAK	BREAK	BREAK	
1900	DINNER	DINNER	DINNER	DINNER —with Sales Director, HQ Sales Manager, Sales and Office Manager	
2030	Talk and Discussion Self-Study for a Career by Personnel Director	Discussion on Salesman's Role as Ambassador, Advisor, Merchant of ideas and benefits by HQ Sales Manager and Sales Training Manager	Talk on Planning Techniques and Decision Making Process by Personnel Director	Informal Question and Answer session with Senior Sales Staff	
2200					

quarters sales training manager has conducted a course of training with salesmen, they go out into the field under the line and staff control of field sales managers working directly under the aegis of the headquarters sales manager. It is the field sales manager who administers on-the-job training.

Diagram 8 shows a typical headquarters induction sales training school programme. It is formulated in this fashion to show the various topics which the newcomer to the sales force may have to consider either superficially or in depth. This scheme allows for the course members to be addressed by the board members and senior managers of a company on their own specialised activities and areas of responsibility. This not only impresses the newcomers with the importance of the selling role; it also gives each member of company top management the regular opportunity of meeting each newcomer to the sales staff, and of keeping himself abreast of sales department needs and duties in pursuing and attaining overall company aims, return upon investment and growth in capital value and market share.

Pages 100–101 extend diagram 8 into the detailed activity of a typical intensive ten-day induction sales course.

Here the newcomer is introduced to the policies, plans, and personnel of his new firm, from board level down to the individual departmental members, who will work with him once he takes up his duties in the selling field. This course helps the newcomer and company personnel to exchange ideas, and meet on an informal basis, professionally during the training sessions and socially during meals and discussion periods. It helps the newcomer to appraise both his new company and his new colleagues as well as his career opportunities. It helps him to feel that he belongs to a company team with corporate aims whose work and rewards he can admire and share. Each item in the course has been proved by actual field work to be both essential and practicable in a soundly based induction process, yet it can be varied to an infinite degree to meet the demands of each company organisation.

For instance, a food manufacturing company would be less interested in their sales personnel having a technical knowledge of manufacture and much more concerned that they were really red-hot merchandisers. A manufacturer of sophisticated machine tools would be much more interested in their salesmen's technical expertise, their knowledge of industrial processing, etc. A manufacturer of equipment sold by speciality means would be more concerned with the salesmen's capacity to open buying doors by cold canvass, to be able to demonstrate expertly, to have an unrivalled knowledge of cost/benefit argument plus investment benefits, and the ability to clinch orders on the initial sales call.

This scheme can be made as flexible as required in content, time given to each subject, and total time coverage of the course itself. Again, the research and development department would be much more interested in the training of salespeople who are graduates selling sophisticated systems where individual design is of great importance to both buyer and seller. Similarly, salesmen selling products which need the recommendation of, say, architects or consulting engineers would preferably be trained in part by such professional folk to meet the particular craft skills and know-how to exploit their product sales. Manufacturers of ethical pharmaceutical products using medical detailers to call upon the medical profession would obviously give specialised training in the knowledge of the disease syndromes their drugs would ease or for which they are a specific cure. They would also train men in the conduct and behaviour suitable to laymen handling briefs direct to qualified and seasoned members of a proud profession.

Lastly we come to the equipment for a modern training room. It can be costly and sophisticated for a large and well-heeled company, or simple and inexpensive for a small firm. It must be sufficiently large to accommodate in comfort the usual number of course members. Speakers need to be comfortably housed so that normal lecturing and demonstration equipment can be deployed without crowding anyone. And it should be easy for members to watch and to participate. Light, warmth and adequate ventilation are absolute musts. Comfortable seats and desks for easy note taking or making sketches are equally imperative. Comfortable and adjacent rooms are necessary in which the members can take tea, coffee, and meals without distraction and upheaval. This can double as group discussion accommodation. Film equipment, audio-visual equipment, video-tape, closed television equipment—all have their appropriate roles to play, according to the money available and the number and types of technical staff to be trained. For example, it is vital to have proper training rooms for even a handful of newcomers and for men on refresher courses. Their luxury depends upon company policy and the cash allocated to the training function.

Conclusion

We should be clear about our semantic terms. Education is held to be that lifelong system of helping a man to realise his full potential by revealing his true capacity to him by help in stretching his capacity to the full continuously and progressively. It certainly is not pumping-in information. It implies two-way communication and interpretation of ideas. Training is usually held to be intermittent instruction in the handling of equipment, methods of doing jobs of work and controlling and validating their efficiency.

Oxbridge which believes education to be associated with the conscious pursuit of excellence contains more esoteric wisdom than the traditional educationist might readily acknowledge. Teachers, at least by definition, try to teach, while educationists are now more concerned with the problems of learning. Of what use is teaching if the pupils will not, cannot, or do not learn?

Theories about learning are ten a penny. Some modernists have ideas that children should do only what they want to do, and not be disciplined. How in the future they will, by the mercy of Providence, find a way to discipline themselves, is a very nice question. Yet, learning is based upon the keen desire of an individual to acquire knowledge that he can use and by personal discipline become expert in its applications to his benefit and satisfactions.

This is the company training problem. To encourage people who want to learn when they feel this psychological urge to do so, and to go on doing so, so that they can acquire the know-how, skills, rewards that they crave. We do not as yet really know enough about the urge to learn. Yet if we study the selling élite, we find a deliberate desire to excel in their chosen profession, and always to be in a winning vein. In simple terms it would appear that we must find ways of finding men who not merely can achieve, but are determined to win their way to the top, and by sheer willpower and devotion to their jobs keep at the top. We can almost hear the slogan muttered beneath their breath in any difficult situation: we can, we must, we will succeed!

If we could bring the performance yields of the majority of our sales forces to within hailing distance of those of our élite (10% of our whole) the selling millenium for many sales managers would be just around the corner for the first time in modern marketing history. This is the training aim. It will be a long haul. But in face of the competition from the Common Market this is what we *must* set out to achieve. Failure to do so could usher in troublous times for delinquent companies and their salesmen!

PART TWO

The Company Headquarters' Role in the Making of a Modern Salesman

CHAPTER FOUR

The Salesman's Relationship with the Marketing Function

The Salesman and His Company's Public Relations Operations

Company Public Relations activities are of great importance to the sales force. They are primarily concerned with the deliberate creation of a favourable public corporate image for the company and all its operations. In a secondary sense, they are concerned with the company's continuous need to get its messages across to the public at large. In this sense also public relations is an integral part of a company's communications mix.

What is the public? And what is an image? Simple enough questions with complex answers. There are in fact many different publics to influence and many images to be projected.

A Favourable Company Corporate Image

An image in broad terms is a picture that each member of the public sees on the telescreen of his individual mind when the company's name is mentioned. It is a picture that is conjured up by the individual recollection or impression. It shows precisely how the company, its products, its services, its staff, registered— as being worthwhile, admirable, disreputable, or poor—on the watching or listening mind. If the impression was favourable it is likely to remain so unless or until something happens to change the individual's attitude to the company.

This is the basic reaction that the public relations function seeks to create in the public mind—an attitude of benevolence, of admiration, towards the company and all its works. For if the reaction is unfavourable, it will tend to remain so until or unless the company public relations activities can change the attitude to a more favourable one.

Clearly, if the image is left to fate and to time to establish it may take ages for a good reputation to emerge and be publicly recognised and accepted. However, this hard-won prestige can be destroyed overnight by a mere breath of scandal or a rumour of failure.

In a competitive economy, companies have to take short cuts to fame. This is the main task of the public relations job. It has to create and stimulate artificially a current continuing interest in a company, its products and its aims. To do this it harnesses every artifice, device, skill and art of the publicity media to give power to its elbow and to win speedy recognition for its quite expensive efforts. Public relations deliberately create the basic backbone of a company's public reputation for its excellence and its standing.

The Institute of Public Relations defines its practice in the following terms : Public Relations Practice is the deliberate, planned and sustained effort to establish and maintain understanding between an organisation and its public.

This brings us to a consideration of the nature of 'public'. This term public conjures up a complex conglomeration of people whose actual make-up is as variable as its membership and whose reactions to stimuli are unpredictable. The word 'public' is a nice cosy word to use. It is a convenient generic term to refer glibly to the world at large, as though the world and his wife were identifiable as individual persons. A man is at one and the same moment a member of a family, a member of differing groups, both trade or professional, and social ones also. Thus a public relations man must remember precisely which man he is cozening when he utters a public relations spiel. A public relations man, although sometimes he may not recognise the fact, is a salesman of ideas and benefits. He must project the ideas he wants to put over with charm, accuracy and in-built benefit if he wants to make the impression he desires on a particular public. Words, angles and slants are ground-bait in a public relations operation. Where does the salesman impinge on public relations?

Let us take a sales force example. A salesman represents a company that supplies the building and construction industries.

Its public relations manager attends any number of public and trade dinners where the company's customers consort, and tries to get invitations to speak, so that he may project a favourable company image. The sales manager carefully places advertising for company products in all the relevant technical and trade journals that customers read. The salesman calls upon each builder's merchant to ensure that there are adequate stocks of his products to satisfy builders' requirements. The salesman knows that quite apart from the builders' merchants whom he has to jolly along in his favour there are other men in the wings who do not place orders but specifically influence a large number of orders which will be placed with his company. Such people are architects, designers, consulting engineers, etc. These are the valued advisers of the clients who place their instructions via builders and constructional engineers, which ultimately find their way to the salesman's order book. The salesman will have to make diplomatic calls upon such advisers and advisory bodies. He must make sure that they are aware of his full product mix, and his capacity and willingness to provide excellent follow-up service to the advisers' clients. At the same time, his public relations man should be cozening these separate publics of the professions—the advisory bodies, the companies and the householders who are the source of the ultimate orders. Although some of the purist pundits in the public relations world see themselves as a race apart, the salesman has a definitive role to play in public relations. This is his company's public relations projection in the selling field in contact with buyers and users. If he sets out to do so he can achieve prodigies of valour in the creation of favourable company images that the public relations department will never in a month of Sundays be able to approach. He can cement the costly impressions created by public relations people by the use of personal influence on the spot, at the psychological moment that is most opportune for the purpose.

THE SALESMAN AND IMAGE PROJECTION

A salesman needs to use a special technique in creating and projecting the right images in his contactual field work. It will help him to know precisely how people in general see images. For example:

1 People prize safety and stability above all else, even though they may not be willing to admit the fact. Hence the shock of

the Rolls Royce RB 211 débacle and the consequent company failure.

2 People appreciate and like to see and to feel dynamism in marketing ideas and activity. They like to feel that a company is forward-looking in its thinking and dynamic in its support of the customer and user of its products and services.

3 People like to deal with successful companies which market successful products. It implies product excellence and business expertise. The publics on the whole do not want or like to be associated either with second-raters or failures. They appreciate the leadership of the successful. They achieve a measure of psychological glory reflected back from such companies to the users.

4 People like friendly and co-operative attitudes to be extended to them by companies. It not merely gives them pleasure in the daily round. It adds a spice of being a member of a family or group—a company and its faithful users image.

5 People value integrity in their suppliers. Guarantees that mean what they say and say what they mean with no restrictive small print get-out-of-trouble saving clauses.

This may seem mere commonsense to the experienced salesman. But good relationships in human affairs are built on commonsense—the little courtesies, the gestures of kindly feelings. However there is a world of difference between knowing what should be done and how to do it simply and well. There are obviously skilled techniques to be used in the putting over of public relations spiels by salesmen, and especially so in image creation.

Here is a short list of vital operational techniques:

1 Like all good selling, a capacity to 'inform' must be combined with a delivery that is never brash, boring, noisy, pedantic, nor condescending.

2 The capacity to 'interpret' ideas and to get them accepted is vital; but in the role of ambassador rather than pontiff, with authority rather than dictation.

3 Again like all good selling, a capacity for creating friendly relationships is imperative. In a friendly atmosphere opposition can be pleasantly neutralised. Cynics can be led to discern more favourable views of a topic, a plan, an intention, a product, a service, a proposition involving co-operation. It has to be done without pleading and without cajolery.

4 There should be an implicit, latent, spot of 'genius' in a capacity to paint a picture or to present a case; to project ideas; to

put over propositions. Genius in this context being merely an empathetic assessment of what a salesman must do to be able to persuade his listeners to see the merits of his viewpoint; and the benefits to be gained by following it.

Epilogue

We hear so much about public relations as an external activity. It can thus be easy for a sales manager to overlook the fact that internal public relations techniques practised with his own sales staff and with other company departments can pay very handsome dividends. Relationships between sales offices and sales forces in the field often leave much to be desired. They are not so supportive as they should be, and in the process customers lose the supportive services to which they are entitled.

The sales force is the public of the sales office, and the customer is the public of the sales force. This fact needs to be faced more realistically in many companies. Similarly, each company department is the public of the sales department. And they need the appropriate informative and supportive services that any public needs of a public relations operation. Therefore every sales manager and each salesman must get the most out of public relations operations.

The Salesman and His Relationship with Company Advertising Activities

Advertising is a persuasive communication aimed by a supplier (a seller) at potential buyers to make them aware of any special features, implied benefits and advantages implicit in the purchase. It is based upon a pious hope that potential buyers will indeed remember the persuasive message sufficiently to trigger-off buying action at any early date. Advertising is a non-personal, non-contactual, selling message contained in a mass communication vehicle. It sells ideas about purchase into a potential market. Advertising can be described as salesmanship in print so far as the press is concerned or persuasion via sight, sound and motion in a television context.

A sales director, on the other hand, would see advertising as a device by which his company publics are made aware of the attractiveness and benefits of buying specific items of his product mix at a given time, at given prices. Advertising is the primary publicity weapon in the sales managerial armoury. Its shotgun technique of spraying information about the product far and wide paves the way for the sales manager to follow up the initial impact or penetration with the rifle techniques of sales promotion and merchandising in retail outlets. Advertising is a selling out of products from the factory to the stockholder and into his inventories. Sales promotion expressed in merchandising is a selling out of the products from the retail store shelves and fixtures into the shopping baskets and the homes of the public at large. Where a manufacturer sells direct to users, advertising makes the user aware that a product is available. Sales promotion in the shape of direct mail shots or a salesman's literature clinches the deal.

Advertising is a process. It uses communication, psychology, buying behaviour, persuasion, information, media, salesmanship to get its messages over, so that people are motivated to purchase a particular product. Advertising expenditure in this country is estimated to exceed £500 million per annum. In the U.S.A. figures in excess of 15 billion dollars are bandied around. In one year General Motors were reported to have spent 200 million dollars, whilst Sears Roebuck (mail order operators) were reputed to have spent 125 million dollars.

In the light of such expenditure we must see advertising as a mass persuasion device created to shift mass production to mass markets in the minimum time at considerable cost. Pundits are often moved to distinguish between initial advertising and reminder advertising, the first to get a brand established, the second to keep a brand going, particularly towards the end of a product life cycle. In effect, the principle is the same: to get an optimum response in purchases, however much the copy and its slant may vary.

The salesman whether industrial or commercial is only too well aware of how his efforts to get a new product known to potential buying outlets can be quickened and consummated in orders by punchy advertising with dynamic cutting edge. Here again there is no difference in principle between initial and reminder advertising. Initial advertising is aimed to get optimum distribution coverage in the quickest time at least sales force support cost, whilst reminder advertising seeks to ensure that the current distribution coverage is maintained.

The public and the direct user-buyer are not easy pushovers. They look for buying benefits. But they are rarely willing to buy products which conflict with their inner beliefs or pre-conceived standards, both personal and professional. In fact there is a similar pattern between the advertising persuasion process and that used by salesmen to present a selling presentation, in direct pursuit of the order. It follows a wellworn path of :

Impact of credibility, acceptability, relevance, timeliness

Awareness of product desirability

Comprehension of buying benefits accruing from purchasing decision

Conviction that purchase is justified, even imperative

Action to put buying decision into order form, there and then.

A Company Advertising Function's Typical Structure

In many small companies the advertising function is but an adjunct of the sales managerial responsibilities. In large companies it is usually the purview of the marketing director. What an advertising function invariably needs irrespective of its size (and often does not get), is a specialist in charge, even though he may have to report to the marketing director or sales manager.

This is the day of the competitive specialist in the publicity field. Company marketing executives are rarely so specialised in publicity that they can meet the company's advertising agency specialists on terms of professional parity and esteem. Yet this is vitally necessary if the company is to get the best out of the agency.

Advertising is not for enthusiastic amateurs, however gifted. It is both a significant social and economic factor in the business equation. Obviously the advertising policy and copy must not be anti-social. Equally obviously the advertising policy and copy must offer pronounced financial and economic benefits, or there would be no point in purchasers indulging buying whims. Efficient advertising can and does help to create an optimum production and sales volume for a product mix. It can materially help a company to expand its market share in those segments where it is advisable. It can play a role in the expansion of company profitability and capital growth. In short, it has a demonstrable economic value. It can build up the total market value of a company as a going concern. Whilst doing so, the passive value of advertising is not always realised. This is a spin-off. It is its denial of current business and capital growth to competitors it hits in the marketplace. It also has a public relations value of promoting a company image of successful achievement and leadership in the market economy.

People do not (if they ever did) automatically cut a path through the woods to the maker of an outstandingly good product. Products need to be exposed to the vulgar and common gaze in the home, shop and industrial plant if they are to be given proper consideration and then bought for their outstanding value analyses. Advertising is the easiest weapon of publicity open to every manufacturer to bring about public buying changes.

We can define advertising in simple terms such as the following:

Advertising is a remunerated (paid for) method of publicity communication that seeks to project, present and promote ideas, products, services by and through an identified source called a sponsor.

Advertising informs people, and makes them aware of the use of mass media as a means of projection of existing opportunities for them to buy. Advertising *SELLS*. It persuades people to buy, to consume, to use the recommended commercial, industrial and technical products and services rather than others (by implication).

Advertising not only creates demand, it creates changes in demand. And this is its principal purpose.

THE ADVERTISING PROCESS

1 Advertising is used mainly to persuade populations and people to change their buying habits in favour of the product or service being specifically advertised. We try to switch non-users to the brand advertised. In a secondary role we try to keep users loyal to the brand and to resist the temptation to switch to other advertised brands.

2 Advertising uses communication with an inbuilt psychological and sociological flavour aimed to influence readers' buying behaviour in favour of a switch to the advertised brand. It does so by a cycle of stimuli, response, motivation, and reward. Recipients of the message need to be stimulated to gain the reward of a greater enjoyment or other benefit by switching to the brand advertised.

3 Advertisers realise from bitter experience that creating buying change in favour of a new brand takes time, patience, the use of the right stimuli and cash. They recognise a syndrome such as the following:

E

(a) *An Awareness Creating Stage*

(b) *A Familiarity Creating Stage* the looker recognises the 'ad' from stage (a).

(c) *A Breakthrough Stage* the buying benefits are bull-dozed in the copy.

(d) *A Conviction Creating Stage* lookers become convinced of rightness of selling copy.

(e) *Buying-Action Provoking Stage* lookers feels that they had better get stuck in and begin to get the buying benefits right now.

ADVERTISING APPROPRIATION POLICY

Apart from pure hunch tactics still carried out in a number of company board rooms, the majority of companies now try to work according to a rational policy. This is to allocate cash to advertising media, that seem to be the best for the company's purpose and standing.

For example:

1 An arbitrary figure is chosen that seems to meet the consensus of board opinion.

2 An arbitrary percentage cost figure related to previous year's sales is chosen.

3 An arbitrary figure of percentage cost related to current sales forecast is chosen.

4 The task method is selected.

5 The advertising/profit residuum is opted for.

6 Method No. 3. is extended and applied to each product in the mix. But flexibility is given to the marketing director to switch allocations to meet situation changes.

Methods 1 and 2 have little appeal to efficiency-oriented sales executives. They savour of the future being hopelessly shackled to the past. They are defensively erected structures. They have no built-in flexibility to optimise upon unforeseen opportunity or to combat unexpected competitive threats.

Method 3 is better. It is at least harnessed to a current sales and profit forecast. It however lacks flexibility, and therefore has similar failings to the first two methods in being unable to exploit opportunity or to combat an unexpected threat.

Method 4, the so-called task method, is not easy to work.

Its task is to aim to fix a specific arbitrary appropriation that is deemed to be the minimum necessary to achieve a predetermined forecasted sales volume. Within strict limits say of a new product launch, it indeed has merits mainly because the initial time period will be short and the board will be forced to become flexible where conditions dictate if the launch period takes longer than forecast. Its real Achilles heel lies in a virtual impossibility to assess probability factors in a market with any true degree of accuracy for other than a short time period. This is especially so in times of rapid market change and competitive ferocity. In fact, unforeseen speed of expansion can pose as many headaches as unforeseen speed of market regression.

Method 5 is used by a considerable number of British companies. It is based upon an effective and highly detailed accounting system. This can produce quickly and regularly exact figures of the net profit that is accruing to each product in the mix. Thus (the theory goes) it is easy to switch allocations rapidly from one horse to another because, one horse is carrying more profit than forecast whilst another is lagging behind. This is a deliberate milking technique. Heavy milk-yield producers are made to subsidise those whose lactatory processes are temporarily deficient. The technique does need considerable mental, even psychic legerdemain in the process of robbing Peter to pay Paul, or the rich to support the poor—a kind of Robin Hood technique applied to advertising. The idea may be a good one, when used in small doses, for short periods, under the control of an astute sales director. In general however subsidies of this kind do not seem to the author to tally with good housekeeping practice whether in the home or in a company.

Method 6 does attempt to get the best of all possible worlds in its capacity for flexibility. The author recommends extending its methodology. This would be to link the appropriation to each product to its life cycle position as well as to its forecasted sales volume. In this way it is possible to create both a long term and a short term approach to advertising exploitation. In short, we can create a hierarchy of planning priorities. We can make a decision whether to give preferential support to product 'A' rather than to product 'B'. This is a logical and sophisticated approach to allocating advertising expenditure precisely where it will do the most good, according to the state of the game. And re-allocating it, when and where desirable to meet the fluctuating competitive market scene. It is essentially profit-oriented via the

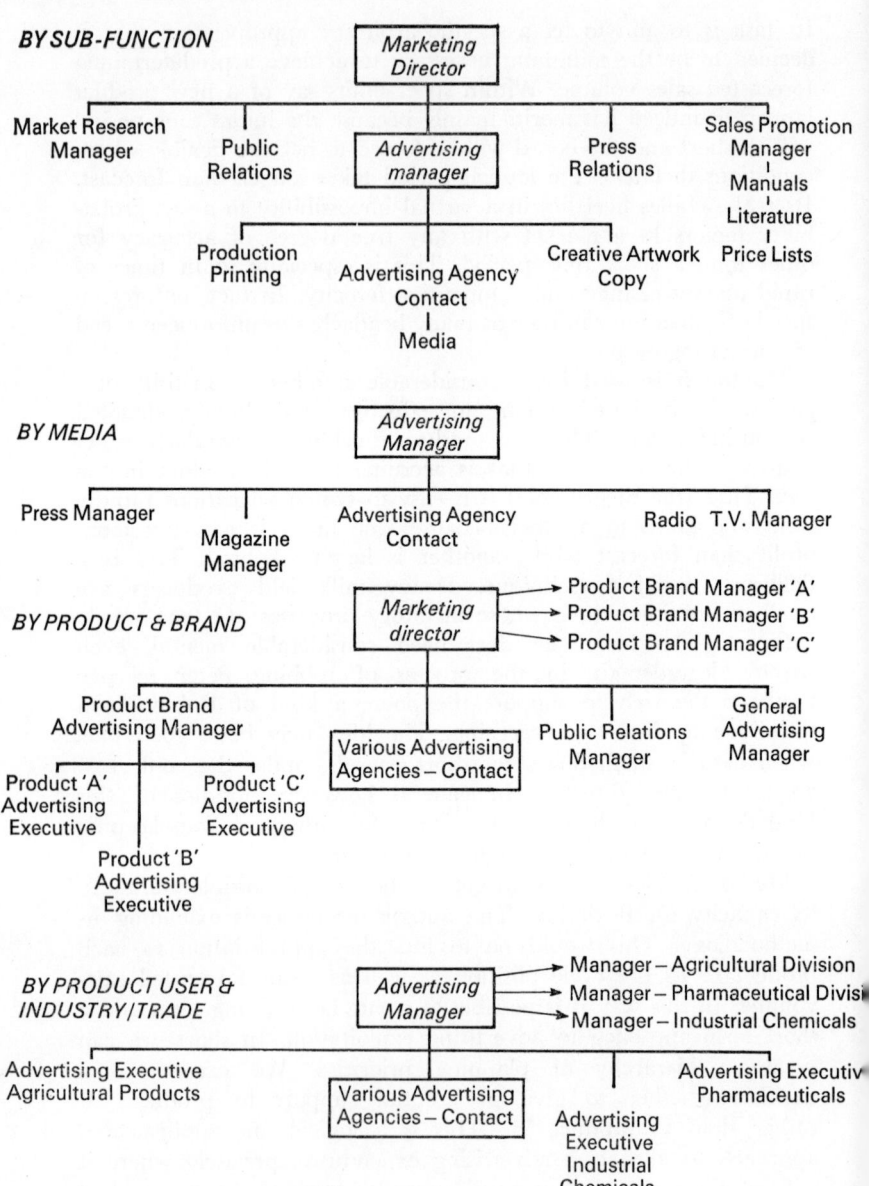

Diagram 9   Advertising function structure

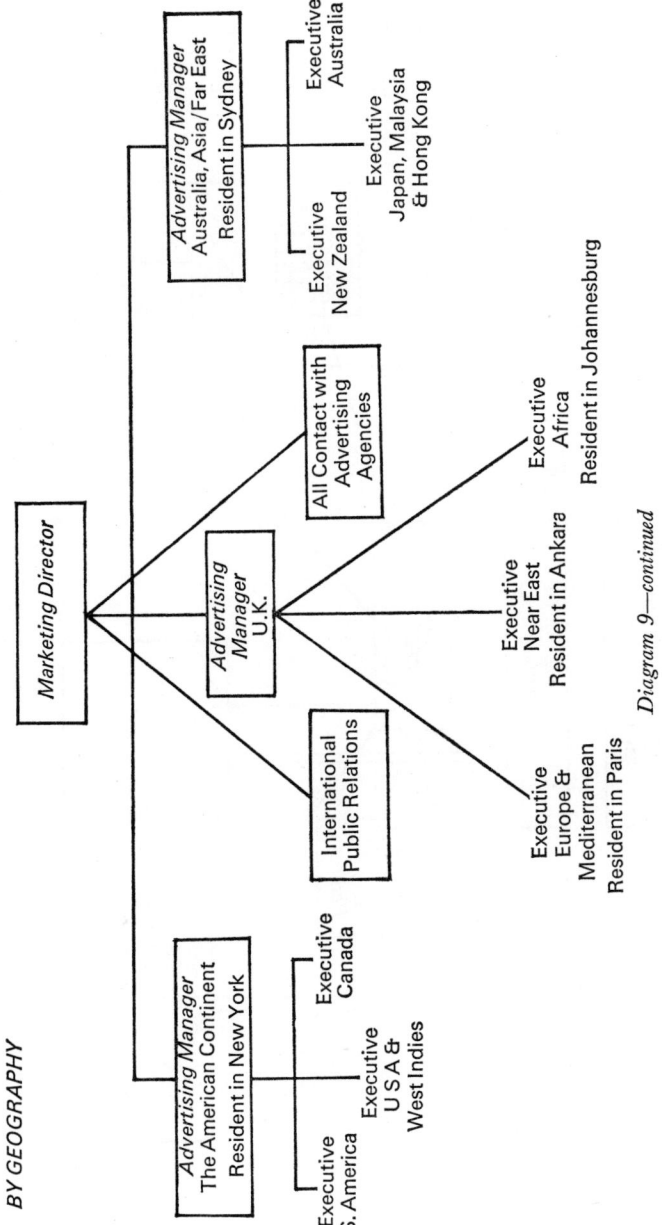

BY GEOGRAPHY

Marketing Director

Advertising Manager
The American Continent
Resident in New York

Executive
S. America

Executive
U S A &
West Indies

Executive
Canada

Advertising Manager
Australia, Asia/Far East
Resident in Sydney

Executive
New Zealand

Executive
Japan, Malaysia
& Hong Kong

Executive
Australia

All Contact with
Advertising
Agencies

Advertising
Manager
U.K.

International
Public Relations

Executive
Europe &
Mediterranean
Resident in Paris

Executive
Near East
Resident in Ankara

Executive
Africa
Resident in Johannesburg

Diagram 9—continued

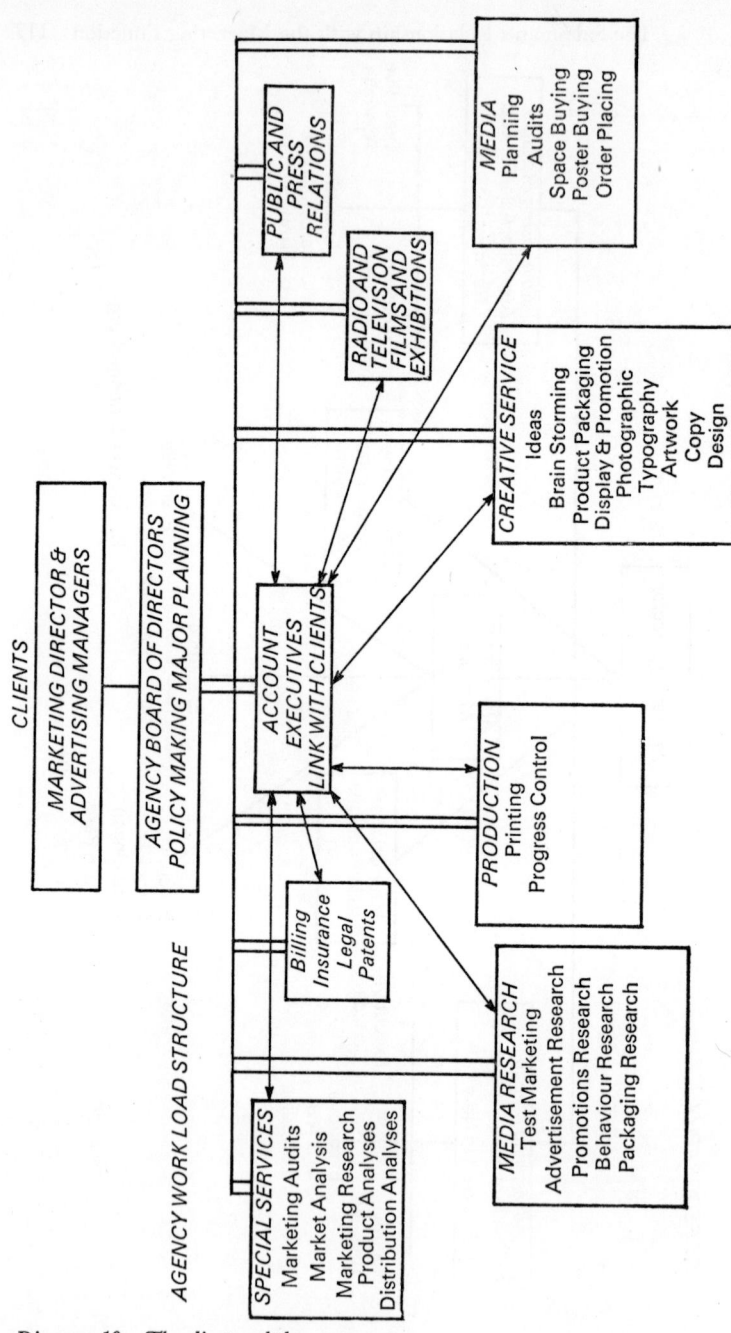

Diagram 10   The client and the agency

attainment of selective sales volume from selected products in the mix.

To complete this chapter it may help the reader to be given a short description of the organisational structures of advertising department functions within a company and those encountered within a typical advertising agency.

Company Advertising Department Structures

There are as many as five identifiable types of structure:
1 Function expressed in terms of sub-function
2 By Media
3 By Product
4 By Geography—market or market segment or country
5 By Product User, by Industry/Trade

The diagrams of these differing types (pp. 116–117) are self-explanatory.

Each type of structure assumes that it will be the company link with its chosen agency. Where a company makes a wide product mix of diverse products or of ranges of products which compete with each other *indirectly* for mass purchase but in different market segments, e.g., high price cosmetic brand for higher middle class markets *and* low price cosmetic brand for the schoolgirl and teenager, *companies may well use different agencies for separate products or products groups.*

ADVERTISING AGENCY WORK STRUCTURE

The diagram depicting the working structure of a typical medium-sized advertising agency is self-descriptive. What an agency does for a client is to provide—even create—specialised advice and services. They may be restricted to advertising alone. They are more likely to include marketing research, test marketing, sales promotion and public relations advisory services. The major services offered will include :

1 as *Agent*   — placing advertisements in selected media.
2 as *Advisor*   — on all communication matters, campaigns, research.
3 as *Creator*   — of ideas, of campaigns, promotions, and materials to support them.

4 as *Researcher* — of markets, media, distribution channels, competitive effort and threat.

5 as *Tester* — of markets for product potential (old, current and new) of market segments for viability and exploitation, for projected campaigns and products and promotions and promotional material.

Agencies usually work on a commission of 15% upon all advertising placed in media, plus special charges for extra services rendered. In large manufacturing companies the inter-company/ agency contacts will be at director level. In smaller concerns where the company director is not a marketing sales—oriented and experienced individual, the sales manager has a special responsibility to keep company-agency affairs on the rails. He should manoeuvre matters so that he is accepted as the company contact man with the agency. He can then try to keep advertising on a strictly cost-benefit basis by constant market study, by audit of advertising effectiveness. For he knows that his sales force will be the perpetual can-carrier for advertising effectiveness in terms of increased business volume and profits. He must get his advertising right in style, content, media, and cost—and prevent overkill.

Sales promotion in all its aspects, direct mail, exhibitions and couponing and sampling, are dealt with under Sales in the following chapter. Some pundits prefer to keep the discussion strictly within the advertising context. However the whole consideration of its structure and operation within this book is sales-oriented. Hence the decision upon where it should be placed.

CHAPTER FIVE

A Salesman's Relationship with his Company Headquarters' Sales Function

AN OVERVIEW

This should be in the fashion of a family relationship, friendly, understanding and mutually co-operative in working together for the common weal. It is also that of a family member who is often separated by distance from the centre of operations, who needs to be in close regular touch by telephone and by letter, and to be kept fully informed of day-to-day happenings. Where this is not the case sales will be certain to suffer, and profits will be lessened. Failure to carry out such a simple relationship negates the essence of good teamworking. And company, salesman and customers suffer from such neglect.

A salesman also needs to know precisely how his company sales function dovetails into the company marketing set-up. Although the umbrella of marketing Diagram No. 11 shows the relationship of sales functions under the overall marketing aegis it fails to show how the two separate functions are co-ordinated within the marketing structure, chaired by the marketing director.

Diagram No. 12 gives a very clear picture of a large company at work in daily or weekly committee discussing company marketing policies and plans. Every company function is represented. Each branch of selling and marketing have representation upon the committee, thus ensuring that each relevant voice is heard and considered in the day-to-day tactical handling of company matters within a long term programme.

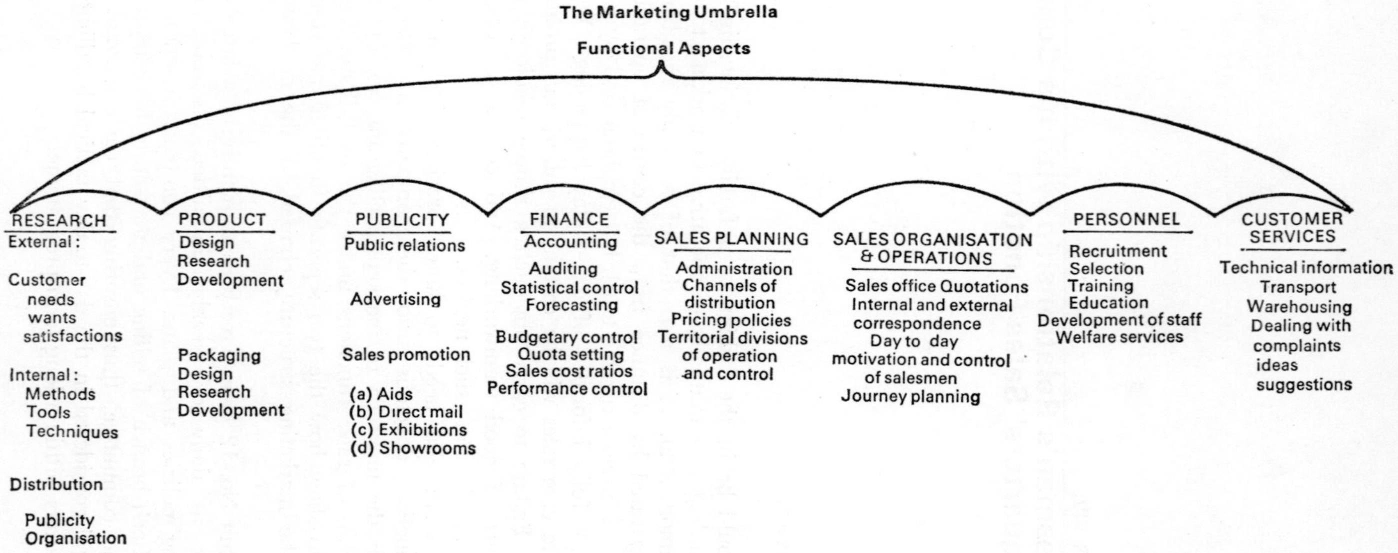

The Marketing Umbrella

Functional Aspects

RESEARCH	PRODUCT	PUBLICITY	FINANCE	SALES PLANNING	SALES ORGANISATION & OPERATIONS	PERSONNEL	CUSTOMER SERVICES
External: Customer needs wants satisfactions Internal: Methods Tools Techniques Distribution Publicity Organisation	Design Research Development Packaging Design Research Development	Public relations Advertising Sales promotion (a) Aids (b) Direct mail (c) Exhibitions (d) Showrooms	Accounting Auditing Statistical control Forecasting Budgetary control Quota setting Sales cost ratios Performance control	Administration Channels of distribution Pricing policies Territorial divisions of operation and control	Sales office Quotations Internal and external correspondence Day to day motivation and control of salesmen Journey planning	Recruitment Selection Training Education Development of staff Welfare services	Technical information Transport Warehousing Dealing with complaints ideas suggestions

Diagram 11   *The marketing umbrella: functional aspects*

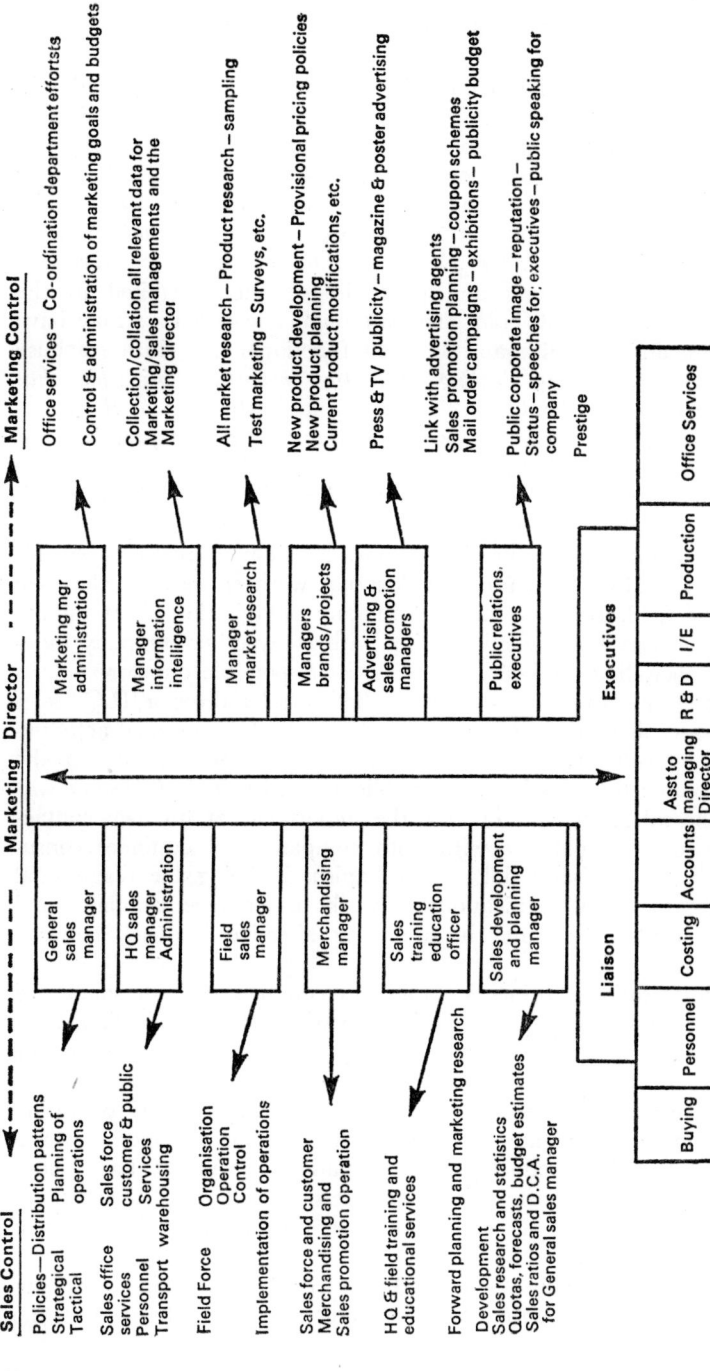

Sales Control

Policies—Distribution patterns
Strategic Planning of operations
Tactical

Sales office Sales force
services customer & public
Personnel Services
Transport warehousing

Field Force Organisation
Operation
Control

Implementation of operations

Sales force and customer
Merchandising and
Sales promotion operation

HQ & field training and
educational services

Forward planning and marketing research

Development
Sales research and statistics
Quotas, forecasts, budget estimates
Sales ratios and D.C.A.
for General sales manager

Marketing Control

Office services – Co-ordination department effortsts

Control & administration of marketing goals and budgets

Collection/collation all relevant data for
Marketing/sales managements and the
Marketing director

All market research – Product research – sampling

Test marketing – Surveys, etc.

New product development – Provisional pricing policies
New product planning
Current Product modifications, etc.

Press & TV publicity – magazine & poster advertising

Link with advertising agents
Sales promotion planning – coupon schemes
Mail order campaigns – exhibitions – publicity budget

Public corporate image – reputation –
Status – speeches for: executives – public speaking for
company

Prestige

Marketing Director

Marketing mgr administration

Manager information intelligence

Manager market research

Managers brands/projects

Advertising & sales promotion managers

Public relations. executives

Executives

General sales manager

HQ sales manager Administration

Field sales manager

Merchandising manager

Sales training education officer

Sales development and planning manager

Liaison

Buying | Personnel | Costing | Accounts | Asst to managing Director | R & D | I/E | Production | Office Services

Diagram 12   Marketing/sales co-ordination and control committee

Of course, in smaller companies the structure of sales and selling co-ordination with marketing will be much less sophisticated. In a very small company marketing and sales may well come together under a common director whose chief function may be either finance or production. In many medium-sized companies marketing is still handled by a sales executive or manager and the office work and services telescoped into one function. Nevertheless the co-ordinating and controlling services itemised in the diagram should still hold good, although one executive may have to don and to doff many different functional hats during a busy day. *Here we are dealing with the important principle that every salesman should be clear in his understanding of the ramifications of a typical company headquarters' selling function and how it works. Unless he does, he will be unable to know precisely how his role works and should dovetail effectively into his company's sales structure.*

To complete this brief overview, a salesman realises that his company H.Q. sales function does not work entirely for the men in the field. Its place in the company organisation chart implies a very close working relationship with every other company function, including the board room via its responsible director.

Diagram No 13 shows the marketing/sales director/H.Q. sales manager as a centre of a complicated web of operational activities and inter-departmental relationships plus those external to the company : the sales force, the public, customers/users/consumers.

The salesman will thus see the importance of his own contactual role—a dual one with both company and customer/consumer/user—the vital linkage mechanism in being the operational centre of a communications network to embrace company and the outside world and in providing effective feedback between them.

Organisational principles apply in common to both small and large company operations. It is the variations in application, their simplicity or their complexity that make them appear to be different.

1 Take a company complex and diversified selling operation such as the Unigate activity. Each morning milkmen leave a range of dairy products upon the nation's doorsteps. Each shopping morning or afternoon, van salesmen call upon the nation's food stores selling an equally diverse range, but under different branded names.

2 Take a company such as the Avery Group selling weighing equipment to factories, to shops and to offices throughout the

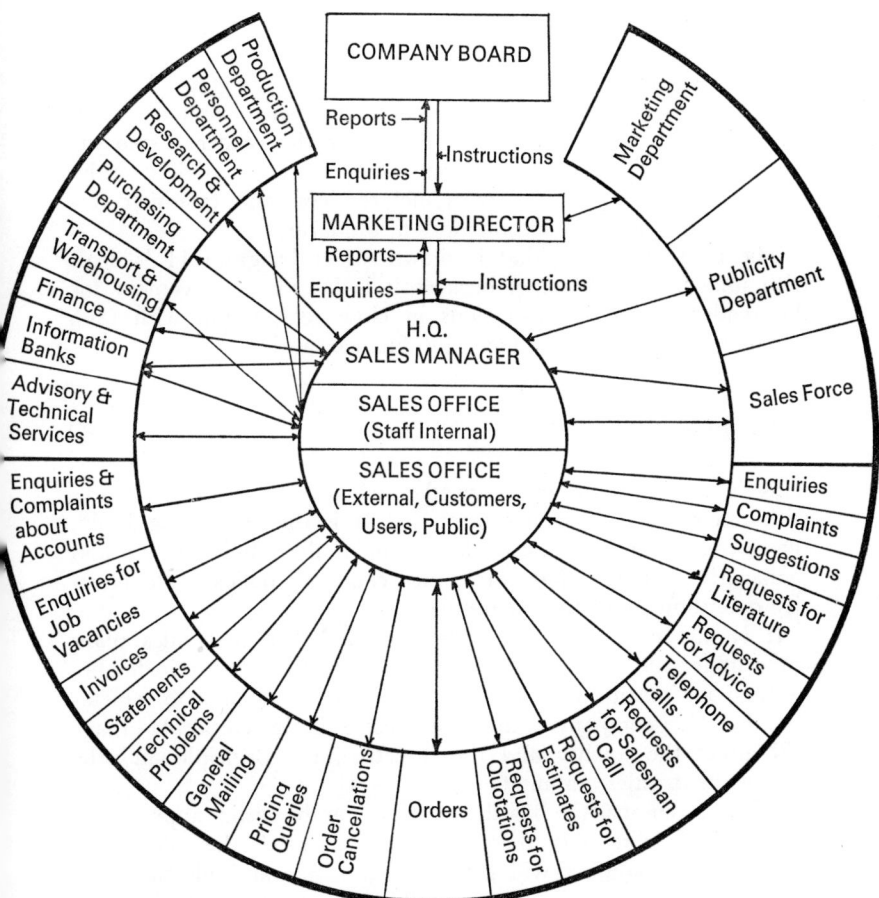

Diagram 13   Sales department functional communications network: spectrum of operational activities

United Kingdom, from a complex of depots. Such weighing equipment coming under Board of Trade regulations has to be installed and serviced by skilled trade unionist craftsmen, working from the same depots.

3 Take any of a handful of leading food manufacturers selling branded merchandise through one or more sales forces to the nation's food outlets, through wholesale and retail channels via a complex of van selling and direct representative calling.

The principles underlying Diagrams 12 and 13 apply however much the applications may differ.

The Marketing Umbrella Diagram No. 11 segregates the sales function into four main areas. This chapter will examine each of these areas in turn in sufficient detail for the reader to see the close cohesion that exists between each of these activities—sales planning, sales operations, personnel services, and customer services—as they work in a company's headquarters.

The area of finance that is shown under Diagram 11 is dealt with under sales planning, because it is far more convenient for the reader to see its operations in close relationship with sales planning than strictly under the finance aegis.

Sales Planning

This is a vital area of knowledge wherever the reader works within a company's selling spectrum. It is the computing brain, the power house of activity, the centre of the administrative and managerial network that transmutes company policies into effective operations, growth and profits.

It is important for the reader to remember that sales plans come under the company hierarchy of plans for priority in financing and for putting into operation. It is also important to remember that the company attitude expressed in its corporate image will affect the quality and the direction, the principle and the content of its sales planning.

When a company's board has given enthusiastic approval to its activities being customer-satisfaction oriented, the sales function and its planning will get a much easier and pleasant ride within the company because all other departments will be fully supportive to the selling role, whereas if the company's board is still production-oriented the sales function will have an uphill fight continuously upon its hands to carry through a forward looking customer satisfying planning activity.

PLANNING OF SALES OBJECTIVES

Marketing planning covers three main periods of time scale: long, medium and short.

Sales planning on the other hand is mainly concerned with the short term span, and the tactics, rather than the strategies necessary to achieve the targets set. A sales manager may well realise that a given product in the mix may take another two years to reach a maturity position in its life cycle. This will be kept well in mind for future planning. But his immediate thoughts will be concentrated on getting the optimum sales for the product during the next trading year, using every tactic in the book to achieve them.

This business of the planning of sales objectives is inexorably tied in with accurate information about markets and competitive activities and their likely trending for a handful of years ahead. In the light of such information a sales manager can assess the financial and productive capacities of his company, its major policies and its hierarchy of corporate plans. He can then make a sales forecast for the coming trading year covering each product's potential sales in the light of the support his company's finances and production will give. He will then match a budget of cost to the obtaining of the sales forecast, which will allow for optimum sales growth within the company capacity laid down. He will, with the co-operation of the marketing manager or director, experiment by fitting a variety of prices to each product with a view to finding which price would favour optimum production for market acceptance and competitive chagrin, and yield an upsurge in the life cycle and profit picture. He may well have to bring in the management and cost accountants with their slide rules to give financial authority to the practicality of the pricing structure chosen.

For this is not just a mere exercise in imaginative brain-storming. It will, when finalised within the company board room, shape the master forecast and the master budget for the company's trading year ahead. Each departmental target and budget will have to be supportive to the sales forecast and budget so that the sales force will be given a scalpel-keen cutting edge in the market-place against all competitive effort and bring in the sales volume and profits the company's target and budget demand.

We have already looked at the marketing research picture and its role in the creation of an up-to-date information bank. What we should now examine in some detail is the sales forecasting and budgetary control aspects involved in all sales planning for future growth and profits.

Sales Forecasts—Their Nature and Operational Use

A sales forecast is not intended to be a prophecy. It is at best a carefully compiled prediction. It is in reality a very brave try to remove risk from any contemplated future activity. Any sailor or airman knows this form quite well. It is the calculated difference between success and disaster, life and death. For example, who but an irresponsible mariner would leave port without having in his possession the latest information upon navigational hazards, and the short and long term weather reports that affect his planned course? Similarly, who but an irresponsible pilot would land his aircraft without having got up-to-the-minute reports upon ground visibility, wind direction and force?

So, a responsible sales manager, before even commencing to plan for the future, demands the latest market information, the latest competitor information, the latest information upon the economic climate that could in any way influence the line and direction of his thinking. Having all the known and relevant information that could affect the plan under consideration, he will also want to know whether there are any as yet unknown or unforeseen contingencies as factors that might inhibit or assist success.

Together these factors should form a basis for a viable approach to planning, via forecasting and budgeting. The forecast is a final assessment of what the sales manager hopes and plans to achieve within a specific time span in a specific market or market segment. The budget is the final assessment that the sales manager considers appropriate to the achieving of the forecasted target set, in terms of cost. Forecasting, budgeting and planning are a tripartite activity : an insurance policy taken out to underwrite the success of a projected enterprise.

Forecasting is something more. It is the key to balanced, integrated, successful sales activity. Forecasts are also the key to successful operation of a whole company's business operations. A sales forecast and budget once accepted and approved by a company board form the masters for all the other departmental forecasts and budgets. Each department will have to orient its forecast and budget to ensure that it is fully supportive to the accomplishment of the company targets exemplified in the sales forecast and budget.

For example:

Production schedules and inventories to be forecasted and budgeted.

Financial budgets to be created to be fully supportive.

Personnel budgets to match sales organisation's needs in manpower.

Purchasing budgets to match production scheduling and inventory needs.

Research and development budgets to deal with any short term sales function's needs.

Marketing budgets to support sales role.

The Sub-Divisions of a Sales Forecast

The example above shows clearly that sales forecasts can never be the sole province of the sales function. The impact of the sales forecast and budget can clearly be seen in the following more detailed examples of inter-departmental activities.

1 *Production* has to make a capacity and output performance to match the sales forecast. Production must schedule output so that an adequate buffer stock of finished goods can be created against unforeseen customer demands in excess of forecast.

2 *Finance* must create overall forecasts of expenditure split down to departmental activities, so that weekly progress against standards laid down can be monitored, on the policy of management by exception. Finance must monitor particularly the expenditure of purchasing and production. So that whilst best quantity bulk purchasing is obtained in terms of price, there are neither positions of glut nor shortage of materials to hamper the smooth flow of the production process in its support of the sales programme. Finance must ensure that sales department (especially in matters of sales promotion) is not hampered in its promotional selling activities by any shortage of liquid cash. Finance must ensure an adequate supply of liquid cash to finance all the requirements in all departments to support the sales forecast and budget achievement. Finance must check at least monthly on the progress of the forecasted and budgeted plans for viability against total planned progress. A monthly trading result in the form of a profit and loss account is adequate.

3 *Personnel* must make a forecast and budget of the numbers of trained workers and supervisors needed by sales and all other departments to match sales forecast implications. This may at times have to be stretched to the ranks of junior and middle managements. This must include the cost of recruitment and selection of such staffs. Personnel must make a forecast of the cost of training such persons so that they are ready as needed to support the sales effort either directly or indirectly through employment in other company departments.

4 *Purchasing* must forecast the quantities and cost of all materials, components and equipment/products that must be bought to ensure that the sales and production forecasts and budgets are met. This places a heavy responsibility upon purchasing expertise to have supplies on tap as required at the prices most favourable to the company.

5 *Marketing* must forecast not only the total number of units of each product of the mix needed week by week to meet the forecast made by sales. They must arrange adequate buffer stocks at the company's warehouses so that there is a smooth uninterrupted flow of finished goods in the pipeline to the customers and users. Marketing must ensure an adequacy of the right type of transport vehicle (whether company owned or hired) essential to the efficient smooth flow of products from the factory to the depots and thereon to the customer and user, in undamaged condition.

Hazards to Successful Forecasting

There are five main kinds of occupational hazard in sales forecasting for sales managers and salesmen (for that matter) to beware. They are:

External   The economy at large
Technology, automation and innovation
The specific market vagaries in demand
Competitive threat and innovation

Internal   Company inanition; sloth; inefficiency; lack of cash; lack of imaginative creative ideas, research and development; introspective management and direction; the defensive attitudes to life, business and competition.

External Hazards

A sales manager can ensure that at least he is aware of what is happening externally in the economy, in the market, in technological innovation, with competitors. Each potential hazard to the sales manager's company competitive selling edge must be carefully identified, evaluated and, where possible, quickly nullified. This can often be accomplished by persuading the marketing director to provide increased buying benefits on relevant products in the mix. This gives added value to a salesman's presentation and proposition, and can ensure that the sales force keeps its nose in front of competitors.

However, where a potential hazard is clearly due to regressive influences in the economic climate, it would be a rash sales manager who rushed incontinently in, to throw good money after that which was already turning bad.

Each hazard must be dealt with individually upon its intrinsic merits, both for the short and the longer term. For example, hazards posed by competitive use of technological innovation may often be countered by carefully mounted launches of new products in the mix with even more buying appeal.

Hazards Susceptible to Company Counter-Attack

Competitive hazards can be overcome often by the simple device of persuading a marketing director to create added values to products in the mix which competitive action or threat is placing at risk. Alternatively, they may be overcome by persuading the production director to shade manufacturing costs to give the sales force a keener competitive pricing-edge in the market. Again, it may be possible for the production director to offer a slightly better product specification or performance at no extra cost. This would give the sales force a powerful differential to sell. The potential competitive hazard may spring from its having a larger sales force in the market, thus giving them a higher calling rate and greater coverage of potential buyers. This too can be redressed should it seem to be viable financially by persuading the board to increase the company sales force to meet the threat.

Internal Hazards

There can be internal hazards operating often unsuspected within a company, that can be controlled, reduced or eliminated altogether. These occur where a company's board permits departments to work in self-created vacuums of their own comfortable choosing. For example, the Research and Development programme is either non-existent or not playing a practical short-term role in technological, product, or processing development. Production department may not be designed to be sufficiently flexible to take advantage of changing market opportunities. Therefore its prices will be too high to be really competitive. The company's distribution channels may be outmoded or insufficiently spread through available market segments to exploit market potentials. The marketing department may not be giving proper attention to the optimisation of all available product life cycles or to the fully representative range of the mix. The transport department may not be offering adequate delivery schedules, or they may be wrongly phased to meet the market's requirements. Personnel department may not have procured salesmen of the right dynamic quality to ensure effective selling efforts in the field. Or, the payment structure may not offer sufficient inducement to obtain or to keep the sales force at the peak of operational condition.

The moral is to remove potential hazards. Operational effectiveness will then rise.

A Salesman's Guideline to Sales Forecasting and Budgetary Control

Obviously responsible and reliable sales forecasts do not merely happen, nor are they conjured magically from the empty air. How are they conceived, researched and built up into the documents which a salesman so often gets with his christmas card, giving him his required target for the year ahead? The answer is twofold. There is a general background to sales forecasting that every company takes into its ken. There is also a specific background of knowledge which a company studies in order to draw up a forecast for the particular market segments in which it plans to operate with profit on a pre-conceived growth curve.

The General Background

1 Economic and political forecasts for the countries concerned and the time period to be covered by the forecast.
2 Specific governmental publications that cover general trades and industries in the countries concerned, public body information about projected development programmes, and the construction and building industry forecasts for the relevant countries to be covered.
3 Bankers' forecasts for trades and industries concerned, technological reports upon current developments and future innovation in the countries outlined.

These reports give the sales manager a general picture of the economic, political, fiscal, legislative and technological scene for the time period ahead for which he has to forecast.

The Specific Background

Trend patterns of the particular products in which a company deals, trend patterns in the particular industries and trades in which the company and its customers operate, trends in particular market segments in which the company will be particularly involved...all these will give the sales manager a shrewd idea of what the stars foretell for the short term future ahead. In this connection, input-output tables can be of considerable use to many companies.

Methods of Forecast Preparation

There are several semantic terms with which most salesmen become familiar but rarely have explained to them in the realm of forecasting techniques: extrapolation, trend analysis, regression analysis, tied indicators.

The extrapolation concept is the simplest of all, and would appear to be most used. It assumes quite blandly that the future will grow predictably and directly out of the present, as the present has grown out of the past—almost on an arithmetical basis. It exemplifies the French *bon mot* that the more things change, the more they remain the same. Arithmetical progression indicates expansion at a uniform rate, and shows up as a straight line on a chart. This assumes neither obstacle nor regression, things neither remaining static nor suddenly expanding at a different speed. Everything should be predictable, moving forward at predetermined speed, in a straight line, in the best possible of all economic worlds. This is of course, far too simple and far too good to be true. The devotees overcome this impediment by what they call weighting. This is a recognition that extrapolation without strings is rarely a viable basis for accurate prediction. Weighting is a simple guesstimate whether produced statistically or by sheer guess. It assesses the possible hazards that might occur to prevent the forecast coming true. It assesses the unforeseen opportunities that may occur in the market that would enhance selling potential. It strikes a balance between evil and good and loads the extrapolated line to take account of the balancing factor.

TREND ANALYSIS

Trend analysis is simple in its concept and detailed in its study and application. It uses a company sales chart that ideally covers at least a five year period prior to the year to be forecasted, and preferably in some industries a seven or ten year back history. These charts can cover total sales *ad valorem;* regional sales *ad valorem;* individual products *ad valorem;* and key outlets *ad valorem.*

The charts operate on a moving annual total basis. They offer each month's sales, each year's sales in a perfectly normal manner. However, there is a trend line at the top of the chart which operates strictly to show at any monthly point the actual sales for the previous twelve months as distinct from those of any calendar or trading year. Thus, the sales manager looking back has a form-at-a-glance line moving in a steady or hazardous trend pattern. This is in addition to giving all the usual data about each month and each year's sales which are readily comparable.

Trends are subtle things. They can change so slowly that unless they are meticulously examined a sales manager can live in a fool's paradise of unalloyed bliss, when in fact his product mix expectancy of life is slowly declining, and the sands of his commercial life are being blown away relentlessly on the winds of competition and market change.

Trend analysis offers a sales manager the best bet in these difficult days, particularly when he is ready to weight the trend by what is termed exponential smoothing. This is a simple mathematical device by which it becomes possible to even out short term variances in a sales/time trend graph, so that the true trend is more easily seen. Seasonal variances in product demand are a fair example.

Regression analysis is an algebraic technique for investigating the effects of one variable upon another.

Tied Indicators and Correlation Analyses

Correlation analysis is a procedure based upon the belief that one company product's sales can be affected by the sales of other products, whether of their own or competitive manufacture.

Simple examples are :
The Birth Rate effect upon sales of baby foods, clothes, etc.

Slimming craze   effect upon dietary foods, fashion clothes, etc.
Building   effect upon sales of all relevant material fittings, appliances, furnishings, furniture, etc.

Tied indicators are a special form of direct and very close correlation. They occur particularly in industrial marketing situations where the sales of one product definitely dictate the sales of others which are dependent upon it. The motor car industry is a typical instance. The sale of individual cars dictates the sales of all components built into the car, especially the fittings, furniture and accessories. In short, sales forecasts and budgets of accessory makers must be linked closely to the trade barometer for motor car sales forecasts and budgets.

The sales manager can now make two estimates from the external sources of market information. The first is his company's *sales potential* for the period involved. This amounts to an estimate of his company's share of the total market available to products of the type his company markets. The second, is his shaded bid of what he considers to be a fair sales forecast of achievable sales, making due allowances for his company's productive and financial capacity; his sales force strength; the likely sum that will be made available for publicity; new product lines to be launched during the period concerned; and likely competitive effort.

A wise and prudent sales manager will want to make an effective check of this forecast from company internal sources. This is often referred to as a composite checking device. It consists of three separate bodies:

1 A *composite* of sales force opinion and territorial sales estimates for the period.

2 A *composite* of dealer opinion made up of customer, consumer and user views obtained by the sales force of the likely trend of their ordering for the period envisaged.

3 A *composite* of top and middle departmental management (a forum of executive opinion) with a special knowledge of sales, and a specific interest in their optimisation in prevailing market conditions.

This gives the sales manager a trinity of expertise and knowledge, pragmatic though it may be. It also gives him a three-point navigational check upon the viability of his preliminary forecast from external sources.

In practice, it has two main advantages:

(a) It tests and crystallises sales managerial opinion formed purely upon outside information.

(b) It offers a practical corrective check from those people who will be required to carry out the forecast once a final decision has been made.

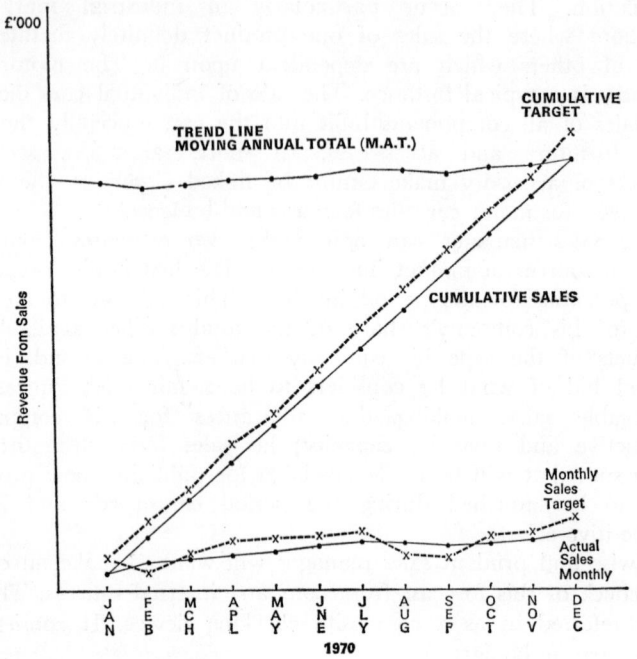

Diagram 14   Trend analysis

The Salesman, The Forecast, the Break-Even Point, and Budget Creation and Control

From the foregoing activities, the sales manager now knows the limits of his company's productive capacity and the financial support available. He knows too his sales force's views upon the part they will be called upon to play to achieve the target once he has made the final decision. He now must concentrate his activities upon devising a budget of cost to fit the forecasted achievement, whilst allowing for a profit that will satisfy the board. Simultaneously, he must build into his organisation a control mechanism that will fix standards of performance, monitor variances from it, and remedy them, in order to keep the ship on course. Thus we have a duality, of management by objective accompanied by management by exception working side-by-side.

The business of profit is of course an overriding preoccupation. For, ultimately sales management is judged by its capacity for planned growth accompanied by the required contribution to company profits. This is a vital exercise a sales manager must carry out in the linking of optimum production and optimum sales obtained at the prices that yield the optimum profits. This exercise is a matter of finding the best price for the product, that will create optimum production and sales, and begin to yield profit at the earliest possible time in the trading year.

THE BREAK-EVEN POINT

The break-even point is reached when the revenue from sales exactly balances the costs incurred. This is the moment in time when profit begins to accrue. The sales manager will ultimately reduce the list of alternative product prices down to two, from which he will have to make a final decision. This will be his estimate of that price which will be most acceptable to the market, most damaging to competition, and will create the optimum sales that production can conveniently handle, whilst beginning to show a profit at the earliest date.

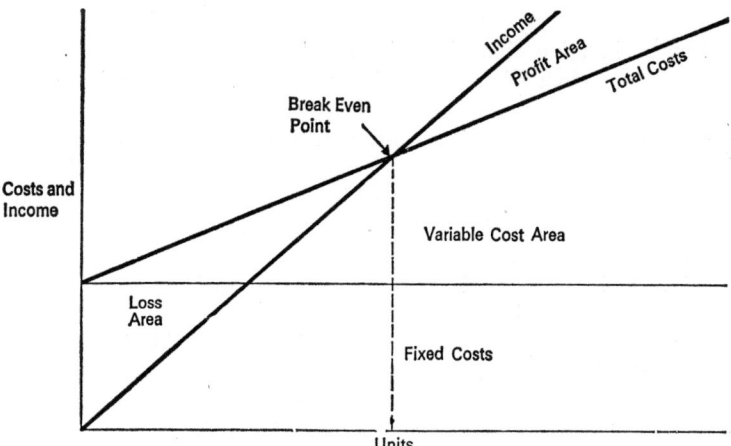

Diagram 15   The break-even point

A Salesman's Exercise in Price Fixing and Early Break-Even point Achievement

There are four main factors to be taken into account. They are:
1 Fixed cost of company operation
2 Variable costs of company operation
3 Sales volume in individual product units
4 Sales volume of (3) in pounds sterling.
Fixed cost includes all items inseparable from company operation that will not change with any alteration in output volume. Variable costs include all items that change with alterations in output volume.
Examples of fixed cost are factory buildings, plant, essential services.
Examples of variable cost are raw materials, components, packing, transport and warehousing of goods, labour rates and selling costs.
Example—A small power machine tool

The formula for establishing the break-even point is:

$$\frac{\text{Sales Value} \times \text{Fixed Cost}}{\text{Sales Value} - \text{Variable Costs}}$$

Let us imagine that the salesman has a possible span of unit price per product of between £10 and £20. This will have been established by research. The ceiling will cream the market, but the floor price will achieve optimum sales volume from a larger number of outlets. The mean price of £15 would superficially seem to offer the best of both worlds, comfortably in the middle bracket for market appeal and profit performance on a reasonable production capacity.

The fixed cost is static at £60,000. The variable cost per unit is £5. The sales volume value aim is £1,200,000.

Let us work out the break-even point. It should then be easy to depict the entire progress of sales per unit compared with sales volume value and cost, showing the break-even point and the upward curve of profit starting from that point.

Once past the break-even point profit making is relatively easier. For only the variable cost acts as a brake.

Salesman's Check on Computation
Data

Fixed Cost	£60,000	Selling Price per Unit £15	
Forecasted Sales Volume	£1,200,000	Number of Units	(80,000)
Variable Cost per Unit	£5		

Formula

$$\text{Break-Even Point} = \frac{£1,200,000 \times £60,000}{£1,200,000 - £400,000} = £90,000 = 6,000 \text{ units.}$$

Headquarters' Sales Organisation and Operations

Most of the companies selling in Great Britain are small ones. Their H.Q. function may be managed by two key personnel; a manager looking after the sales force: another managing the office and the flow of paper between company and customer, and between company and sales force. In larger selling organisations we encounter a growth in numbers of managerial personnel. These numbers are roughly related to the company's size and types of marketing and sales activity. In very large companies we may meet very imposing personnel pyramids indeed. A general sales manager, a sales promotion manager, a sales planning and development manager, a sales office manager and a sales training manager operating under the aegis of a sales director.

A Purpose of Sales Organisation

Many salesmen take their headquarters' sales structure for granted, without reflecting upon its purpose. In effect, they will not know how to make the best use of its services. *A sales organisation should exist to form a framework within which people can work effectively. It should be deliberately created to do precisely this job in both width and depth.* For instance, the organisational pattern must enable people to operate effectively, to communicate clearly, to co-operate intelligently. In turn, it must enable management to plan, to operate, to audit, to co-ordinate and to control both people and their work so that the company aims and objectives can be achieved on course, on time, and on target and budget set.

This emphasis upon effective organisation and operation has resulted in the choice of paper as a communicating, co-ordinating, recording and audit-cum-control tool. Paper is a tyrannical master, but a useful slave. In many companies the elevation of the computer to stardom has resulted in paper becoming a swash-buckling boss instead of a willing and invaluable servant. Hence the derisive term, the paperwork explosion. It behoves every employee of the company to reduce essential paperwork to a minimum, in the interests of efficiency and cost. *There is a golden rule about paper.* Is each piece of paper essential? Does it work well, completely and comprehensively? Can it be ruthlessly costed and controlled by regular audit for its viability? It is surprising how little paper is absolutely essential and comprehensive in action.

Alas, we must reluctantly face the fact that many headquarters' sales functions use a plethora of paper forms. Data processing systems and organisation and methods engineers can produce paper so easily about every facet of company operation that there will soon be an occupational hazard known as strangulated hernia by paper.

It should be a sales manager's vow that so far as he is concerned paper will be absolutely minimal consistent with efficiency in volume, usage and application. In this way paper can be made to offer maximum benefit at least cost. This applies particularly to statistical offerings from the computer. Unless the piece of paper has a valuable checking or application purpose, cut it out. Otherwise sales office costs will rise with lip-service to a dreary, boring, expensive, unwanted, soul-destroying chore.

The Company Sales Office

Just as the sales force is the field communications network between company and customer, the H.Q. sales office is the company communications network between company sales force and customers and users everywhere. In a small company the sales office may have no separate existence, being part of the general office structure, often with the company secretary in charge. This is usually the case where there is no sales manager as such. One of the partners or directors looks after sales under one of his many interchangeable departmental hats. Larger companies insist upon a clear demarcation between the sales office and the general offices. They are frequently in different and separate office blocks. In such cases, there will be a sales office manager in charge of clerical activities with senior status in the sales managerial hierarchy.

We shall use such an example as our model for the discussion of sales office structural activities.

The sales office manager in this example will be directly responsible and fully accountable to the company general or headquarters' sales manager for the following services.

Ten Commandments for Effective Sales Office Operation

Information upon paper for forecasting, budgets, quotas, territorial planning and control, including distribution cost analyses and sales control ratios.

Quotations, estimates, contracts, queries, enquiries, complaints, suggestions, order processing.

Customer credit control, invoicing, statements of account.

Liaison with other company departments (including a complaints ombudsman).

External communications with public customers, users, etc.

Customer information and technical advisory services. Customer list on addressograph plates.

Sales force control and servicing. Sales force reporting and information collection.

Sales personnel services: welfare, payment, expense control, salaries, career rewards, promotion, manpower development, training and education services, managerial development, recruitment and selection services, performance standards setting and audits of performance appraisals, competitions. Training of customer salespeople.

Sales promotion servicing of sales force : merchandising, exhibitions, mailings of promotional literature, direct mail shots, competitions involving public.

Sales information bank, reporting to sales director on matters of boardroom interests and concern. Information service to sales planning and development manager.

A Functional Analysis of a Typical Sales Office

Most H.Q. sales offices cover the following daily stint:
1 Correspondence with the external world of customers, users, enquirers, complainants, makers of suggestions, external sales forces both home and overseas. Internal memos to other company departments are also extremely important both in relaying

information to them, requesting co-operation from them, and gaining their co-operation in matters affecting the external worlds of customers, users, and the sales force. Correspondence in this sense includes communication by telex or telephone. How else can the H.Q. sales function operate as the company's communications centre of a network covering customers, users, publics, and sales forces everywhere?

2 A corollary of the preceding paragraph is the daily emphasis upon everything that concerns the processing of enquiries, estimates, quotations, which we shall deal with under a generalised heading of quoting services.

Quoting services are in so many cases, particularly in industrial and technical selling, the prerequisite that can pre-empt an order in the company's favour. Quoting is an art as well as a pricing science. Far too many companies are still satisfied with a purely straightforward quotation on a quarto sheet of standard office paper, giving the essential facts of price, specification, delivery period. They overlook the significant fact that the enquirer always wants to be sold by the quotation, accompanying performance criteria and all the persuasive promotional literature that will help him to justify the purchase to both his personal and professional conscience. This will be dealt with later in this chapter in some considerable detail.

3 Contract and order processing are two of the most important company procedures in sales office routines. They give each contract and each order a birth certificate in the guise of an order number and reference that govern the contract or order's life whilst it remains in the company's records. Once having been numbered the contract or order is checked for credit viability. Once this is passed as O.K. THE CONTRACT OR ORDER HAS A PASSPORT AS WELL AS A BIRTH CERTIFICATE. Little needs now to be done except to check correctness of customer's name and address, the availability of the ordered goods and their prices, as a first step to despatch. The final steps are to transfer the logistics of each contract and order to invoice sets that establish the official existence of the contract and order as they progress to goods outward and accounts. The order or contract number and reference enable it to be picked up in any stage of its process from factory to customer.

4 Sales ledgers—Invoice and account procedures Statistical Section—Forecasts, budget, quotas, sales cost ratios, etc.

Once the orders and contracts have been invoiced and ledger

entries made for subsequent rendering of statements of account to customers concerned, the order copies form the basis of a wealth of information that can easily be abstracted for statistical purposes. High among these purposes is the abstraction of material about salesmen's targets, and any variation from the standards of performance laid down. Similarly essential data for distribution cost analyses can be painlessly abstracted for immediate confirmatory use in the sales control function. Important trends of customer demand can be detected quickly. They can offer the general sales manager information about unforeseen opportunities to be exploited, or sudden competitive or market threats to be offset and thwarted. In short it has the capacity for the production of a running commentary upon shortfall or over-spill, each of which will need immediate sales managerial attention. Even where the ship is merely upon its predicted course, there is the satisfaction of knowing that no remedial treatment is necessary, for at least the short term ahead.

5 Personnel services. This in many sales organisations is a neglected, undermanned and underrated sub-function. This is a nonsense if ever there was one. Here is the function that provides the information and the paperwork for the seeking, the selection, the education, the motivation, the development of the sales force, and its career rewards, welfare, and promotion. This should be a particular adjunct of the company general sales manager in his responsibility for the making of manpower throughout the sales activity. Here he should be able to browse and to dip into records that indicate the real strength of the selling operation in both the short and the long term aspects of company activity. Here should be the information that separates the men from the boys. The information upon which he can shape all plans for future development that envisage the use of specifically trained and competent manpower at every field sales level.

6 Credit control and factoring. Credit properly handled is an effective sales developmental tool. Wrongly accorded and it is a heavy contributor to the loss sector of the sales cost centre. There are two main ingredients to the credit mix: individual credit ceiling for each customer and length of credit time to be given. Customers will almost automatically take the fullest advantage of both credit limit and time extension. Provided that (a) they do not add to the cost of trading with a supplier, (b) they do not cause unpleasantness or embarrassment, (c) their name for prompt payment does not suffer in the trade or industry, and (d) the manu-

facturer does not embargo his supplies at an unpredictable moment because the account is outstanding.

To do so is an obvious benefit. The customer can trade upon the suppliers' credit, and turn over his inventory more than once before paying for supplies. It does in fact amount often to an interest-free loan, which the customer can use to make money for his business.

Credit is still established by an exchange of references from reputable suppliers in the particular trade or industry. Bank references are in the main worth very little unless the company has a very bad record. Credit agencies are becoming much more used—Dun and Bradstreet for example. Here for an annual subscription the subscriber gets the loan of confidential credit worthiness lists. They cover most of the companies trading in the United Kingdom of average size to the very large operators. Very small companies can be reported upon by Dun and Bradstreet for a small additional fee.

Time extension is a matter for individual supplier judgement. Here the ideal is one month, but two to three months is common. Beyond that period the risk would appear to grow in geometrical progression rather than arithmetical progression for short time periods. Whilst longer terms of credit may seem sometimes to be justified and sometimes undoubtedly are: the old adage that short credits make long friendships is undoubtedly apt. Taking chances without any means of underwriting the risks is scarcely the recipe for sound trading in the longer term. Credit extension costs the supplier money. (If it were to hand he could be using it.) It amounts to a form of price and profit cutting!

Factoring is a financial service which a small supplier may purchase in order to reduce his costs of sales office operations, whilst reducing the risk of loss by extended credit or by bad debt. The factor buys the supplier's outstanding customer balances for an agreed discount, and settles in cash on agreed dates. The small trader hands over the invoice sets on completion, and the factor then takes over the collection of the debts. The liquid cash savings to the small trader are obvious, and so is the peace of mind the operation creates. He saves on office staff, machinery, accommodation and supplies. He pays for the privilege in the form of a commission upon the amount of work and the size of the debt handed over to the factor. The factor makes his money upon his judgement of the traders he helps and his own judgement of the bad debt liabilities and his costs of collection in terms of risk and loss.

Three Vital Sales Office Functional Areas

There are three particular areas of sales office handling that are of special concern to the salesman's interests and to his peace of mind. They are:

1 Speedy handling of all correspondence, telephone calls, or personal visits from the external dimension of customers, potential customers, users, the publics, the sales force and agents.

2 Speedy handling of all matters that affect the sales force or agents whether from external sources or from departments within the company itself.

3 Speedy abstraction of all material from information banks, research operations, the press, libraries, television, radio that should be referred to higher sales department authority for onward routeing to the board.

Speed is of the essence. Yet the actual timing of the information is also important plus the vital documentation to validate the contention of the sales function that top management needs to read it, mark it and inwardly digest it, for immediate or for future action.

Speed is equally important in dealing with correspondence or telephone calls from the sales force, agents, customers and the publics. It is not merely a matter of good manners, important although such courtesies are. It becomes a matter of ignoring the importance, the standing, the status, the prestige, the *amour propre* of either a member of staff, or of a customer unless every contact is acknowledged with expedition and the contents dealt with both intelligently and sympathetically. Actually, it is the basic attitude of a sales function that is at stake each time a member of staff deals with the sales force or a customer, or a member of the public. However much the public relations officer may labour in his vineyard, all comes to nought if a member of the sales function shows an attitude that is less than perfect, in his concern for the company's image for excellence of service to its publics. Sales training should include every member of the sales function as well as the sales force. It could with benefit include every telephone operator on the company's staff who speaks to the outside world.

Speed of telling sales force staff of H.Q. contacts of any kind with the outside world of public, customer and user is essential. Imagine the chagrin so many salesmen feel when the customer being contacted knows more about a situation with his company's

F

headquarters than the salesman himself. Similarly, imagine the chagrin, the acute feeling of distaste, the wondering lack of confidence seeping into a salesman's mind, when a report made with great care on a vital subject remains unacknowledged weeks after. No sales function has a moral right to ask its sales force to make carefully considered reports unless it is prepared to have the interest, the efficiency and the courtesy to thank the salesman immediately for his report and to tell him what if any action will be taken, of what magnitude, when and where. Or if it has to lie on the table for further consideration. Or even more tactfully, why H.Q. will not be taking action upon it for the moment.

Anything less than this creates a lack of confidence in his H.Q. in the salesman's mind. It reduces the risk of his bothering to bother H.Q. in the foreseeable future with any more cerebral contributions.

We come now to the vital matter of complaints handling. And this deserves several paragraphs of its own because of its vital bearing upon company goodwill. In every way a complaint contains a time-bomb ticking away in its interior, ready to explode to the company's detriment unless it be dealt with in friendly, firm and forthright fashion forthwith.

The Handling of Complaints

In this connection there is a close affinity between actual complaints and suggestions. Because a suggestion in its way contains a request for a change for the better, which is a tacit complaint with the present and the past.

Nobody takes the trouble to write a letter, to telephone, to make a personal call upon a company, unless he feels pretty strongly about the matter. This applies whether the matter be suggestion or active complaint. The caller wants something to happen immediately upon his call. That would appear to be elementary justice. He wants attention and empathetic attitudes to the reason for his call. He wants his complaint or suggestion to appear to the company to be fully justified. He wants a change to be made in the company's product, service, value, methods, quality, pack etc.

Rebuff such a caller, and the company will get no second bite at that cherry. Give him less than he thinks to be his due, and the same thing will apply. Fail and the company is on the losing end for a long time, if not for ever. Succeed, and a friend is created and won from the threat of defeat. And such friends prove to be of long standing, once rapprochement has been achieved. And it can be done for little cash, time and effort. But it is the direct fruit of a customer-satisfying sales policy, no more, no less. It takes imagination, it takes initiative. But what dividends it can pay!

Complaints Ombudsman

It is clear that such a vital area should be under the control of an ombudsman. He should be at least a senior company sales executive. This is not a new idea. The Rowntree Sales Organisation used this methodology in the early 1930s, under the guidance of their farsighted Chairman, the late George Harris. It was under the direct control of the H.Q. Manager of the Sales Office Administration. The author and he were involved in the creation of a simple form that could ensure immediate handling of complaints, with an inbuilt alarm that sounded out loud and clear when for any reason a complaint was not handled with expedition. This occurred forty years ago, yet modern methodology would appear to have little extra or new to contribute in this vulnerable area of public and customer/user relationships.

Complaints Procedure and Organisation

Complaints are threats to the prestige of our company image. What simple procedures should we adopt? Who should handle these hot potatoes, and be responsible for their happy endings?

Complaints come normally under a series of visible headings, such as:

Dissatisfaction — with service, product, performance, usage, pack, price.

Disgust — with any of the above, plus personal handling by company staff.

Discourtesy — arising from actual or imagined lack of respect for recipient, from letter, telephone call, letter content, staff rudeness.

Damage — product or pack on arrival at recipient's place of business or home.

Deterioration — product in transit, in store, in use.

A Viable H.Q. Organisation for Complaints Procedures and Handling

(*Note: In this context enquiry and suggestion handling can take an identical course.*)

Record and acknowledge immediately by letter (or telephone if urgent) the receipt of the complaint, enquiry, or suggestion, whether from public, customer, user or own sales force.

Make a book entry of it, and give it a number and code, as in order and contract registration. This gives it an official existence and record.

The letter of acknowledgement or telephone call will primarily express pleasure or regret according to the nature of the enquiry, suggestion or complaint. Especially, it will give an expression of intent to meet the content of the communication to the satisfaction of the originator so far as is legitimately possible. Always the acknowledgement must end with an expression of thanks to the originator for bringing the matter to the company's attention, so that proper satisfaction may be achieved.

Where there will be a delay in producing the information and its attendant satisfactions to the originator, the company should clearly say so, and if possible indicate when the next communication will be made.

The letters should be signed by an ombudsman or at least a senior sales executive, and not by a mere clerk. There can be no quicker way of intimating to the originator how important or how trivial his communication seems to the company than by the rank of the signatory of the letter.

If the matter could be handled better by a personal visit from a company official then a salesman or agent should be properly briefed to call and do the public relations job of assuaging hurt susceptibilities, administering verbal soothing syrup and aspirin, to expedite the originator's ultimate satisfaction. Or, it may seem better to call to clarify a point made in an enquiry or suggestion. Whichever may be the case, a tactful pleasant visit can take the heat out of a misunderstanding or a fancied slight. Equally it can prevent a company 'boob'. It can also make an enquirer or a person making a suggestion walk ten feet tall. Overall it can create a feeling of trust and confidence in the company that was previously either not there or not so strong.

S.E.C. FORM

Tick relevant heading

Suggestion √	Enquiry	Complaint
Originator's 2 Reference C.40	N.A. 2	N.A. 2

Sales Office Number / Date	Originator's Name
X. 4 A 50 9.7.71	Salesman D. Stoddart

Name	J. Binks & Co.	Tel. No.	of Complainant
Address	4 Shipley Place	Bacup	Enquirer
	Bacup	06795	√ Suggester

Nature Suggestion	To improve pendulum mechanism in Scales Model − X. 7

Details

Detailed Specification,

and Drawings

Action Proposed
    Send to R. & D. Dept. for investigation, evaluation,
    and recommendation by 31.8.71.

Action Taken   *Date*   12.7.71
J. Binks & Co. − Sent letter of thanks and intention of
writing further in Sept./71.   Copy to Salesman Stoddart.

Disposal date sent to Information Bank.

A Central Complaints, Enquiries, and Suggestions Registry (Internal Handling)

1 The registry gives each complaint, enquiry or suggestion a number and code.

2 The creation of inter-departmental channels to get accurate and rapid answers to the complaints, enquiries, or suggestions, for onward routeing to originators.

3 The creation of a progress-chasing section to ensure that no matter, however trivial, can get lost in the pipe line, or an an originator could be kept waiting for his answer. There is one golden rule. No originator should ever be left in doubt or in mid-air about any matter that demands explanation, apology or information.

4 A form in triplicate should be designed to suit the company's style and procedures, which will be the vehicle through which all questions are asked and answers made. The diagram offers an extremely simple layout.

The originator of the form, a salesman in the field, the ombudsman or one of his staff, gives the name, address and details, written or typed in triplicate. The two top copies are sent through the registry to the department within the company that will have to give the gist of the reply for onward routeing to the actual originator. The third copy is kept either by the salesman or the member of registry who originated the form. This third copy remains like a festering sore on the day-to-day file of salesman or registry until the query, suggestion or complaint is cleared and answer sent to actual originator. This simple procedure is water-tight in any normally efficient organisation and pays quick and growing dividends in customer, user, public and sales force esteem.

5 *There is another quite different built-in benefit. It enables the information bank to whom the third copy is ultimately sent to keep tabs on potential trends in complaints and enquiries. These can be of exceptional importance to the sales and marketing directors. They can indicate areas in which customers, users and publics are unsatisfied or dissatisfied with products, services, prices, terms, sales contact, product performance criteria, new usages, new market segments, new product requirements, competitive threat or innovation.*

An isolated item of complaint or suggestion in any firm can be easily overlooked. With this system nothing that indicates an opportunity, a threat, or a potential trend can be overlooked, unless the ombudsman is wearing blinkers.

Sales Office and Sales Force Interrelationships

The company H.Q. sales office is the vehicle of communications and should be the creator of empathetic understanding that makes the sales force tick as an integrated and balanced unity, an effective happy whole—in fact a real team. This demand that the sales function should be seen to act as a closely co-ordinated whole in the creation of business through customer satisfactions is a wholly rational one. It means that there can be no gaps of understanding between sales office and salesmen about planning, calling, business seeking, business promotion and overall operational effort. Each side to the company equation has a responsibility to see that they think, talk and act as a viable entity in the determination to achieve the company's total objectives. This is not a pie-in-the-sky prescription for the millennium but the brass tacks of successful selling activity.

Sales Planning

'Pertinent and required Information, properly communicated, is the basis of all effective action and drive'—Callaby

In most companies the overall responsibility for the planning of national operational selling activity is vested in the sales director and operated via the H.Q. sales office. This is mainly strategic planning of the choice of market segment to be developed, the type of distributor channel to be selected. And the size and shape of the average sales territory, method of remuneration, and basic minimum standards of salesman performance enshrined in minimum norms that are vital to the success of sales forecasting, quota setting and budgeting. Along with this overall responsibility for operational planning, is a similar one for sales promotion and sales control. The tactical planning of every day operations of the sales force is usually entrusted to field sales managers, and in many cases to the salesmen themselves. It is the sales office responsibility to act as an effective promulgator of all instructions and information concerning H.Q. planning, promotion and control down to the sales force via field sales management, where there is such a managerial level of activity. And the instructions and information must be sufficiently clear, comprehensive and detailed for instant and total understanding by those who have to act upon them. Further, the instructions and information must be given in sufficient time, and rightly timed, so that two-way feedback upon any misunderstanding or queries can be effectively sorted out. Nothing less than 100 per cent comprehension should be the aim in two-way consultation. Thus each member of a sales force knows exactly what he is expected to do, where, when, by what method, to whom, in order to get a precisely tailored target result at budgeted cost. This is quite additional to the job description which covers the main lines of strategical concept, reporting and operational routines.

The Bible has many matters of interest that reflect directly upon the selling job; for example, the epitaph of many an unsuccessful sales office. 'For, if the trumpet give an uncertain sound, who shall prepare himself to the battle?' (Corinthians 14:8.)

Note: Tactical planning is dealt with in a subsequent chapter within the role of the field sales manager.

SALES PROMOTION

'Sales promotion is the "moving" of the company's products to the consumer or user, in contradistinction to advertising which is the "moving" of the consumer or user to the company's products.'

'Merchandising is an integral part of sales promotion. It is an "inducing" activity at the actual point of sale to get people to buy the products on offer. It is an additional inducement to any attractiveness of the normal price.'

The chief sales executive, whether sales director or general sales manager, is responsible for the budget for promotional and merchandising activities. He is equally responsible for the actual operational activity in the field, although he will usually delegate the field activities through a sales promotion manager via field sales managers to the sales force. The sales promotion manager or the sales office will be responsible for passing down to the sales force all instructions and information necessary for effective promotional activity in the field.

Such information and instruction may well include the placing of show material in shops or other outlets to support particular company publicity campaigns. It may include the distribution of special literature in similar support of local or national advertising, or precise and comprehensive details of merchandising tactics to support campaigns in special outlets, involving information upon inventory control, profit margins, shop and window lighting, aisle bins, shelf filling, and a host of ancillary detail.

It may be the issue of special and costly portfolios involving either the whole product mix or special items in the mix, which form a powerful presentation of a selling proposition to the dealer or user.

It may be leaflets to support a national user and dealer competition in the press or on television, which the sales force will have to place with dealers. This will almost certainly involve the supportive action of the sales force in getting special retail displays to enhance the value of publicity at point-of-sale.

Listed below are a mere 27 separate and important aspects of their part in the total company's selling operational role.

The overall purpose of sales promotion activities is to enthuse dealers, their selling staffs and users about specific company products and services. The objective is two fold: to sell more into the shops and to sell more out of the shops; and to get the user to consume more, more rapidly than heretofore.

The merchandising activity is to encourage all potential purchasers to become so eager to buy, that they do so on the spot—a true impulse purchasing result of the selling behavioural drive.

SALES PROMOTIONAL ACTIVITIES

1 Design and Production of Advertising and Sales portfolios for Sales Force usage

2 Point-of-purchase material—Showcards, Leaflets. Display Containers, Literature

3 Direct Mail Shots to Customers, Users, Consumers, Dealers, and others

4 Design and Execution of Premiums, Coupons, etc.

5 Trade Shows and Exhibitions

6 Special Occasion and seasonal Promotions

7 Demonstrations—Store, Factory, Office, Home—Goods-on-Approval

8 Lectures to Public, Professions, Trades, Industries, Clubs, Organisations, etc.

9 Sampling to Customers, Users, Consumers, and the Public

10 Tie-Up with Trade and Public in National and Local Events
11 Sales Meetings and Conventions
12 Sales Training of both Company and Dealer Sales Forces—including Retail Staffs
13 Sales Contests—Sales Force
14 Dealer Contests
15 Consumer, User, and Public Competitions
16 Sales Bulletins
17 Sales Films and Audio-Visuals
18 Sales Manuals
19 House Publicity Organs—Magazines, etc., Notice Boards, Meetings of Staff
20 Within-Company Training in Customer and User Relations, Correspondence, Telephone
21 Merchandising
22 Packaging and Design
23 Improving Sales Distribution Coverage
24 Increasing Buying Response
25 Optimising Customer, User, Consumer stock inventories by Promotional Inducements
26 Optimising Display in Trade Outlets
27 The deliberate reinforcement of Company Advertising Policies, Plans, and Operations with Sales Promotional Support, applied to relevant Purchasing Outlets, at carefully judged times—either to precede, to synchronise with, or to follow up Advertising Campaigns.

Sales Control Activities

Arising from the company sales forecast, quota setting, and budget setting, it is vital that the sales director should know not only how the company is faring sales-wise, but why it is doing either well or badly in terms of sales force activity. Only in this way can he take any necessary remedial actions in good time to get the ship back on course. Only in this way can he hope to raise the performance of individual salesmen or sales areas up to the highest standards of the selling élite. Thus sales volume, selling of the product mix in balanced fashion, sales costs and effective performance of the sales force for a host of contributory reasons are all involved in this matter of sales control.

It is exercised by the chief sales executive via the sales office and in the field by field sales management. It is carried out by the imposition of a series of standard control ratios and sales force performance related to them.

Budgetary Control

The sales budget of expenditure fixed to match the cost of achieving the sales forecast (now the sales target) is a twin accountancy tool. First, it is an auditing tool. Second, it is a control tool. It measures the progress of the cost of selling activities in pursuit of its target. It shows the variances from the norm and thus invites corrective action to be taken.

The sales budget contains every item of fixed and variable cost. On the sales side it supplements the manufactured cost of the finished goods delivered to factory warehouse for onward routeing; with the full inventory of costs incurred in getting the goods promoted and sold, the costs of delivery and branch depot warehousing, the full sales departmental costs at H.Q. and in branch depots and offices. And of course the cost of the sales force in every nook and cranny of activity and any technical or advisory servicing required by the customers or public.

Budgetary control offers in a very broad context the effective control mechanism that covers the achievement of the sales target and costs in accordance with the figures set by the board and approved as the basis for the achievement of the company marketing and business objectives *in toto*.

In actual operation budgetary control provides a continuous running commentary and comparison of forecasted revenue and expenditure with the actual results obtained. It does so at sufficiently regular and close time intervals to detect variances immediately and to remedy their deficiencies. Budgetary control is a company fire alarm system that detects the flames before they can take charge and destroy the organisation.

A very important subsidiary application of budgetary control is effected in the sales field by distribution cost analysis and by sales cost ratios. As these cost control techniques are used also in quota setting, performance standard creation, and field control through the sales office at company H.Q. their consideration takes place in the discussion upon sales organisation and operation later in this chapter.

DISTRIBUTION COST ANALYSIS

Salesmen should never forget that the cost of distribution is a heavy one for the sales function to bear. In fact, in many organisations it exceeds the cost of production of finished goods delivered into company warehouse to await orders from customers. Obviously any practical ideas for resolving these occupational hazards by a significant reduction in such cost centres could have an important bearing upon a company's marketing competitiveness in the pricing of its product mix.

Distribution cost analysis is the traditional auditing way of throwing up, in clear relief, each major contributory cost of the sales activities. This enables a sales director to compare one type of cost with another on a regional and area basis. He can compare each single kind of cost in each area throughout the country, and compare each area cost with the national average. In this way he can see by this form-at-a-glance method precisely where the company's sales costs lie, which are too heavy, which are not heavy enough, and take remedial action. Exact costs of this kind are also extremely useful in sales budgeting by geographical area.

There is an activity of inter-firm comparison which the salesman should know about. Its joint sponsors are The British Institute of Management (B.I.M.) and The British Productivity Council (B.P.C.). Subscription to this service enables a company to compare its departmental and functional costs with others, both competitive and non-competitive. Although in its infancy, its worth is clearly beginning to show.

A salesman can see by reference to page 157 the type of significant activity that needs to be analysed for any exceptionable item of cost to be thrown up for attention.

Sales Analysis

The purposes for which sales analyses are regularly required include:
1 Comparisons with budgeted objectives and with previous results and trends.
2 Speedy recognition of change in trend so that opportunity can be exploited and threat nullified.
3 Careful comparisons with the assessed market potential for a product mix (e.g. input-output analysis tables might offer a trendy clue) to determine the company's real market share.

SUGGESTED FORMS OF ANALYSIS FOR SELLING AND DISTRIBUTION COST AND SALES

| Expense Analysis only | Expense Analysis only | Expense and Sales Analysis | Sales Analysis only | Sales Analysis only |
By nature of Expense	By Functions	By Locations	By Individual Products or Product Groupings — With regard to Purchase Basis	By Individual Products or Product Groupings — With regard to Prices and Terms
Direct Materials	Selling	Customers	Purchase Outright	Net Prices
Direct Labour	Advertising and Sales Promotion	Towns	Hire Purchase and Deferred Payment	Quantity Rates
Indirect Labour	Transportation	Counties	Rental	Wholesale Prices
Indirect Materials	Warehousing and Storage	Countries		Retail Prices
Services	Credit and Collection	Markets		Sale or Return (Consigned stocks or on approval)
Packaging Materials	Financial	Agents		Special Prices
Freight, etc.	General Administration	Representatives' Territories		Rebate on Turnover
Travelling Expenses		Departments such as Counters, Warehouses, Showrooms, Depots and Head Office Depts.		Cash Settlement Terms
Communications				
Information				
Advertising				
Other Charges (in detail)				

4 Relationship of sales with promotion costs can be examined with a microscope—cost per unit sold etc.—in order to determine promotional effectiveness and method.

5 Determination of cost of order collection to total sales revenue, i.e., the value of the sales force's contribution to profitability.

6 Measurement of effectiveness of sales by different outlets. Cut out dross.

7 Contributions made to total sales revenue and profit by each member of product mix. Cut out dross and loss leaders where wisdom indicates.

SALES CONTROL RATIOS ANALYSES

Clearly there must be ratios which can vitally affect the successful achievement of company sales forecasts and budgets and thus seriously influence company sales policies, planning and control at administrative top level.

For example: let us look at company budgets for the distribution cost centres.

We need therefore to create control ratios for the following cost centres of sales activity:

1 *Publicity Cost*—Public relations, advertising and sales promotion (including merchandising). The effectiveness of each component and that of the total needs to be checked against sales revenue and profit as acceptable cost.

2 *Sales Force Operational Costs*—here again the validity of each salesman and each component of sales force cost must be subjected to the closest scrutiny for validation purposes in terms of revenue and profit directly gained.

3 *Warehousing and Transportation Costs*—depots and transport can be of the wrong type and incorrectly located. Validation must be shown of their contribution to cost of sales and the viability of operational effectiveness established.

4 *New Product Development Costs*—are the costs acceptable in terms of the speed of break-even point reached, and their speed of climb into maturity phase of the product life cycle? In short how are they carrying their share of product mix cost and profit?

5 *Marketing Research Costs*—are the costs acceptable in terms of benefits clearly gained? For example, an investigation into the optimum work-load of a territory should quickly show a profit, or its implementation will have been made at too high a cost in terms of cost/benefit ratio.

Check ratios

There are a number of obvious check ratios that will quickly reveal whether a company's sales function is working profitably and well. For example:
Publicity cost to sales value
Production cost to sales value
Inventory level of finished goods to sales value
Bad debts to sales value
Profits to sales value
Contribution of key products to sales value and profits
Research and development costs to new product sales value and profitability
Sales volume per individual of work force
Profit per individual member of company.

Sales Analysis and the Computer

The essential volume of information data flowing through the average sales office is such that a computer or the hired services of a computer become daily more desirable to offset the delay and inaccuracy of purely manual means. A programmed computer can give quick, clear answers to problem areas such as the following:
1 Shall the company continue to service customers below a stated annual sales volume? Or continue to accept individual orders for less than an arbitrary value related to an actual loss on handling?
2 Shall we raise minimum order values to certain minimal figures? If so which?
3 Shall we service only large accounts and hand over the rest to middlemen?
4 Are there customers whose potential business (obtained by trend analysis) entitle them to special services to develop their potential? If so, how far can they go?

5 Applying the thinking of para (4) above to market segments, to products, to geographical areas, to countries, to types of outlet, to markets by usage.

6 Applying the thinking of para (5) would the profitable yield be speeded up by the use of carefully devised publicity campaigns?

Almost any question affecting sales analysis can be answered fairly quickly.

Market Models

Mathematical models can be constructed to deal visibly with many of the answers given by initial reference to the computer. The computer in such cases is not a decision-maker. It is a mathematical device for yielding information upon which experience, information, wisdom and further research can create provisional answers to the viability of carrying out certain operations. A well produced market model throws up the possibilities and constraints into clear perspective. It enables a worthwhile value judgement decision to be made.

Note The sales force control ratios will be dealt with in the following chapter dealing with field sales management where they operate in the search for business and the satisfaction of customers.

The Field Sales Manager's Overall Role in the Making of a Modern Salesman

Part Three

The Field Sales Manager's Overall Role in
the Making of a Modern Salesman

CHAPTER SIX

The Field Sales Manager's Overall Role

Clearly the actual sales force activity is the crucial operational centre where a company's sales plans succeed or come to nought. Hence the quality of field sales management is equally crucial in the attainment of company sales targets and budgets. We could say that it is in the cauldron of competitive activity in the marketplace that a company's sales policies and plans will come like Daniels to judgement. It will be the field sales managers who will largely be responsible for the company's return upon investment and its capital growth, represented in a larger market share. Field sales management will achieve such results in direct ratio to their success in the making of the salesmen they control into first class professional operators. In oversimplified terms it boils down to a managerial pursuit of salesmen who can and will excel.

With the trend towards organisational decentralisation top management is tending to look beyond its ivory tower at company headquarters. They want to see how their best laid plans are being put into action at the periphery of the markets they serve by the sales force. With the trend towards tighter costing of operational activities, top management is beginning to take a closer visual interest in checking how their cash is being expended, particularly in the contactual activities between the sales force and customers at large. For the sales cost centre is indeed a large and crucial one to company prosperity. In fact in far too many companies it is the largest company cost centre of all.

How then is the field sales manager to achieve his aims of making and developing the sales manpower in his charge so that

they reach as quickly as possible the peak of excellence in performance that is his main goal? In the majority of companies which
the author has contacted in this context, there seems to be a touching belief that competent performance of the sales force as a whole
is the most that any sales director can reasonably expect. In effect
they already accept that some 10% of their salesmen will be in the
top flight of performers because they possess an inward itch to be at
the top of the heap. The performance of the remainder will vary
from moderate in the case of some 60% of salesmen, to unsatisfactory in the case of 30% who constitute a flotsam and jetsam of men
who come and go without leaving any trace of success behind them.

This 30% failure rate represents one of the most costly ingredients
in the overall cost centre in the sales organisation. It is a tacit
admission of our national failure to select and interview realistically
in our search for top-notch salesmen. Even when such men with
high potential are found and recruited there is a potential failure
rate. Because field sales management has not been given an
adequate overall authority and responsibility to direct their
imagination and energies to manpower development as an absolute
operational priority. It can also be said with a strong degree of truth
that far too few field sales managers have been specifically trained
to do this important job with true expertise. Nor, have they been
trained in a methodology that makes this vital job easier to achieve.

The author has devised as a result of many such researches into
field sales operations a simple processing procedure called
PRIDOSAC. This makes the building and development of salesmen
easier to carry out. It is important to note that PRIDOSAC itself
does not contain any specific training or educational elements for
the salesman's development. What PRIDOSAC does is to provide a
working operational framework within which the specific needs for
training and education become manifest for each salesman
according to his need and the state of his professional expertise.

The PRIDOSAC Umbrella

The reader will spot at once that PRIDOSAC is in many respects
the marketing umbrella translated into specific terms for field sales
managerial guidance for operational activities. It starts with a plan
for each salesman's optimisation of the sales potential within his
territory related to specific time periods that will in due course be
geared to a target and a budget.

The plan is based upon detailed research carried out by the

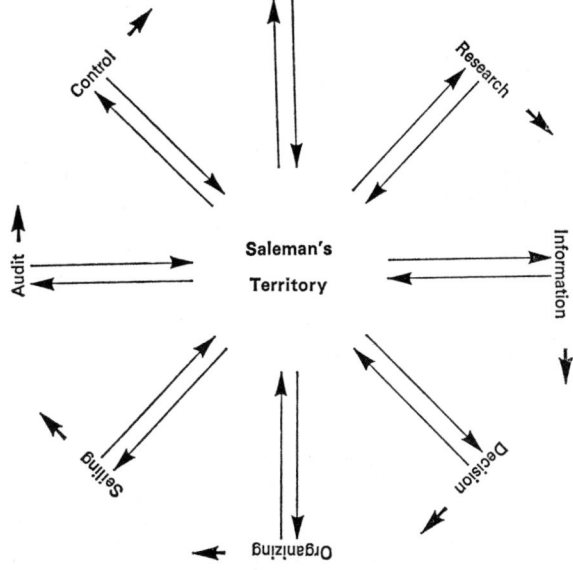

Diagram 16   The PRIDOSAC spectrum

salesman and his field sales manager, sometimes aided and abetted by company H.Q.

The research provides the necessary information upon which the salesman can mount his individual selling campaign ideas for optimisation of sales by product, by market segment and by key outlet.

The alternative ideas are examined, evaluated, and the best selected for the organised selling that will have to be done in the period and areas chosen. This is decision-making, taking and organising for success.

At this stage selling sweeps into action according to plan, forecasts and budgets for the time period that have been made and the campaign gets off the mark.

So far we have dealt with field sales management by objective. There must clearly be an auditing system continuously applied to ensure that the plans are achieved as stated, in the time allocated, at the cost envisaged. This rarely happens owing to the paucity of our predictive skills and market vagaries. So we must monitor any

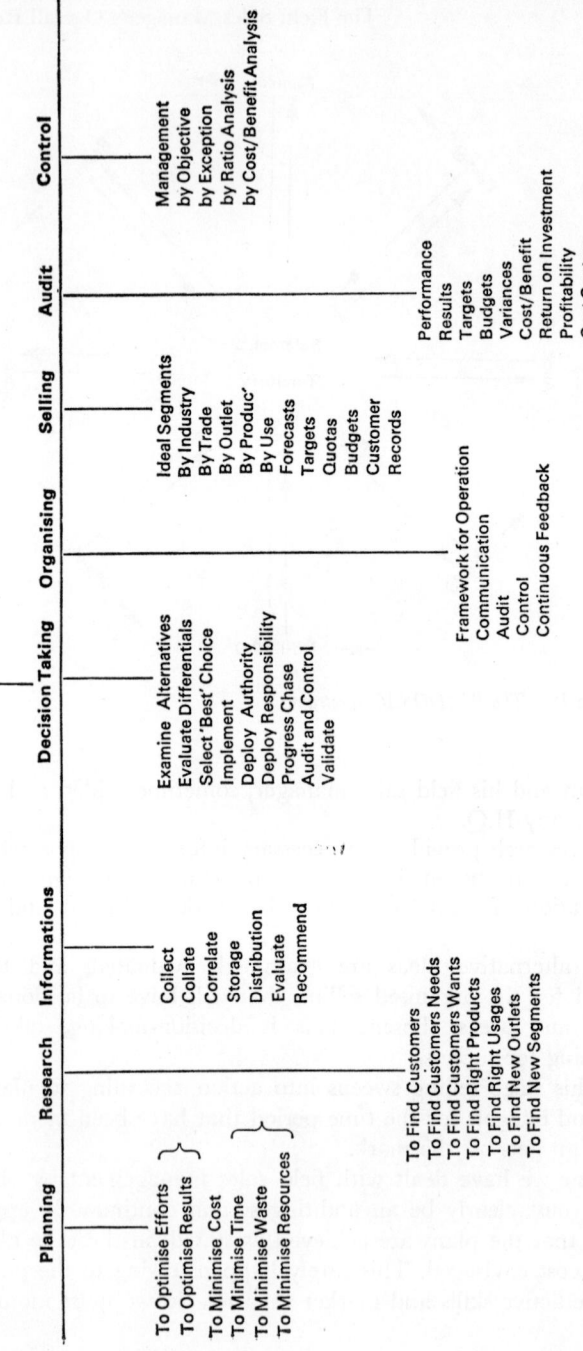

Planning	Research	Informations	Decision Taking	Organising	Selling	Audit	Control
To Optimise Efforts	To Find Customers	Collect	Examine Alternatives		Ideal Segments		Management
To Optimise Results	To Find Customers Needs	Collate	Evaluate Differentials		By Industry		by Objective
To Minimise Cost	To Find Customers Wants	Correlate	Select 'Best' Choice		By Trade		by Exception
To Minimise Time	To Find Right Products	Storage	Implement		By Outlet		by Ratio Analysis
To Minimise Waste	To Find Right Usages	Distribution	Deploy Authority		By Product		by Cost/Benefit Analysis
To Minimise Resources	To Find New Outlets	Evaluate	Deploy Responsibility		By Use		
	To Find New Segments	Recommend	Progress Chase		Forecasts		
			Audit and Control	Framework for Operation	Targets	Performance	
			Validate	Communication	Quotas	Results	
				Audit	Budgets	Targets	
				Control	Customer	Budgets	
				Continuous Feedback	Records	Variances	
						Cost/Benefit	
						Return on Investment	
						Profitability	
						Cost Centres	

Diagram 17   The PRIDOSAC umbrella

variance so that remedial action can be taken without delay to get the activity back on its planned and scheduled course. This is field sales management by exception.

This control of variance and planned activity is made much easier by the usage of sales control ratios, specially slanted to the selling activities face-to-face with competitors and customers.

Note
Each of the more significant activities is dealt with in some detail in the following chapters.

This chapter continues with a survey of the managerial arts, skills, attitudes and outlook essential for the making of modern salesmen.

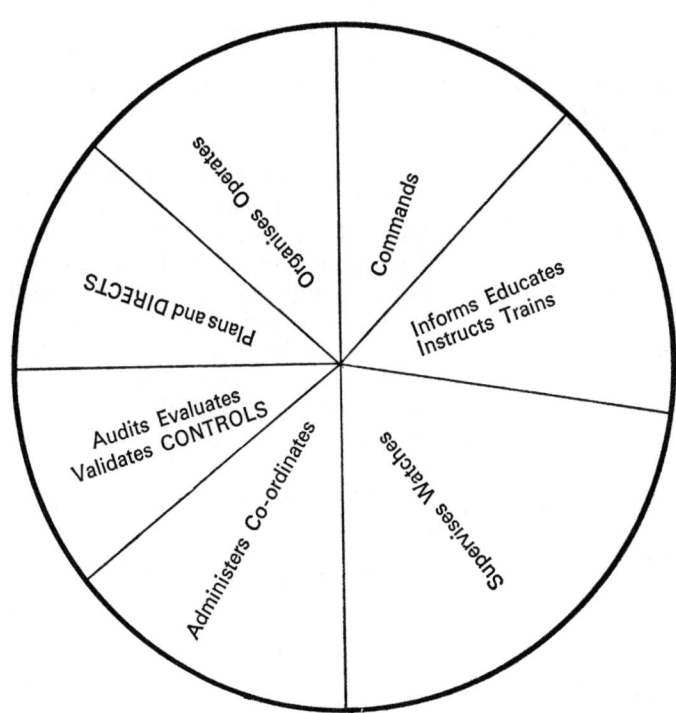

Diagram 18   Line responsibilities of the field sales manager

THE CYCLE OF FIELD SALES MANAGERIAL ACTIVITY

A field sales manager is thus a projection of headquarters' sales management into the market, where he manages a territorial region, and the men within it. The field sales manager is thus a central core of a communications and managerial network in a geographical region between company H.Q. and his sales force. And indirectly between company H.Q. and the market segments within the region that he manages. However, it would be a cardinal error to visualise the field sales manager as being a purely line manager between H.Q. and field. Relaying instructions down to the sales force and reporting the results back vertically in an upwards direction to the sales director or general sales manager, as shown in the diagram.

The field sales manager is that *rara avis* a staff adviser as well as a normal line manager. He carries a most important responsibility for the development of the total resources in his control: money spent, materials used, methods operated, men managed. Thus at one stroke we see the field sales manager wearing in quick succession a number of professional hats to match a number of advisory roles. For example:

An Accounting Hat	— to oversee the return upon investment made in his region for which he is the trustee. He follows this up by underwriting the capital growth of the investment by planning profitable activities and development of men and sales.
A Planning Hat	— to make all the pipe dreams come true in terms of sales exploitation of market and manpower potentials.
A Research Hat	— to ensure that all relevant and obtainable information is registered, recorded, evaluated and used to achieve the optimum results from selling efforts.
An Organisation Hat	— to ensure that each territory is properly organised in terms of securing the optimum profitable work-load, of methodical calling, intelligent reporting, optimum development.
A Control Hat	— to ensure proper performance standards being instituted for each salesman, regular audits of performance being made and

variances both qualitative and quantitative being controlled.

An Auditing Hat — to evaluate the needs for training, education and development for each man revealed by control of performance.

A Training Hat — to ensure that training, education and development are carefully tailored to the exact measure and need of each man at any given time. And that it follows a pattern for each man's career development in time.

A Motivation Hat — to ensure that each man is motivated according to the needs of the man, his customers and his company. A most difficult and self-crucifying task.

A Leadership Hat — to ensure that there is always an enthusiastic, positive, creative attitude to people and to work in the field organisation—a constructive approach to every problem, difficulty, and opportunity.

A Tutoring Hat — the role of elder brother and statesman is a vital one in the creation of morale by which a salesman and a sales team grow and thrive. It is a role sadly neglected both in our educational system and in field management. It must not be confused with motivation, training and leadership. It is concerned with the development of each salesman as a balanced, integrated man for all seasons and occasions. It is far too often forgotten that when we hire a man's services, we take the whole man, his family, his social side, his professional abilities, the total man. Each aspect of a man affects all the others, either to his benefit or to his detriment. Field sales managers are thus in a unique position to get the best out of each man because they know how each man thinks and acts in each of his portfolio of skill and activities. And they are concerned in helping him to blossom to his fullest potential as salesman and as an individual.

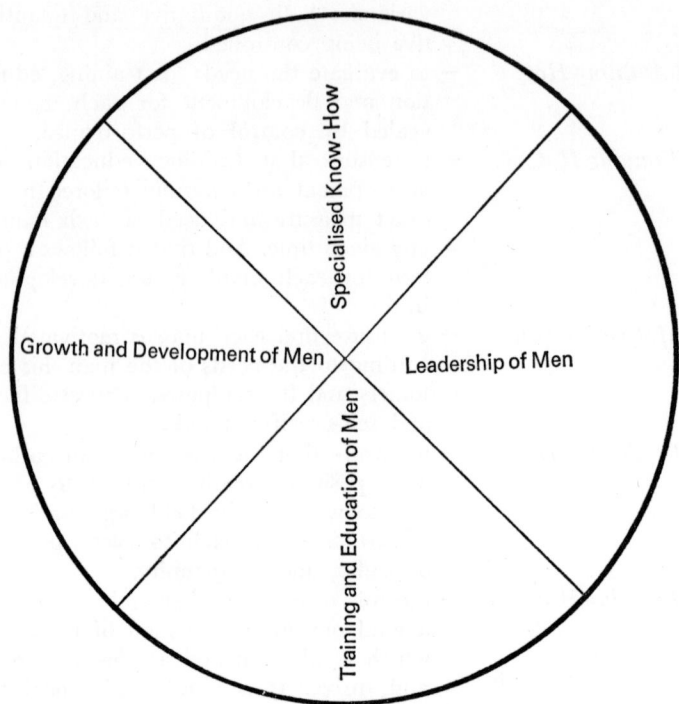

Diagram 19   Staff responsibilities of the field sales manager

Note
So far we have been concerned with the manager managing his
men. There is another aspect of field sales management that is
crucial to his success with his men. This is the self-management of
the manager himself. There are three broad areas of self-management we should study.

A FIELD SALES MANAGER'S SELF-MANAGEMENT ROLE

A field sales manager needs to manage, audit and control three areas
of his own activities:
Self-organisation; management of time and effort, coupled with self-
development; and management of the danger zones to successful
operational activity.

Diagram 20   Human responsibilities of the field sales manager

Self-Organisation

Self-organisation can be roughly divided into two very broad areas of planning and control. The pity is that far too many field sales managers get so bogged down in the detailed running of routine trivia. Thus they do not see the absolute necessity of spending a part of each day thinking about better ways and means of self-organisation that will lead to an all round improvement in field operational efficiency. For example, as a consultant I find that field sales managers are often concerned about the unproductive way in which many of their men spend their time. Yet, most of them have not carried out an audit of their own time usage for years past, if at all.

Self-organisation is the essential first step in self-discipline. It is not easy to understand how field sales managers can talk about discipline to salesmen unless they practise this most difficult of arts themselves, and upon themselves.

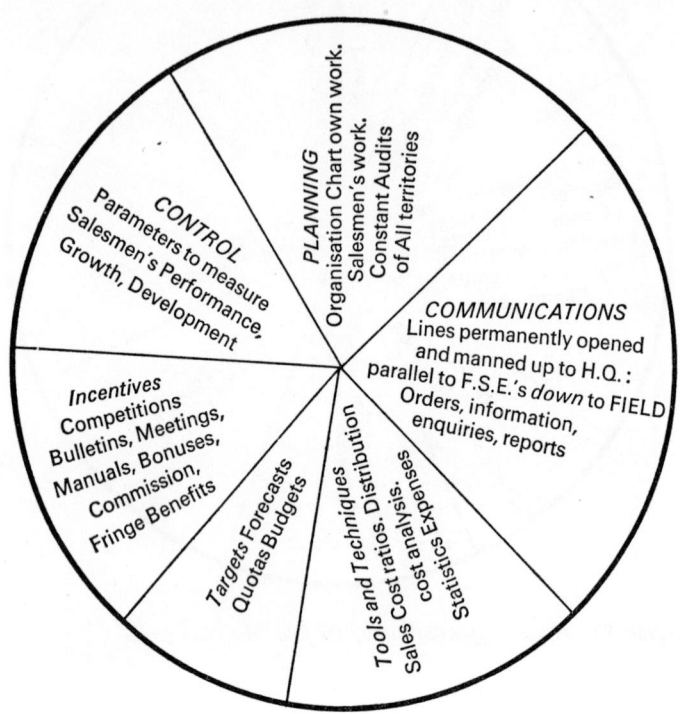

Diagram 21   Self-organisation

Diagram No. 21 shows the principal areas in which a field sales manager should be regularly and patiently involved. When this pie chart is considered in conjunction with Diagram No. 22 we can see more clearly how vital it is for each field sales manager to create an accurate split between the demands that are made upon him.

There are field sales managers who have not found the time for years to read a book about management, or selling, or training. Their out-of-date effects upon forward-thinking and new techniques can be imagined, with the sales force the inevitable sufferers. Apart from the obvious fact that a field sales manager is going to find it difficult to keep on top of his demanding job without finding time

Diagram 22   Managerial split of time and effort

for study and self-organisation, there is the vital matter of promotion.

Promotion for both members of the sales force and for its field management is a natural phenomenon. It is a vital part of a career escalator. The essential requirements are that a candidate for potential promotion must have made himself ready for it by previous study, experience and judgement. To do this it is vital as a principle of management that all suitable men should force themselves to find the daily time for study for this purpose. Management must set the example. Hence the emphasis upon self-development and all its implications mentioned in the Pie Chart Diagram 22.

MANAGERIAL SELF-DEVELOPMENT

The variety of managerial hats which a field sales manager is called upon to wear provides a happy and apt introduction to managerial self-development. In short he must prepare himself to be proficient enough to wear each separate hat to the manner born, with absolute authority, with competent ease, with dignity and poise. How else can he hope to influence his men effectively?

A field sales manager should ideally understand the whole of his company's operation from board policies down to clerical procedures He should be able to interpret them to his men effectively so that they can admire the company's corporate image and its forward thinking and expertise in general. He should study the simpler applications of psychology and the social sciences as they affect the small change of everyday human relations. He should understand better than his own salesmen the problems they will be called upon to solve, the needs they will be called upon to satisfy. He should know how to help his men to create positive, creative attitudes to life, to living, to selling, to work, so that they may enjoy and benefit from them, just as he himself does.

A field sales manager must develop his powers of empathy, of persuasive communication, of training, of educating, and above all of tutoring his men, so that he and they can get the utmost benefits from working together as a team in search of the attainment of company objectives.

A field sales manager must develop his powers of value-judge-making so that both he and his recommendations for action are fully respected by his men. Above all, he should try to acquire the attitude of championing his men and their efforts so that they can work for him with pride, as well as the pride that ensues from doing a professional job well. The field sales manager must in effect learn to develop his skills and mind in the pursuit of excellence.

MANAGERIAL DANGER ZONES

Managers quickly learn to appreciate that they work within statutes of limitations. There are limitations forced upon management by their own frailties, or from lack of specialised expertise. There are limitations forced upon management by the weaknesses of the men whom they seek to influence. There are limitations of the surroundings such as the market, or competitive ascendancy which are difficult to counter. A manager does not have to wear the mantle of a modern Solomon or Socrates to realise that there are some limitations that he can overcome. There may be others that for a time he will not be able to circumvent, particularly those that are associated with his own company top management or policies.

There are danger zones that always lurk beneath the surface of most managerial jobs. And many are like icebergs, where the exposed surface gives little reliable indication of their unseen depth. There are many that lurk within the bias or prejudice of a manager's own habits of thought or of action.

Diagram No. 23 offers a representative selection of typical managerial hazards that deserve to have their respective storm cones hoisted whenever the manager comes within their potential range of adverse operation.

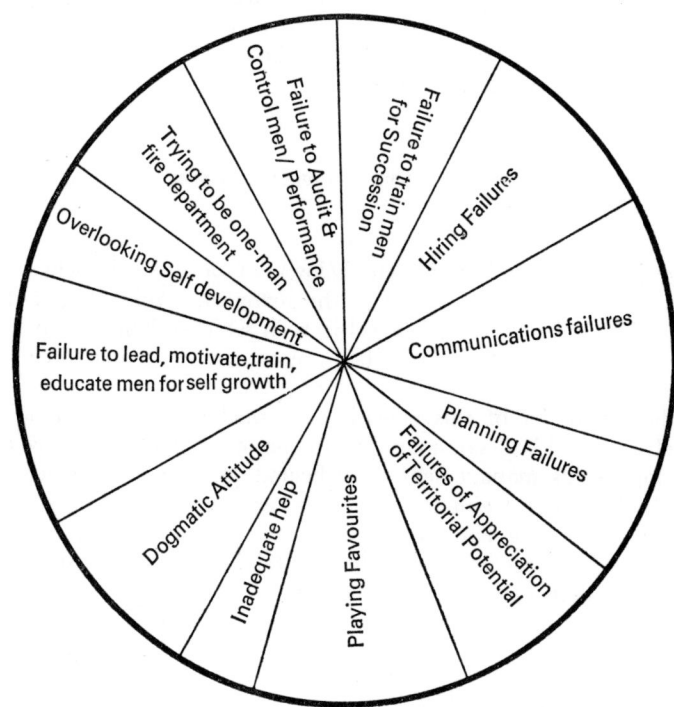

Diagram 23   The danger zones

Many of these danger zones are a menace because of a managerial failure to appreciate how they think, feel and act. They are nearly all hazards only because a manager fails to insist upon high standards of self-conduct, organisation and control. It is the compromise that many managers make with excellence and defeat. They seek to find a safe zone between these two opposite polarities and merely create rods for their own backs by an acceptance of the second rate. Board rooms are concerned with success, with winning, and not being the best of the losers. There should be no cult of the second rate or admission of failure in forward looking field sales managers. But, there can be the opposite danger of over-confidence.

The price of freedom (this country has appreciated through one thousand years or more) is eternal and unceasing vigilance. A field sales manager can expect to pay no smaller price for peace of mind. Hence he must be prepared to accept nothing less from himself than first class operation. And be unwilling to accept less from his men. Only the cult of operative excellence will suffice, however hard and long it must be worked at and for, to ensure its continuity in any circumstances.

A TYPICAL COMPREHENSIVE JOB SPECIFICATION FOR FIELD SALES MANAGEMENT

The job specification (given below) of a typical field sales manager indicates the stretch of the managerial role. But, it does more. It implies the range of subjects in which salesmen will need to be continuously trained if they are to carry out their own jobs expertly.

The remainder of this book is concerned with selling activities which the budding salesman has to master, if he is to grow and develop as his management is dedicated to help him to achieve. On-the-job sales training is the master tool in the managerial armoury to create effective modern salesmen. It is dealt with in great detail in accordance with its vital importance to successful sales operations carried out by modern salesmen.

JOB SPECIFICATION FOR TYPICAL FIELD SALES MANAGER

1 To *achieve* all Targets, Quotas, and Budgets set within stated Time periods

2 To *organise* Manpower and Material Resources in area to achieve optimum results

3 To *organise* deployment of selling effort to match increased potential in markets

4 To *achieve* the optimum Profitability of Operation throughout the area

5 To *create* the optimum of Customer/User Satisfactions and Goodwill throughout the area

6 To *create* the optimum of co-operation between Office, Factory, Field, and Markets

7 To *plan* the development of Sales through every actual and potential outlet

8 To *ensure* regular two-way dissemination of Information between Factory, Office, and Sales Field

9 To *grade* both Source and Reliability of Information reported to H.Q.

10 To *ensure* regular and complete returns to H.Q. upon every aspect of Selling Work

11 To *make* proposals for area promotions, advertising, exhibitions as necessary

12 To *prepare* area forecasts, budgets, performance standards, appraisals as required

13 To *keep* a constant check upon customer credit standing and need for extra accommodation as and when deemed to be desirable to expand safe business

14 To *insist* upon the balanced selling and promotion of each product in the mix

15 To *enforce* Company Sales Policies—especially about Price, Terms etc.

16 To *hold* regular Sales Meetings both to promote sales, interpret policy and planning—and to act as Training Sessions in Manpower Development

17 To *supervise* all Education, Training, Counselling, Guidance, Tutoring necessary to ensure the Planned Manpower Development of each Man according to his current needs

18 To *appraise* each salesman's performance against standard norms, to report upon each man regularly to H.Q.—and to *create* remedial projects to *ensure* any defaulter gets back on course with a minimum of delay

19 To *supervise* all company property—cars, samples etc.,—to *ensure* that all Manpower needs are adequately met at least cost with maximum efficiency

20 To *use* Participatory Leadership and Management of Men so that each man feels that he has both a niche in the Team, and a responsibility to optimise company effort.

21 To *manage* both by Objective and by Exception—Control

F

through the constant monitoring of variances from the norm, and their remedial treatment

22 To *provide* the escalator for Job and Career Satisfactions for both himself and for each man—training for the next job ahead on the career escalator—development of potential to match timed career aspirations—to *create* a Happy Ship, a closely knit and integrated balanced Team Effort to optimise the company's Market Share on each salesman's area.

CHAPTER SEVEN

The Field Sales Managerial Role in Sales Territorial Planning, Calling Frequency, Routeing

We shall assume that a new territory is being planned, a new sales-man has been carefully chosen to work it, and together field manager and salesman sit down to plan how the territory can be operated to optimum benefit in terms of progressive development.

A TERRITORIAL SURVEY

Not every salesman is a born planner. He has to be shown how to plan well, and how to acquire the necessary skills and outlook. Psychologically, it is necessary to involve him in his own working future, from the outset of the planning activity. Only in this way will he feel that he has an active role in the shaping of his own destiny, and therefore will work full out on every cylinder to prove the excellence of his own planning capacity.

We must assume also that the salesman will be located at that geographical spot in his territory, that will economise travelling time in the overall working of his customers for at least a five year period ahead. We shall assume that the territory is the County of Hertfordshire. Two actual case histories are involved, one of a salesman involved in technical selling; the other a salesman engaged in a medium priced engineering product.

WORK-LOADING FOR COMMERCIAL AND INDUSTRIAL SELLING

Case A

The actual home of salesman No. 1 selling a technical product by

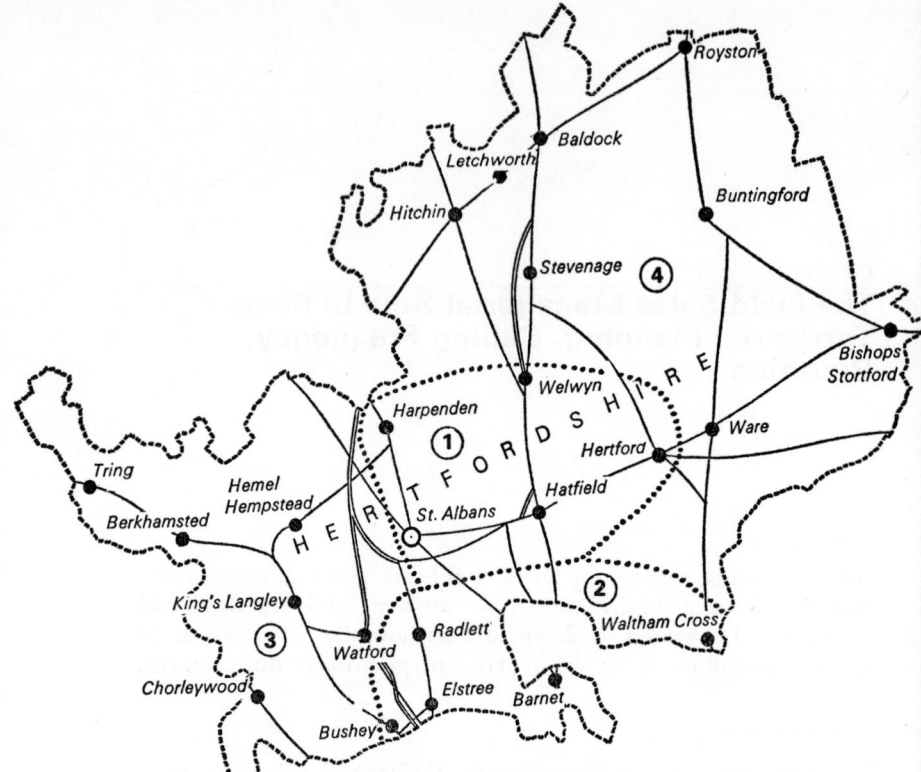

Diagram 24   Hertfordshire: principal towns and roads

speciality method—retail weighing equipment—was in the Hatfield-Welwyn Garden City area. The reader can see at a glance that as the job is one of regular cold-canvass calling on retail businesses, involving much back-calling, it was wise to elect for the County to be divided into four areas of operation (numbered 1–4 on map). The areas were chosen because they permitted calls to be economically arranged around the main trunk roads of the A.1., A.10., A.5., A.41. from which it was easy to programme calls in a logical and sequential fashion. Area No. 1 was designed deliberately around his own doorstep, so that he could optimise upon time when weather conditions such as fog and snow made travel to the perimeter of the County either time wasting, or hazardous.

The County was then reduced to a hypothetical square. Just as a rotations of crops is good strategy for husbandry so is the rotation of calling cyclically so that each succeeding day's work falls in a different sector of the square. For, back-calling can take place

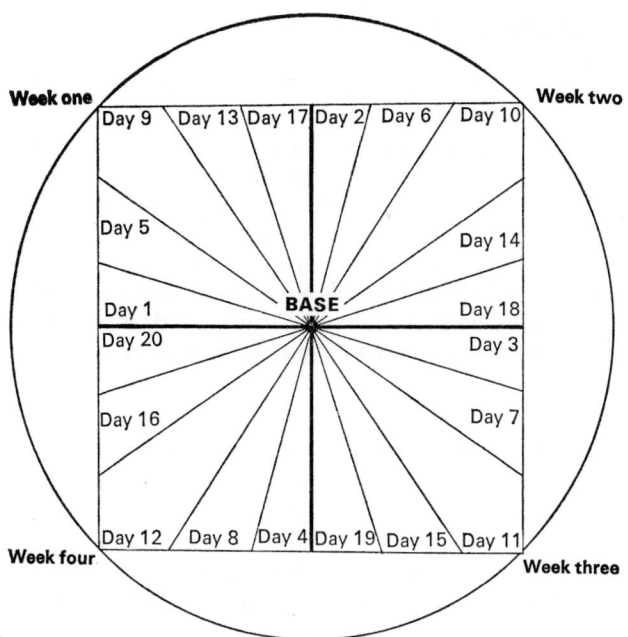

Diagram 25   Distribution of calls: the four-week cycle

economically within a few days, whereas in the traditional system of working through each district at a time, back-calling out of rote into a different district is extremely prodigal with the commodity in shortest supply—time.

Case B

The home of salesman No. 2 was at Enfield, near to Waltham Cross. His problem was similar but different. He needed to contact all the engineering users of his product within the County. A different method of cyclical calling had thus to be designed to meet his requirements. Instead of the square, it was decided to use the four trunk roads as the veins of a leaf, or petals of a flower, along which the salesman could travel with a minimum of time loss and obtain an optimum access to the kinds of industrial outlets he needed to contact.

The petal approach aims to reduce travelling time to an absolute minimum. It makes the farthest point of the day's work load geographically the mid-point of the day's journey. This is the directly opposite method of so many salesmen who make the farthest point either their first or last call of the day. In the majority of cases the petal approach saves time. In some instances savings of up to 33⅓ per cent have been reported. The effect is to transmute otherwise wasted time into productive time that can be used for face-to-face selling to prospective buyers. The *modus operandi* is simplicity itself. Each day's work is within the petal and continues progressively along the spine of each trunk road.

Combining the square and the petal can yield even greater dividends in saved time. This salesman found that by working each succeeding day along a different trunk road, back calls were effected without wasted time or journey disruption.

ALLOCATION OF INDIVIDUAL WORK LOAD AND CREATING A DIFFERENTIAL
CALL FREQUENCY

To revert to the field manager helping the new salesman to plan his territory from scratch, we attack the problem of optimum work loading that each man can efficiently operate. This amounts to an assessment of the actual number of calls that can be made by the salesman upon the number of prospective purchasers during a calendar year.

Here is a simple equation for working out this vital estimate :

The Number of Prospective Buyers × *The Calling Frequency* =
The Number of Working Days per Annum × *The Average Daily
Call Rate*

The new salesman can use this equation in the following way:
1 He needs to assess the number of differing grades of customer call.
2 He needs to establish the number of real working days per annum.
3 He needs to establish a total norm for calls daily allowing for the difference in grades, waiting time, travelling time, meals, etc.

Companies differ enormously in this respect. The criterion is to set the number of worthwhile calls to accept as the minimum and not the number of doors upon which a man can unprofitably knock.

Industrial calling averages some 200 days in this country. Commercial calling averages some 240 days (allowing for holidays etc.). Industrial salesmen tend to become involved in many extra-curricular activities (not related to actual selling) that make their daily score so much less. Commercial sales forces are becoming more ruthlessly routed so that only holidays seem to interfere with working schedules.

Commercial salesmen can make between 15 and 20 calls a day on retail outlets according to size and to the amount of merchandising to be performed.

Industrial salesmen are in the main limited to six good hours a day, and one to ten calls are acceptable according to the company and its product line (including the difficulties in selling and order time lags). Six calls seem in the broad term to be acceptable to a majority of industrial companies.

We now have one of two sums for the new salesman to work out, according to his job type:

If in industry 200 days @ 6 calls a day = 1200 calls per annum
If in commerce 240 days @ 15 calls a day = 3600 calls per annum

Allowing for four grades of call frequency
'A'   48 calls per annum for commerce)
'A'   10 calls per annum for industry   )

'B'   24 calls per annum for commerce)
'B'   6 calls per annum for industry   )

'C'   12 calls per annum for commerce)
'C'   4 calls per annum for industry   )

'D'   6 calls per annum for commerce)
'D'   2 calls per annum for industry   )

The 'new' Industrial salesman can work out a hypothetical pattern
 20 'A' customers @ 10 calls per annum   = 200 calls
 50 'B' customers @ 6 calls per annum   = 300 calls
100 'C' customers @ 4 calls per annum   = 400 calls
100 'D' customers @ 2 calls per annum   = 200 calls
Spare capacity for cold canvass calling   = 100 calls
                                    Total 1200 calls per annum

This new salesman by his attention to detailed research into his potential work load has established exactly what, where, when and with whom his calling activity will be concentrated for the year ahead.

He will avoid the plague of being overloaded or of being underloaded, either of which is a morale-buster and a cause of ineffective working and results below par.

He can now concentrate upon the task of becoming an entre-preneurially-minded business builder, when regularly motivated, helped and wisely led and controlled by his field manager.

The calculation for a new commercial salesman would not be easy to work out as a truly representative figure. This is due to the enormous variations that exist in companies selling through retail outlets. These variations are caused by the differences in computa-tion of work-loading, differential calling frequencies, merchandising duties and the like.

Each commercial reader should work out a figure for his own territory based upon his own experience and the equation offered. This would be an interesting check upon his current working practice.

TIME MANAGEMENT AND MASTERY IN THE MANAGERIAL CONTROL OF
CONTACTUAL CALL COST

Here is our greatest average sales cost centre that offers the mechanics of control by planning and audit. Chaucer hit the nail on the head in his stricture on time usage many centuries ago 'For TIME lost may not be recovered'. This is exactly it. Time is our most precious selling commodity and medium, yet there is little if any published research on such a vital subject.

The author's work in this field is well known. The four pie charts together depict the average usage of time by field sales management and men in both the industrial and consumer goods operations.

The effects of cost can be seen immediately if we look at an average figure of £5,000 per annum to keep an industrial technical salesman in operation. On a basis of 200 working days per annum this represents a working cost of £25 per man per day of six hours. On a basis of 6 contactual calls per day each contact costs £4·16, and on a basis of 20 per cent face-to-face selling time each product-ive hour costs £20 whether an order is booked or not.

McGraw Hill in the USA published a piece of research on some 1,000 industrial sales calls on various industrial outlets, giving figures rarely if ever attained here. For instance, a total working day of over 9 hours; covering more than 8 calls with an average length of 28 minutes each, and including face-to-face exposure to prospective purchasers of 3 hours and 52 minutes.

The effects of cost can be seen equally clearly if we consider an

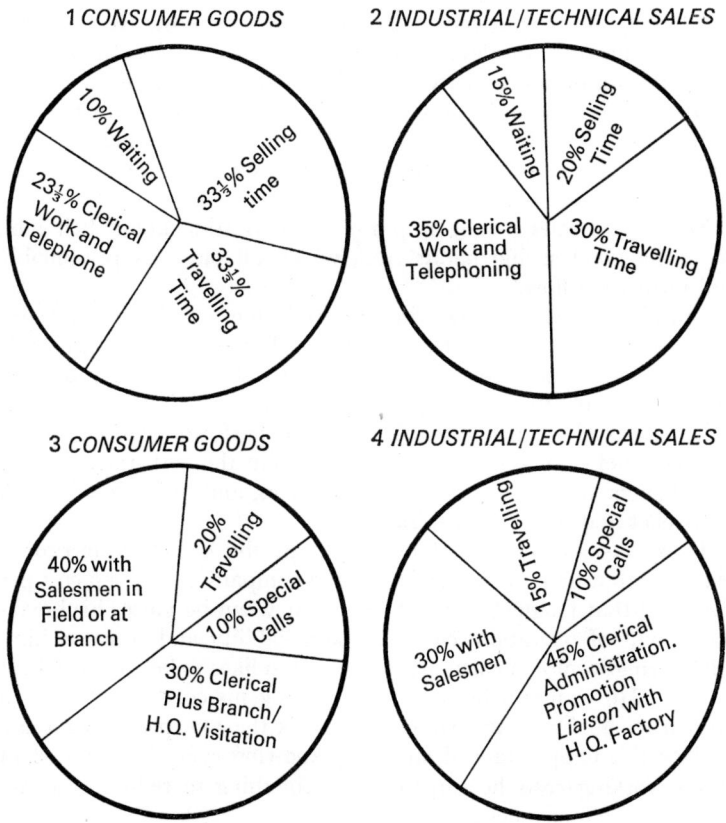

1 CONSUMER GOODS

10% Waiting
33⅓% Selling time
23⅓% Clerical Work and Telephone
33⅓% Travelling Time

2 INDUSTRIAL/TECHNICAL SALES

15% Waiting
20% Selling Time
35% Clerical Work and Telephoning
30% Travelling Time

3 CONSUMER GOODS

40% with Salesmen in Field or at Branch
20% Travelling
10% Special Calls
30% Clerical Plus Branch/ H.Q. Visitation

4 INDUSTRIAL/TECHNICAL SALES

15% Travelling
10% Special Calls
30% with Salesmen
45% Clerical Administration. Promotion Liaison with H.Q. Factory

Diagram 26   Time analysis
1 and 2: the salesman. 3 and 4: the field sales executive

approximate figure of £4,000 per annum to keep a consumer goods salesman in operation. On a basis of 240 working days per annum this represents a working cost of £16·6 per day. On the basis of 15 calls each working day this gives a figure of just over £1 per contactual call. On a basis of 33⅓ per cent face-to-face exposure to prospective purchasers this offers a cost per productive hour of over £6 per 8 hour working day, regardless of the number and value of orders booked. Where a man is involved in a heavy merchandising promotional activity, the number of calls per day will be less, with a higher cost per contactual call.

With such a high contactual cost centre a field sales manager must consider how best, and where best to give his invaluable time in developing the overall regional business at least cost. He must not overlook his role of developing each man under his tutelage to the optimum of his capacity to produce business and profit.

He must for example consider precisely how much extra training in methodical working, plus skill in closing business quickly, might bolster up the daily call rate, and thus produce more business at less comparative cost.

Many field sales managers prate about insisting upon their men acquiring good selling habits from which all blessings presumably will ultimately flow.

Learning, as we shall see when we study the practice under training sessions, does not flow from managerial invocations or threats. It begins when a salesman sees the sense of what a manager is discussing, and relates the suggested benefits to himself. The manager is selling ideas about a salesman's improved performance in terms of buying benefits. The salesman has to see that the best usage of time must benefit him in everything that he does, and ultimately in both his pocket and his career aspirations.

Thus, a salesman should be taught at the outset of territorial planning that he is being carried by the company at a given cost per day until that magical moment each year when he passes his break-even point of operation, ceases to be a liability and converts himself overnight into an earning asset. No man likes to be seen as a kept satellite. He wants to be seen to be paying his corner and to be a growth stock. Once he realises that he is the one person who can achieve this happy state of affairs by knowing every item and slant of his working costs he can then do something to reduce cost and to increase effectiveness.

The author has found it helpful to give salesmen new to a company a time and motion check list of time wasters that insidiously fritter away valuable selling time unless detected and controlled.

A Study of Time and Motion

Typical Time Wasters

1 Leaving home late and getting home early. Customers can be called upon from the minute they open to the moment they close, and many may be seen after normal trading hours.
2 If you visit the branch office or depot, do it before work starts or

after it stops, and never whilst calls could still be made upon customers.

3 Calling upon customers incompletely equipped to show, demonstrate and sell.

4 Unnecessary use of the telephone, and its inefficient use also. Its proper use is to get an appointment or to deal with an emergency.

5 Frequent, long business lunches.

6 Unnecessary conversations with non-customers.

7 Writing detailed reports or making unnecessary notes when there is a chance to sell.

8 Unnecessary calling upon regular customers or upon those where business will drop sometime but not now.

9 Unnecessary visits to branch office or depot to collect material during selling hours.

10 Unnecessary waiting at customers' premises because an appointment was not made in advance.

11 Bad routeing and doubling back. Failure to plan movements.

12 Cosy chats with competitive salesmen under the illusion that they will drop vital information.

13 Wasting effort on fringe business, on doubtful starters, on suspects rather than prospects.

14 Wasting effort on customers whose potential is strictly limited.

15 Waiting at home to collect the morning mail before setting out.

16 Failure to contact the key men in the customer's buying departments and dealing with small fry.

17 Failure to prepare for each interview with selling sentences, sequences, equipment and knowledge to clinch the sale on the call.

This brings us to the consideration of sales forecasting, quota and budget setting for each salesman's territory, and his responsibility to carry his share of the total company sales load with expertise and honour.

THE FIELD MANAGERIAL ROLE IN SALES FORECASTING, QUOTA FIXING AND BUDGETS

It is often overlooked that field sales managers and salesmen have a definitive role to play in assisting the company to make territorial and regional forecasts. They do this through the use of their specialised knowledge of local conditions and actual purchasing potential of key buying outlets.

It is pure wisdom to involve both field management and the sales force in the creation and computation of the selling targets it is intended that a company shall achieve. It can be argued that individual salespeople can be unduly pessimistic in their own target setting in case things go wrong and they appear to be condemned as failures out of their own big mouths. This remark can be applied equally to overcautious field managers too. In practice however sales folk are optimists in the main and are more likely to have to be protected from the results of over-optimism than from errors due to over-pessimism. Wise field managers are shrewd enough to know the score of potential increase on every sales territory they control. And, much more to the point, they know the exact strength and capacity of each salesman when fully stretched—which can be a very rare happening indeed.

A field manager will start to forecast by using the familiar tools characteristic of company H.Q. and of course the information on the sort of year ahead that is expected to be experienced.

The Field Managerial Role in Helping Salesmen to Plan their Approach to Ensure Optimum Business with Buying Satisfactions

General planning of a strategic nature common to most types of selling operations has been discussed. We now approach the point where differences in tactical planning occur in the types of selling and the kinds of buying characteristic of British commerce and industry.

For example, although there are common basics to all selling and buying activities, problem areas and needs, patterns of selling and buying can and do differ in considerable degree.

We can see this more clearly by identifying the principal kinds of selling and buying activities.

THE SELLING PATTERN—DIFFERENT TYPES OF SALESMAN

1 Staple regular repeat selling items to commerce and industry. Examples are foods, cigarettes, alcoholic and soft drinks, nuts, bolts, screws, etc.
2 Semi-durable items to commerce and industry: pots, pans, light cleaning equipment, clothing, etc.
3 General services to commerce and industry: towel and laundry services, janitorial cleansing, catering services, etc.

4 Specialised services to commerce and industry: insurance, fire fighting, consultancy, investment, financial, etc.

5 Speciality serving of commerce and industry: weighing equipment, cash registers, office control machinery, typewriters, duplicating and printing equipment, etc.

6 Industrial sales engineers: every kind of selling where engineering knowledge and experience are essential to a proper handling of the selling proposition and buying needs.

7 Technical salesmen to industry: involving specialised technical know-how, experience, and competence including chemical engineering activity, construction industries, computer and data processing activities, special equipment.

These seven areas of selling can call for very different kinds of salesmen; different kinds of knowledge, experience and skills; different selling approaches, plans, tactics in wooing the prospective purchasers.

We have not mentioned merchandiser as a separate class of salesman; most salesmen in categories one and two are called upon to merchandise their wares.

We have a blurring of outline in categories five, six, and seven. For instance, speciality salesmen are often encountered in industrial sales engineering and technical selling, where the type of product demands it. Similarly, technical salesmen sell engineering goods, and sales engineers sell technical goods. However, in the main the category listing is fully descriptive.

THE PURCHASING PATTERN — DIFFERENT TYPES OF BUYER

1 *Commercial Buying* — retail, departmental store, wholesale, cash and carry, discount houses, direct mail operators, mail order operators, direct-to-householder operations, supermarket, self-service. Salesmen in categories one, two, three, four, and five all serve this buying category.

2 *Industrial Buying* — consumer items, semi-durable items, durables, equipment, plant, machine tools, components, raw materials, general and special services, computers, automated machinery and machine tools, office

machinery, buildings, furniture, furnishings, cars, lorries, mechanical handling equipment etc.

Industrial Purchasing Patterns—A Seven-Way Split

1 Raw materials
2 Components
3 Consumable materials
4 Packaging and wrapping materials
5 Plant and equipment
6 Technical services
7 General services

The length of selling negotiation is related to the longevity of the items to be bought and the unit cost. Nuts and bolts are bought quickly and with regularity, whereas computers costing very large sums of money are invested in but rarely by one company. The types of selling planning and approach are clearly very different. The contactual cost is recovered quickly in the first instance, and the competence of the salesman is easily and visibly apparent. In the second case, the cost comes first, and there is a considerable time-lag caused by the period of the ultimate order's gestatory time in months or years. It is thus far from easy to assess the salesman's professional expertise, except in the very long term.

Although most buyers are actuated by similar syndromes of motivation in their professional roles, the emphasis on individual motivations can vary enormously. A food buyer will be much impressed by the publicity backing, a new wrap, a large discount. An industrial buyer rarely buys on such impulse motivations, but on longer term considerations linked to need, suitability and overall values.

Lurking behind the screen of anonymity lies a host of company officials on the industrial and technical purchasing fronts who can and do materially influence the placing and destination of the larger and more important orders. They are the faceless ones that a salesman may meet on a purchasing committee. Pleasant, often silent men, but, where vocal, the askers of the quiet and awkward questions to which salesmen need to have prepared replies of a highly satisfactory kind, if they are to survive the group interview and come out with either the order, or at least a letter of intent. Each has a functional or departmental role to play in ensuring that the item to be eventually bought meets each man's value analysis needs. And has a demonstrable, competitive, comparative edge on all other available propositions on the market.

There are the peculiar third-party orders which arise via professional advisers. These advisers never actually buy. They recommend and specify the inclusion of certain items of different manufacturers' ranges in purchase contracts issued by a company's buying office. Architects, consulting engineers, designers are typical of this very important and influential purchasing medium of recommendation.

The field manager will indoctrinate his salesmen in all the intracicies of the contemporary and relevant buying scene. He will educate them in the common motivations and needs that have to be influenced in a successful sales interview. He will persuade them of the mandatory need of using an emphatic understanding of the buying role philosophy and methodological patterning. This is a basic factor in selling success. This is unlikely to be a speedy process; in most cases it is a lifetime study, an essential part of continuous on-the-job training.

The Buying Function's Basic Needs of Suppliers' Salesmen's Services

A field manager needs to instruct his men in the following purchasing motivations and needs—

A positive duty to:

1 Get the most suitable goods from reputable suppliers, on the best terms, at the best prices, in the exact quantities against exact specifications, when he needs and wants them and to be able to ensure continuity of supply where needed of the identical or alternative acceptable specifications, complete with advisory and technical services needed.

2 Be his company's defence against unsuitable, unprofitable purchases and against unsuitable suppliers.

3 Be conditioned and motivated negatively against loss, error and risks involved in changes and to be conditioned and motivated positively in favour of buying, owning and using benefits, security of his own tenure and peace of mind.

4 Seek and find widespread contacts to keep his information bank absolutely up-to-date on all innovations, technological changes, new materials, new processing, new machines and equipment that will be

of interest to all departmental managers, so that they can be obtained whenever his company needs to purchase.

5 Ensure that he gets an informed and helpful service from all who call upon him which is utterly reliable in its provision of unprejudiced advice slanted specifically to the buyer's exact needs.

6 Ensure that he gets prompt attention to all enquiries in full, upon which buying decisons can ultimately be safely made. This information will of course include suitable alternative products and propositions where relevant, precise and exact statements of specification. performance, price, delivery, and credit terms. There will be no loose ends that could create misunderstanding or doubt.

7 Establish the credibility and reliability of each prospective supplier as well as the reliability of products under purchasing consideration, including performance specifications and range of usage. Established suppliers should be subjected to a similar scrutiny when they are being considered for the purchase of a new product or an established product for a new usage.

8 Get the very best available competitive comparative, suitable product in terms of overall value analyses of effective purchase, including investment appraisal, operational effectiveness, freedom from trouble, easy maintenance and longevity of active and serviceable operation.

Consumer and semi-durable goods are bought on a different set of criteria from industrial durables, plant, etc. They include *inter alia* —
Strength of demand for re-sale
Profitability on re-selling
Speed of stockturn compared with competitive products
Stability of demand for product and product type
Low prices and length of credit facilities
Satisfactory past experience of supplier
Reliability of supplier's services in delivery and quality specification
Reliability of supplier in dealing with complaints or deficiencies

Industrial or consumer durables, equipment, tools, raw materials, components and plant. Here there are very clear distinctions between product and producer, between purchasing and patronage.

Purchaser's Product Need	Purchaser's need of Supplier to Ensure Patronage
Capital equipment	
Reliability for performance	Reliability of supplier for quality
Low cost of repair	specification and service

Low maintenance, attention and cost

Low operating costs

Good investment values

Price as a cost benefit equation

Suitability, durability, productivity, economy

Co-operation in advisory and technical services

Low prices and long credit terms

Previous satisfactory relationship

Speedy attention to all requests

Supplies and components

Exactly right quality and specification

Exactly right performance criteria

Uniformity, economy, durability

Utter reliability in all respects

Continuous supply at all times

Accessibility, low price and long credit

Raw materials

Absolutely exact quality

Uniform specification and character

Dependability in action and reaction

Economy

Utter reliability for every aspect of supply

Continuity of supply always

Accessibility

Low price and long credit facilities

Equipment, office machinery, data processing machinery, typewriters, weighing equipment come under similar buying criteria imposed on supplies and suppliers of capital equipment, whether bought for industry or for commerce.

Industrial and technical purchasing all rely for their satisfactions upon a totality of buying and usage benefits, calculated as a comparative, competitive assessment of a favoured supplier over all others.

Professional purchasing people keep a league table of satisfactory suppliers and supplies. Thus a best supplier for the best product can quickly be identified upon past experience. It then remains for the prospective purchaser to carry out an up-to-date check to verify his rating on the current scene. By inference, there is a league table of non-starters carefully compiled from a history of unsatisfactory, unsatisfied transactions in the past. A salesman, a company, a product, a service that fails to satisfy, automatically get their names inscribed upon the buyers' role of dishonour.

Professional purchasing people have an interesting habit of chatting about suppliers products, services and salesmen when they meet at their professional institute meetings. Salesmen should again beware of receiving anything else but a highly satisfactory rating of purchasing esteem.

So much for buying psychology—what of a selling psychology to match?

Field management has a positive duty to educate their salesmen in the arts of buyer-seller co-operation. This does not occur naturally. It has to be worked for, and worked at, continuously over a selling lifetime, in order to perfect the subtle scoring of a personal compatibility between salesman and buyer. To achieve this degree of excellence, a successful salesman needs to get the buyer to provide him with the following flow of essential information which is an essential basis for effective negotiations being established:

1 A frank statement of necessary relevant information, in confidence where necessary, so that the salesman can match his services to the buying needs.

2 A clear statement of whether the query in question relates to estimating, for planning, or for actual supply whether in the short or the longer term.

3 A willingness of the buyer to introduce the salesman to the buyer's company specialists when technical problems and data about specification and performance have to be discussed at length and before negotiations can begin on a commercial basis.

4 The earliest possible consultation about future needs so that sufficient time is available for supplier to produce properly thought-through ideas for buying guidance and careful consideration before actual negotiations begin on a commercial front.

5 The earliest possible introduction of supplier's technical people to their opposite numbers in the buying company (where apposite) at and preferably before the design stage in new product preliminary thinking has started. This enables a real meeting of minds to take place between supplier and buyer before the shaping of a new product for the mix actually begins. Here costly mistakes can be avoided, unnecessary time-lags (costly in themselves) can be averted, valuable time can be conserved (often vital in getting an early market launch ahead of competitors) because on both sides the right questions are asked so that the right answers can more readily be forthcoming.

6 The willingness of buyer and supplier to see themselves as essential co-operators in the search for a product and a market

which together can yield mutual growth, profit and success. Here a salesman reaches the ideal projection of his company's marketing objectives in the actual market. He becomes a trusted competent extension of his company within the buying sanctum.

7 The willingness and dedication of the salesman to see himself as the initiating factor in the engineering of agreement in the market place that will make his company both prosperous and progressive.

8 The readiness of the salesman to understand and to appreciate fully that it is only through the co-operation of buyers (which he himself creates) that his territorial sales quotas and budgets can be met and beaten, and profitable growth made in his market share. It is not the salesman who denies sales to competitors. It is the buyer whom the salesman has pre-conditioned in his favour who does the trick.

Some Conclusions

Suppliers' Salesmen and Buyers seem to be fated to become even more than now an inter-locked, inter-dependent, inter-personal combination of business activities. The prosperity of one is reflected inevitably in the other. Mutuality of advantage and benefit is thus a vital ingredient in this partnership mix. Each can be a critical cost-centre. Greater mutual effectiveness should reduce the cost centre of each activity, thus giving each man's company a more competitive cutting edge in price and value and their companies a potentially more profitable operating activity.

However to make the relationship of salesman and buyer more mutually profitable, care must be taken to ensure that the fringe buying benefits (free advisory and technical services, low price and long credit) do not vitiate the salesman's operating costs to an unacceptable degree.

Buyers want their suppliers' salesmen to cosset them, to feather-bed them, in a meld of technical advisory services, consultancy in special areas of operation, guidance in specific aspects of value analysis and engineering techniques, help in problem-solving. These are cost-provoking activities. To neutralise their adverse content, a salesman will have to split his non-productive activities and his productive selling activities in such a proportion that his activity *in toto* can remain a viable, profitable, cost-wise proposition, salted with growth potential for both short and long term. This fact is stressed here, because essentially it is a behavioural rather than an accounting problem. Psychologically the salesman must see himself success oriented. That means a customer-satisfying, yet profit making man. The salesman holds the key to profitable selling.

It is because buyers prefer to purchase through the intermediary of salesmen that the cost benefit ratio of the salesman's operational activity is so vital to a company's marketing performance in pursuit of company overall objectives.

No longer is it a matter of creating a nice and cosy business relationship with buyers, where sheer force of habit will keep it a viable one. This is a relationship where each transaction is good or bad on its merits. Whilst earlier success or failure will condition the next meeting to some degree, it is not necessarily a certainty. A successful salesman is a person who sees that he must woo each buyer like a man seeking to win a bride. And having won the damsel for one order, he has to be just as excellent in his wooing, and no less ardent in his suit, if he is to win the next order—and so on *ad infinitum*.

Purchasing will become even more proficient and professional in its scope and in its expertise due to the increase in competition and the search for ever better values. Advanced technologies, automated inventory techniques, will make the salesman's task progressively harder. Yet, for this very reason, it will sort out the men from the boys and place a distinctive premium upon selling excellence.

Its overall lesson for the field manager training his men in selling skills is that a successful salesman will have to know as much about buying skills, arts, attitudes and practices as professional purchasing officers themselves. Whilst technological and methodological skills have progressed, behavioural know-how in interpersonal relationships remains much the same as it ever was. The way to a buyer's heart is through the creation of trust in the salesman's empathetic attitude to him. Once this has been created, the door is open to an exposition of a salesman's expertise based upon his capacity to solve problems. And to truly serve the potential buyer's interests, through mutually beneficial persuasive activity. And the offer of the right solution to a buyer's need in a competitively excellent package deal of benefits. This is the logic of offering the buyer a totality of buying benefits, values and services that excels anything offered by competitors.

Field sales management has thus an educational task in creating a selling attitude that sees the buyer-salesman relationship not as a confrontation but as an opportunity to integrate the relationship into a mutually beneficial, mutually satisfying business building activity that has a promise of permanence about it.

MATRIX NO. 1 INDUSTRIES IN A CONSTANTLY CHANGING MARKET ENVIRONMENT

Industry	No. Outlets	No. Clients	Product	Use No. 1	Use No. 2	Use No. 3	Use No. 4	COMMENTS
Aircraft			A B C					
Brewing			D E F					
Food			D E F					
Dairy			D E F					
Motor Car			A B C					
Chemical			D E F					
Electronics			G H I					
Shipbuilding			A B C					
Computers			G H I					
Other Industries Not Penetrated								

This matrix is purely descriptive. It should stimulate the Sales Engineering Apprentice to constantly be on the search for new uses in each industry for each product. And it should haunt his dreams that there are still many industries that he has not yet penetrated for his company's product range! Most of all it should *force* him to measure his achievements not just by his results. But negatively, by the number of potential users in so many industries that he is not yet serving ! ! ! It may be salutary, but it is at least constructive, to measure opportunity by the horizons not reached. And to ensure always that the reach forward forces one to extend the range of one's grasp ! ! !

MATRIX NO. 2 INDIVIDUAL CUSTOMER FORM-AT-A-GLANCE—OUTLINING SCOPE OF FUTURE OPPORTUNITIES

CUSTOMER VITAL DATA	EXECUTIVES AND BUYERS	INDIRECT THREATS FROM COMPETITIVE ACTIVITIES	DIRECT THREATS	UNMET WANTS, PROBLEMS, NEEDS
SIZE	Purchasing Officer Production Officer Chief Accountant Research Officer Chief Engineer Systems Officer Office Manager General Manager	WHO? WHAT? Degree of Customer Acceptance? Innovative Reputations? Products? Pricing? Design? New/Alternative Materials? Leasing versus Purchase? Special Credit Facilities?	WHO? WHAT? HOW? WHEN? WHY? WHERE?	
Product Groups				
Type Markets Supplied				
Credit Rating				
PURCHASING POLICIES	(i) Chief Contacts (ii) Characteristics of Each Contact			
MOTIVATIONS	(iii) Buying Patterns			
DIFFERENTIAL CALL FREQUENCY	(iv) Best Times To Call			
PRODUCTS USED	(v) LIKES/DISLIKES			
X) above/below Y) quotas set Z) for period	(vi) NEEDS/WANTS (vii) ENTERTAINMENT (viii) STRATEGIES/TACTICS DEPLOYMENT			
PRODUCTS YET TO BE BOUGHT	(ix) SPECIFIC SERVICE NEEDS			
LAST ORDER DATE AND VALUE	(x) POINT OF ENTRY			
DATE NEXT CALL				

Again this matrix is purely descriptive. It would ensure that a Sales Engineering Apprentice is continually thinking about the development of each customer's business. And also precisely how this should be done against direct or indirect threats to his share of each customer's business! The Unmet Problems, Wants, and Needs should act as a trigger mechanism to sell the complete product line. And, of formulating further Field Intelligence Reports to H.Q. about 'new' products and services needed to ensure that their share of market is kept intact and developed. Similarly it should result in requests for more H.Q. research to develop new uses for existing product line. Each Sales Engineer must construct his own matrices to cover his own job!

MATRIX NO. 3 OUTLET TYPES IN CHANGING CONDITIONS OF MARKET

Product lines or groups	Supermarket Chains	Symbol Groups	Co-ops	Wholesale Outlets	Cash and Carry	Independent Retailers Hoteliers etc.	M.A.T. trend	Period total value
A								
B								
C								
D								
E								
F								
G								
M.A.T. trend								
Period total value								

MATRIX NO. 4 TECHNICAL AND INDUSTRIAL SALES REPORT

1 Negotiation phase	2 Description	3 New product Name	4 New use Identified	5 Current customer Names of important personnel	6 Prospective customer Names of important personnel
1	Identification of problem				
2	Examination of factors				
3	Provisional evaluation				
4	Search for alternative solutions				
5	Researches and tests				
6	Selection of best solution tested and proven				
7	Statement by value analysis of features and buying benefits				
8	Provisional presentation created				
9	Demonstration and proof for customer				
10	Proposition costed. Estimate and quotation made				
11	Salesman calls to clinch order				
12	Buying satisfaction created good-will built				

Name of salesman and customer

Insert call dates in 5 and 6 and progress of proposition.

O.K. Ahead of Schedule. Hiatus. Refusals. Acceptances.

Developmental Selling

Developmental selling means exactly what it implies. It is not interested in a *status quo*. It bears no relationship to the so-called maintenance selling that some authors and pundits prate about. Maintenance selling has a true Alice-in-Wonderland air about it. It assumes that an activity like buying and selling in a mobile market, full of competitive activity, can yet guarantee a company a stable demand for its products. Market demand ebbs and flows like the tides. There is always a state of flux. Developmental selling is a belief that to try to maintain a *status quo* in a market is doomed to defeat. Only the deliberate policy and planning essential to progress can ensure company stability. Provided only that it is geared to the making of adequate profits from which to finance its future growth.

Developmental selling is a policy and an activity that together are geared to a product mix, expansionist marketing and sales policies, to ensure a steady building up of a company's share in the totality of market segments in which it operates. Developmental selling meets its private Waterloo in the field. It is field management's job to see that the policy and the company are the winners in each gladitorial contest with competitive activities. To accomplish this the field manager must ensure that he can educate his salesmen in the entrepreneurial attitude of developing the sales of each product through each suitable outlet to the optimum that his territory will stand in both the short and the long term.

Developmental selling is thus a positive creative productive approach to selling. Maintenance selling is a defensive approach to both life and to expansion. And in today's markets, chock-full of competitive activities, it is an anachronism with little hope of survival in the face of progress and competitive challenges of change. Developmental selling aims at the steady expansion of revenue, profits and growth in market share as the result of very detailed strategic and tactical planning of the potential sources of additional revenue and by each product in the mix, each market segment, each industry and trade, each territory and each individual outlet of size.

The field manager's approach to the education of his men in this particular technique must be one of detailed examination of territorial records. He will want to have a record and a trend for each of the above-mentioned outlets for expansion over a period of some years. Where trend charts have been kept on a territorial basis, the problem poses few difficulties. Having established the trend line for each of the types of outlet, the field manager can compare them with those for his sales and national teams. This will give a guide line to the potential expansion in the individual sales territory.

Having carried out a detailed autopsy on the territorial figures of achievement for the past, the manager will have to make a forecast for the year ahead, for the additional sales volume to be gained from the development operation.

It might seem heretical to infer that many companies have an insufficient knowledge of their potential markets, even in this country. This particularly applies to industrial and technical selling, where new product applications, and new uses for products are discovered daily. In this way, a number of new market segments can be opened up quite rapidly, where field sales managers and their men have the skill to see that modern technologies have opened up entirely new vistas of selling.

Using page 197 depicting the market segments of industries and trades shown under input-output tables—a field manager can make a start by comparing his actual market coverage with the revealed potential. He could then make a realistic forecast of the additional development of sales that could be gained from these additional sources in the year ahead.

By examining each product in his mix in a similar fashion and by relating this exercise to each salesman's area he has a team prescription for extra sales. By extending this examination to each key outlet on each salesman's area and to each potential new outlet that can be gained a future forecast much nearer the true optimum can be made.

Field sales managers and their salesmen can help themselves to see what they have to do, and how they are faring against their true optimal potential, by creating a number of matrices which will give them form-at-a-glance. The four matrices, on pages 197–200, are typical examples, of which, although Nos. 1 and 2 refer specifically to industrial selling, No. 3 has a commercial flavour. Each man should construct the ideal kind of matrix to suit his own situation best.

At a recent conference when this question was raised many members of senior sales management who should have known better felt that developmental selling was automatically practised by their sales force already. Any experienced field sales manager worthy of his salt who really has his eyes on the stars and his ears to the ground knows better. He knows that developmental selling is generally not being practised, and, even where it is being used, it is rarely a developed technique.

How then should a sales director or a company sales manager know whether his field sales managers are really doing their stuff in this subject area, whatever they may protest? Here is a simple 20-point check list for questioning field sales management:

1 When was a detailed audit last carried out on each sales territory to assess potential additional growth?

2 How many field sales managers or salesmen have produced recently a sales forecast and budget of cost for each key outlet on their territories for even one year ahead?

3 How many field managers and salesmen have done so, product by product, and use by use?

4 How many field managers and salesmen have produced a detailed survey industry by industry and trade by trade (particularly those to which they do not supply or do so marginally) and seen the potential expansion as a harvest to be gathered in speedily?

5 How many field managers and salesmen have made even provisional plans for bringing in those prospective customers to the fold who currently deal with competitors and have produced a forecast, budget and time schedule for the operation?

6 How many field managers and salesmen as yet are not using gridded territorial maps for forward developmental planning? Or, are using differential calling frequency, squaring the circle or petal calling, to get the optimum result from productive time management and conservation?

7 Have we analysed each market area with a view to setting up the most profitable type of salesman—e.g., our own salesmen versus manufacturers' representatives or agents?

8 Has the job of the salesman been defined specifically and in writing?

9 Is our field sales staff organised in keeping with the potential market in each geographic area?

10 Can the flow of communications between our field sales force and the home office be improved?

11 Have we kept sales paperwork to the right level—neither too much nor too little?

12 Have we provided for optimum supervision of our field sales force—neither too little nor too much?

13 Are we certain that each customer is getting coverage in proportion to potential volume in terms of number and frequency of calls made?

14 Are our salesmen welcome callers with something worthwhile to talk about?

15 Is our sales training programme adequate in providing product knowledge, the skills of selling and the way to organise a territory?

16 Have we set up realistic targets for each individual salesman?

17 Would it be desirable for us to raise the calibre of men on our field sales force by getting better educated, more experienced men? Or lower the calibre of men in our field sales force?

18 Does the compensation plan we offer our field staff and its management provide optimum incentive and optimum security at reasonable cost?

19 Can we improve the selling aids and sales tools we provide for our field personnel?

20 Is each area on or above target, at or below prescribed budget levels?

No sales director or company sales manager should be satisfied, whether his sales force be large, medium, or small, until each field manager and salesman has produced an anatomical framework for each territory as a working background for the detailed developmental planning described. Such developmental planning is utterly essential to the balanced development of any business large or small. It is the only way in which a sales director or company sales manager can begin to hope to get value for money from his investment in manpower and expectation. It is the only way to keep sales force cost down to reasonable proportions in the total sales cost and marketing cost mixes.

Cold Canvass Calling

Cold canvass merely means what it says : calling from scratch, without prior warning or appointment, upon people whom one has not met before. The cold component of the canvass is the alleged frigidity of the buying atmosphere extended to those who come unknown, unhonoured, unsung and uninvited. By implication, the salesman in such circumstances has to provide the warmth that would be necessary to thaw the icicles from the entry to the buyer's citadel.

Some pundits still smarting from the bitterness of their own experience refer to the process as raw canvass. This rawness lies in the mind. To some it still is the rawest and toughest assignment known to the newcomer to the selling profession. For the salesman has to bridge the gulf that extends from the gate to the private secretary, to get inside the buying sanctum without prior invitation or appointment.

In a recent survey carried out by the author with the Purchasing Officers' Association, now the Institute of Purchasing and Supply, no fewer than 82 per cent of a very large and representative sample of prominent buyers preferred to see salesmen strictly by appointment. The reason is obvious. The buyer's day can be meticulously planned with adequate time allocated to appointments, and the remainder to departmental matters. This is a cheering way of taking the cold out of canvass.

However, a great deal of cold canvass calling must still be done, especially in the industrial, technical and speciality selling fields. How then should a field sales manager tackle the training of his salesmen in this difficult technique in communication and human relationships?

Like most difficulties that inhibit human relationship, the causes lie deeply hidden in the participants minds. Salesmen have two basic endemic fears, first of failure in their selling job, second of rebuff in personal relationships. They are a blow to the *amour propre*, to the dignity, the self-esteem of the individual, and of course to his professional self-image and pride of achievement. So the risk of being kicked in the teeth both professionally and socially is a great disincentive to salesmen to cold canvass—unless they are made of stern stuff both morally and intellectually.

The salesman who fears cold canvassing instinctively has a host of evidence that he feels that he can adduce in support of professional salespeople not being expected by their companies to follow this unethical practice, as he would term it. He recalls the foot-in-the-door buccaneer who allegedly terrorises the unsuspecting housewife into buying what she does not want, does not need, and cannot afford, to support his lack of appetite for the tougher side of the selling job.

If a salesman who decries cold canvass calling will pause for just one moment and think *not* of his less well-heeled brethren whose job of selling life insurance (industrial office) and vacuum cleaners makes it imperative for them to sell on-the-knocker, but consider that it is all a matter of semantics and sophistication, we shall be able to look at the problem with unprejudiced unbiased eyes.

The selling of a new technical product of great complexity handled by a chemical engineer graduate is a cold-canvass onslaught (however subtly the material is handled) upon an unsuspecting buying mind. The new usage of an ethical preparation detailed by a medical representative to an unsuspecting G.P. is likewise a knocking from cold upon the doors of a professional mind. Selling computers and automated technologies, even where appointments have been made, still largely amounts to a cold canvassing of far from susceptible professional purchasing minds. Selling any new idea or concept is a challenge to the selling mind. Because he has to sell it from cold. It is a continuous challenge to the exploring mind.

Cold Canvass Methodology under the Microscope

The old traditional approach of sales managers of speciality sales forces was to knock upon as many fresh doors as possible each day. Thus they argued, by some strange alchemy associated with a law of averages, the order rate would be in direct ratio to the number of calls made. This of course is utter nonsense. It would not work with the wrong doors whose owners were not interested in the products being offered. Neither would it work with the wrong products which could not offer a competitive edge at a competitive price and thus competitive comparative value to a prospective purchaser. Nor would it work where the timing of the call was wrong and the people with authority to buy were not available. It certainly would not work if the salesman had not selected his calls as those which offered the greatest likelihood of successful outcomes to his persuasive presentations and propositions.

The crucial factor in successful cold canvass calling is to separate the prospects from the suspects. An experienced field sales manager will educate his men to allocate a similar value of priorities to prospects as he does to actual customers on a differential calling frequency basis. It would be stupid to inculcate a respect for calling upon customers strictly upon a cost benefit basis, then to have a calling roster of prospects which were visited by whim or purely upon convenience.

The field manager must train his men to see that a cold canvass call, which is a blind date with fate, is potentially a waste of valueable productive selling time. This will be avoided by insisting that each salesman has a suspect roster. This he investigates by making enquiries through various channels such as directories with a view either to discarding their names as unsuitable or transfers them to his current prospect list for careful vetting before trying to make an appointment to call. Every effort should be taken to get an appointment (going in warm). Only when this fails is cold canvass calling justified. Further, enquiries can still be made on the telephone, prior to calling, to make sure of the buyer's name, and whether he will be there on the proposed date of call, and at the appropriate time. There are still hundreds of salesmen making blind calls, travelling often 50 or more miles to do so, which prove to be completely abortive.

GETTING APPOINTMENTS—A CONSTRUCTIVE METHOD

Most salesmen seem to be casual in the extreme in this technique. Many seem to think that telephoning the buying office to try to get a date and a time for the discussion of an abstract proposition is the best that they or anyone else can do.

There is a positive and constructive technique that field managers can teach. It stems from having a plan for work, and to work only at a plan. The field manager will insist upon having a list from each salesman for three months ahead of the prospective people he would like to bring into the regular customer fold. Each prospect will be analysed as far as possible (often it is wise to get desk research done at H.Q. for larger firms). A priority list is then drawn up for each salesman, divided into the territorial squares or petals of cyclical working. The list will then be sub-divided into market segments, outlet and user types.

This sets the work-load scene for the deliberate planned cold canvass campaign to developmental selling through new outlets on each territory, under the supervisory aegis of the field manager.

A provisional promotional plan is then drawn up for making the best calculated approach to each prospect. It is based ideally upon the securing of appointments to call, rather than to risk the costly disappointments associated with straight cold canvass calling. The field manager should then arrange to have the campaign backed by H.Q. which will write special letters to tie a proposed appointment in with a promotional letter of introduction, stressing a product or service felt to be of special attraction to the recipient in each case. It is important in this context for either H.Q. or the salesman to get the buyer's name correct in every detail, in initial, spelling and title. Then a personal and individually composed and typed letter can be sent for the buyer's own attention and not handled by subordinates.

If a reader thinks that this is a tortuous procedure, and prefers to take his daily routine of hit and miss as his guide he is only handing a hostage to Fortune who rarely smiles for long on the sheer opportunist or unimaginative uncreative operator. This troglodytic attitude of chancing one's arm perpetually is a direct cause of a high sales cost centre in the growth stakes and this in the long run can make a salesman and his company uncompetitive in the markets of his choice.

There are of course many instances where and when a salesman must make cold calls, because attempts to make advance appointments fail. There are vocational hazards to be respected and circumvented. Here again the field manager can educate his men in the best methodology of getting in to see the buyer.

GETTING PAST THE THREE VOCATIONAL HAZARDS

The three traditional watchdogs surrounding the buyer, and protecting him from unwanted and unnecessary callers, with unwanted and unnecessary propositions are the commissionaire, the receptionist and the private secretary.

The drill is simple if lengthy to hoist in. It consists in trying to get as much advance information as possible, that will oil the wheels of conversational cut and thrust and make it easier to charm one's way in, past the human barriers. Correct information handled with a right blend of authoritative charm is the open sesame to most buying sancta. It is important to get the closest co-operation and friendliness of the keepers of the three doors en route. This enables them to help you on your way to the salesman's goal, the buyer himself.

A typical conversation would go on the following oiled wheels : 'Good morning, Sergeant-Major.' (Even sergeants like the sweet taste of status and promotional prestige.) 'My name is Smith. Would you kindly help me...? Can you tell me...' Few commissionaires are averse to giving their help on demand via the medium of a charming request for their assistance. (It ministers kindly to their egos and their importance.) The conversation now established on a friendly co-operative basis will go something like this : 'Will you kindly ask Mr Jones (the buyer) whether he is now free to see me?' Usually, this results in the salesman being directed to the receptionist's desk for onward routeing towards his goal—the buyer's office.

The receptionist is the buyer's second line of defence. She either gets rid of the unwanted quickly by saying that the buyer is not available, or, under pressure, gets on the inter-com to the buyer's private secretary, to pass the responsibility for rejection or acceptance onto her shoulders. This is where the salesman without an appointment is really at hazard and must box both cleverly and truthfully. He will if he can say something on these lines: 'Good morning. I've a complex proposition to put before Mr Jones. I'm sure that you would prefer me to tell his secretary about it, and she can then arrange for me to see Mr Jones.' Well done, this usually receives an invitation to talk to the lady in question on the inter-com.

Here there are no grounds for anything other than truth charmingly and directly put. 'I've a special proposition I would like to put to your chief about... When would it be most convenient to you both for me to see him. About 15/30 minutes would be ample.' Once the secretary has satisfied herself that the salesman has a genuine prima facie case for taking up the time of her chief, she will usually make the next step towards getting the salesman his interview. Charm her and she can become a fine ally. Thwart her or let her down and you have an implacable enemy situated strategically and tactically in precisely the spot to do the maximum future harm.

Where a salesman fails to get past hazard No. 1 or 2 he need not give up the ghost either initially or finally. It is well worth while leaving the premises, getting into the first call box, and telephoning the buyer's secretary, to express your regret for calling at an unpropitious moment. Usually she has not been told of the rejection and may often resent that she was not invited to express her view. Here is the chance to try to get another bite at the cherry and an appointment at an early date.

SURVEYING

Surveying may be an unfamiliar activity to some salesmen. But in speciality selling, and in selling to industry it is familiar enough. It is based upon the simple fact that a salesman who only gets into the buyer's office, and fails to penetrate further into the company's factory, warehouses, etc., has only a second-hand view of the buyer's problem areas and needs. Many salesmen fail to get orders that they should do because they are not made aware of the company problems. Hence the vital need for a salesman to get on to the factory, warehouse, or general office floor so that he can see for himself at first hand what the problem areas are that he can solve. In simple terms, salesmen need to be educated by field managers in

G

the subtle art of estimating through visual survey the scope, shape and size of buying power of each key outlet for some years ahead. This is the basic pattern for developmental selling. It is a survey of buying intent for a period of years ahead for sales planning purposes.

We can get this vital information in two different ways. The first is by question and answer usually at top managerial levels. The British Insulated Callender's Cables Ltd. example is a text book case of what can be done to create an exact pattern of future business through a simple survey technique carried out at top levels. In 1961, they were considering the introduction to the British market of a revolutionary mineral cable. Simple questions were asked of leading potential customers and users to predict their requirements progressively until 1966. The replies were clear enough for B.I.C.C. to go right ahead at full boost with production planning. We can call this strategical surveying on a grand scale.

The second way is a tactical one. It falls to the salesman to initiate such surveys as a subtle service to the customer and user; in the guise of reporting back for free the state of existing equipment and its true capacity for effective future use. Or, it may spring from a buying enquiry about equipment (in the usual vacuum). Let us take similar cases of a departmental store needing a cash control system with immediate visual indication, minute by minute, in the managing director's office, of the cash flow through the store, and a large industrial plant in which processing leads to considerable shrinkage in its departmental flows towards completion. Here visual controls of value in terms of weight can give effective control.

The salesman asks politely that the buyer allow him in complete confidence to render both him and his company a signal free service. This would be to examine each machine item, its location, effectiveness in use, then to report back to the buyer, and to survey what could be done by contemporary machinery to show a worthwhile improvement in efficiency at little cost. This is the only way for a salesman to get at first hand a proper appreciation of the equipment in use, the problems unsolved, and the potential miracles that could be wrought, by the introduction of new equipment to meld with the most effective items in actual usage.

This is creative selling and developmental selling at its tactical and ultimately strategical best. Had this technique been followed out by all computer salesmen it is probable that our national computering effectiveness would at this moment be much higher than it actually is.

There is an important spin-off benefit to the salesman's developmental planning for increased sales per key outlet. Not only can the salesman see precisely what his sales targets should really be, but he can estimate clearly the strength and potential threat posed by competitors and their innovative and selling expertise.

There is also an important indicator of the potential shape of future selling itself in such fields where systems selling will become more operative. This is the need to get suppliers' design teams of engineers to talk with buyers' design teams at an early stage of developmental selling to a key outlet where innovation or at least considerable change in systems control and analysis is contemplated in the individual selling or buying plans.

CHAPTER EIGHT

Setting Performance Norms for The Sales Force

INTRODUCTION

Setting performance norms is the first of a trinity of managerial activities. Together they are of vital importance to the capacity of a company to meet its targets, budgets and long term profitable growth in its market share. The other two activities are the control and appraisal of the sales force activities, man by man.

The sales forecast and the budget are the master documents against which most sales directors set their activities and the other company departments in turn create their own standards of measurement in order to play a fully supportive role in the attainment of the company sales objectives.

Just as a sales director breaks down the company sales forecasts and budgets to field and territorial levels, so that each man knows the share of the company sales task for which he is personally accountable, so must he get his field sales management to create individual performance norms for each member of the sales force, in support of those ends.

THE FIELD SALES MANAGER'S ROLE

A field sales manager begins with the local knowledge of each sales territory and the man who is its trustee. He begins also with the definitive knowledge of the ways and degrees in which each territory differs in character and sales potential from all the others. He begins again with the personal knowledge of the ways and the extent in which each man differs from every other salesman in the region.

We have already reached a basis for one overriding conclusion: that sales directors who merely divide their total company target and budget equally between all the salesmen on a population or sales value basis are not being realistic. In short, a total company target and budget must be divided up strictly according to the potential of each territory and man for the period in question. This decision in turn calls for a most careful assessment of the sales potential in each territory, each product, each usage, each type of outlet in each kind of market segment. Further, the capacity of each man to work his territory truly effectively must be taken into the calculation.

We now reach a second important conclusion. This is that the performance norm set for each man in terms of quotas and budget will be a reflection in competence of the amount of time the field manager spends getting to know intimately each territory and man and the training and education he hands out to make each man as effective as possible in terms of job attitudes, job aptitudes, working efficiency, etc.

Performance norms are built up in each territory upon basic criteria including:
1 The greatest potential productive time usage
2 The most effective planning of each territory's working activities
3 The most effective planning of each day's optimum work-load
4 The optimum selling effort at each day's calls
5 The creation of satisfactions and goodwill
6 The optimum effective use of selling tools and techniques
7 The share of the regional quotas and budgets allocated to each territory.

We thus have a blend of quantitative and qualitative norms. Far too many field managers are apt to neglect the qualitative in favour of men getting their quotas and budgets above all else. This is false doctrine, for the excellence of the qualitative factors in a salesman's performance usually determines the fate of the quantitative results. For instance, poor selling techniques and poor usage of selling tools almost predict poor results against quota. Or at least poorer results than would have been the case if the man excelled in his professional arts and skills.

Performance norms must be properly and carefully set. They reflect directly the management skill in the task. They assume that managerial supervision, training on-the-job and control will ensure that the norms are met on time and in detail. It can be a great mistake to set merely a total quota and budget. It can be very limiting and myopic, particularly when a salesman (through judgement and good luck) beats his overall targets with a flourish of gentlemanly élan and *joie de vivre*.

Performance norms are set not merely for tidy bookkeeping and their subsequent confirmatory and congratulatory audits of effectiveness, heady wine though this be for the ambitious field manager and salesman. They are deliberately set in the more thoughtful managerial circles to create a viable basis for effective developmental selling. So we reach another conclusion : that performance norms need to be set for a whole range of selling activities and qualitative skills and that they must be regularly audited to show variances from standards set so that remedial treatment can be put into immediate operation. In short, management by objective neatly blended with management by exception.

Typical Performance Norms
 1 Each product of the mix *in toto*
 2 Each outlet for usage *in toto*
 3 Each industry, trade, and market segment *in toto*
 4 Each key outlet for each product and usage
 5 Number of new customers gained against those lost for period
 6 Number of orders to calls for periods
 7 Cost per £100 of order value
 8 Number of effective calls per day
 9 Number of quotations to enquiries
10 Conversion rate of quotations into orders
11 Bad debt ratio to sales volume value
12 Total quota in sales value and total budget
13 Reporting effectiveness
14 Presentation and demonstration efficiency
15 Overcoming objections and order clinching prowess
16 Communication effectiveness
17 Confidence shown by customers in salesman's judgement, skills, and service
18 Self-confidence and self-education of salesman
19 General development
20 Potential for promotion and for managerial development

RELATIONSHIP OF MANAGER AND MAN IN SETTING UP PERFORMANCE
NORMS

Many companies and their field managements make their own
computations quite exclusively of the salesman's views or ideas
upon these subjects so close to a salesman's self-confidence, self-
esteem and ambitions to shine in his profession. He is thus a paid
vassal of the management in search of a progressive career, in
the detailed management of which he has no voice or influence.
This is not only undemocratic, it is both unwise and un-
professional.

A salesman is in a position where he can do enormous good
for his company in his contactual calls upon prospective and
actual customers and users. He can of course be a passive wrecker
or a destructive influence if he is not properly motivated and
controlled. In many cases (except those of the myopic, the
miniscule-minded, and the naturally lazy) a salesman is much
what management motivates him to be. Management can work
wonders by getting the sensible and ambitious salesman personally involved in the arithmetic of his own career accountancy by
consulting him upon the standards of performance the company
expects him to honour, if not actually to excel.

Salesmen are not fools, although there are people who thought-
lessly treat them as such on occasions. They know their own
limitations pretty well. What they rarely know and too often
guess is their performance potential when fully stretched. This is
the norm the astute field manager must try to get the salesman
to accept as his contribution to his own career and the team pool
of regional effort.

Salesmen must also clearly understand that performance norms
are expected to be at least as progressive as the performance of
the company they so proudly represent. This is what a career in
selling is all about : the planned development of profitable
performance in the company interest as well as the salesman's
own.

Salesmen must therefore realise and accept that the performance norms set specially for each aspect of his activity for a
given period are not the maxima their companies are willing to
accept from them. They are minima. Similarly, salesmen must
accept that the performance norms set individually against their
personal skills and standing, are those which will automatically
be appraised on the regular manpower appraisal form that field
management fills in at regular intervals.

The way and the extent by which a salesman beats his norms is a yardstick of his potential career progress within his company. It is a regular record of his personal development in his professional expertise.

Human Motivation, Job Enrichment and Their Effect upon Performance Norms

This is one of the most important, yet most thinly researched areas of selling and sales development. Most salesmen get through their lives without any close knowledge of or attention to psychology, and the behavioural and social sciences at first hand. Yet what motivates or drives men to sell and others to buy is of profound importance to every man in the marketing arena. What motivates or drives a man to become a member of a selling or buying élite has not yet been scientifically established. Yet how very much all of us concerned with business would dearly love to know the simple blunt answers to what makes each man tick.

Although many widescale industrial researches into the working environment have been published—and it has been established that money and rewards of a financial nature are important—it has been proved also that there are many other rewards of a very different kind which motivate men to follow one career rather than another or belong to one company rather than another. Men in the main like teamwork and the fraternal solidity and mutual identity and identification that ensue from joint effort. It has been established that employers do not merely get a worker when they take a man on the payroll. They get a man of parts—a family man, a social man, a sportsman of sorts, a political animal and sometimes a philosopher or barrack-room lawyer to boot. In short we get a whole man. Sometimes one facet of a man's interests is in the ascendant and sometimes another. Which roles he regularly plays will determine the consistent value of his services to a company. There have been many costly attempts by employers to try to match indirect and direct rewards to the effort that management requires from its workpeople.

JOB ENRICHMENT AND HUMAN MOTIVATION AND DRIVES

Most people accept already that pleasant working conditions

within a stimulating environment are conducive to higher and better standards of work output. This is irrespective of the monetary reward and incentive that have been woven into the working structure. In short, environmental enrichment can be seen as a bonus extra to that of monetary reward in raising output and production standards.

Psychologists, sociologists and social scientists have not been backward in jumping onto this attractive bandwagon, in order to research and to stir the human pudding and to evaluate environmental effects upon employers' investment in manpower at work. Let us not be mealy-mouthed about this exercise. Employers expect each experiment in work and job improvement to raise their return upon investment and to stimulate the profitable growth of the enterprise.

Professor Herzberg's[1] name is the one most closely associated with job enrichment on both sides of the Atlantic, particularly as it affects the selling scene. In brief and somewhat over-simplified terms job enrichers aver that if and when a salesman is allowed and encouraged to take a positive planning role in his daily job, then his increased interest and the challenge to his pride and skills tend to expand his effectiveness. It is implied that a managerial deference to an individual salesman's innate capacity to be a progressively good judge of his job potential will automatically expand his commercial horizons in search of more business. In fact, that a salesman's personal involvement in his job planning and operational structure will raise his productivity and the company's prosperity.

There is clearly much truth in Herzberg's thesis. But the effects of too sudden a liberation can vary immensely with both man and job. For instance, managers know from bitter experience that men, like children, have to be carefully groomed for stardom. They need to be taught the elements of planning theory and to be trained in the effective use of planning tools and techniques before they will even be capable of assuming the mantle of self-management via acquiring the discipline of self-control.

Some salesmen do not want such freedom because it would make them automatically accountable for their actions, and responsible for their own futures. Others grasp freedom far too readily equating it in their minds with a licence to paddle their own canoes, irrespective of skill or suitability. Whilst applauding any general improvement in selling job conditions it is highly questionable whether job enrichment can be seen as a universal palliative for ineffective selling. Rather it should be seen as a managerial responsibility to create the best working environment possible as one of the incentives in the managerial armoury capable of improving a company's sales performance.

PARTICIPATORY MANAGEMENT

Rensis Lickert[2] in the USA has become associated with his theory of 'New Patterns in Sales Management'. It is a most interesting area of research in which a certain personal managerial pattern of attitude and operation is shown (in the research sample) clearly to establish a leadership influence over subordinates resulting in greater job involvement and higher productivity. Lickert favours a theory that field managers who exhibit well thought-through and organised operational plans, set high personal targets of achievement, use group supervision methods of participation by consultation, and offer continuously an older brother's fraternal supportive shoulder get better, if not optimum, support from their men than others who follow traditional patterns of supervision.

Work done by Sadler[3] in this country at Ashridge Management College supports a theory that consultative leadership is a style of management that is preferred by a majority of the managed.

So far we have dealt with the deliberate attempts to isolate an environmental and managerial style that will induce the greatest and most enthusiastic support of salespeople for their employers shown in optimum productivity and profitability of growth. We should now look at the most important factor in the total manpower equation—the Man in the Sales Man himself—and try to see what we can glean from his innate capacity to optimise work and its resultant satisfactions.

MOTIVATION AND DRIVE IN THE SELLING JOB

Most of us love an ordered background. A pattern upon which we can depend. We apply the same standards to people whom we know. We tend to like those who are similar to us in outlook, who follow the same interests, and who make similar judgements upon men and affairs. We feel cosy and safe with such people.

Differences and variants from our usual patterns of outlook and behaviour, particularly in standards, tend to puzzle us. They certainly make us sit up and ponder. They introduce an atmosphere of uncertainty into our surroundings. We wonder what such people intend to do, and where and how they intend to go. And, of course whether their influence upon us will be beneficial or harmful. In short we tend to fear what and whom we do not understand.

Similarity and conformity tend to be binding influences. Differences tend to be divisive, at least until they are proved to be all right. Differences disturb. They have always done so since early childhood, when we found safety within the body of a conforming mass. This is a basic reason why most men wonder what it is that makes others tick. Our bent of curiosity is associated with fear, a basic need to try to insulate it, and to prevent it from being harmful. Until we know what the basic components of human thinking, feeling and action are we cannot hope either to understand others or to be in a favourable mood to co-operate in joint activities.

Psychology is defined by the shorter Oxford Dictionary as 'the science of the nature, functions, and phenomena of the human mind or spirit'. Phenomena are manifestations of causes. So what a salesman in particular wants to know about a buyer or another person are the causes that make them tick.

HUNGER, FEAR, SELF-PRESERVATION, SELF-ESTEEM AND
SELF-ACTUALISATION

Professor Maslow[4] has produced a theory that is exceptionally popular in managerial circles, both here and in the USA. He has cited a number of primary causes that seem to condition human behaviour. They are hunger, fear, self-preservation, sex, self-esteem and self-actualisation.

This seems to be a reasonable approach to the matter. It would appear to cover man from his primitive condition to his most sophisticated present day state. The trouble in such descriptive material lies in the meaning of the words used. For instance, what is spirit, or mind, or nature? Salesmen and managers are rarely trained psychologists or behavioural scientists. They are mostly laymen who apply daily many of the teachings of such scientists. It is a mistake to get bogged down in terminology. Fortunately words like Hunger, Fear, Sex, Survival, Esteem, Fulfilment in Achievement are meaningful and purposeful to us all. Each one of us during a busy lifetime is at one time or another assailed by Fear that we might starve if we were to lose our jobs, that we might die if we were to have serious accidents or illnesses, that we may not be liked, and thus lose our self-esteem, or, that we may fall by the career wayside and fail to achieve and fulfil our potential role (due to fate, unfairness, envy, bad luck, etc.).

David McClelland[5] in the USA is associated with experimentation into the causes which make men work. Some seem to have an in-built desire and determination to achieve pre-set goals, to defy adverse factors, and to exploit opportunities. Others work merely as hard as they must either to survive or to keep the wolf from the matrimonial door. There is a distinct implication that the first group are achievement-oriented, quite apart from the actual monetary rewards, although of course few men really are disinterested in or despise the resultant hard cash. There is a secondary implication that such achievers are also self-observers. They want to know precisely how well they are faring at all stages of the game. A fair guesstimate would be that they are concerned perpetually with an unquenched desire continuously to score better. This is not the usual spirit of competition between people. It is a self-imposed and continuous battle for high performance against steadily higher personally-set standards. Excelsior—he will not be happy until he reaches the highest summit available to him. This is truly a pursuit of personal excellence.

In broad terms there is much common ground of agreement between Herzberg, Maslow, and McClelland, once the academic and somewhat erudite phraseology is translated into everyday simple commercial language. Successful salesmen tend to have abnormally high self-set standards and goals of achievement compared with those who either just avoid the sack or who fail and are dismissed. This is an interesting finding for field management. It is that top-achievers in their sales teams will be largely self-motivating, self-starting, self-energising, and rarely satisfied people. This poses a secondary and extremely vital question. What does a field manager have to do to raise his poorer or middle-of-the-road achiever to a higher standard of performance? Is it a matter of motivation alone? Or, will it be an amalgam of motivation, incentives and training, regularly supervised, audited and controlled?

There has been some research carried out in disparate sectors of the selling activity, mainly in the realm of better selection of salesmen, usually by testing, mainly of a psychological nature.

Robert McMurray[6] has seemed to concentrate his divining activities upon finding suitably equipped men who both can and will do the job impeccably and successfully, given a minimum of enlightened training and supervisory control and help when needed.

Mayer and Greenberg[7] seem to believe that all else is possible, provided only that a salesman possesses in ample degrees both ego-drive and empathy.

The McKinsey Company seems to believe that much can be done by involving salesmen in planned careers.

Samuel N. Stevens points out the twin factors of energy and motivation in successful salespeople. Salesmen possess a higher than average energy compared with other professional groups. Salespeople are strongly self-motivated in their desire for prestige, power and material gain.

Steven J. Shaw believes that successful salespeople are characterised by their exceptional capacity to project personal communication.

Cash and Crissy believe that successful salespeople are particularly perceptive communicators in their unusual capacity to listen and establish mind-to-mind two-way feed back.

Brooks points out that salesmen do better when they learn how to relate their own company's selling effort and product mix to the individual patterns of purchasing management.

The Graduate Centre for Management Studies at Birmingham is reported to be deeply involved in a new approach to salesmen selection which does not centre upon personal traits and qualities but is concerned with three main operational areas: *Exposition* (a man must be able to detail and interpret his product proposition), *Propagate* (a man must be able to sell himself to potential purchasers), *Close* (the discussion to get the order). This should undoubtedly prove both enlightening and useful. Yet even if they advocate in addition the selection of horses for courses, there seems to remain a feeling of a lack of wholeness in the overall approach. It seems unlikely to help us very much in the motivation process.

Some Conclusions

(a) It seems fair to assume that salesmen are heirs to a common hierarchy of needs and wants, posed by Maslow. And that they seek to satisfy them continuously in their daily lives and business operations.

(b) It seems to be equally appropriate to assume that salesmen who are successful are high aspirants to personal achievement—

much in the vein of mediaeval craftsmen who sought future fame in the works they left to posterity, but current personal satisfactions in the public acceptance of their works as masterpieces, and themselves as masters of their crafts.

(c) Modern aspirants are also career seekers in which they can see a visible escalator of promotion lying ahead, which they will achieve step by step on a planned and carefully timed basis.

(d) Trying to equate selection techniques with performance motivation is surely trying to match unlike with unlike. The former details an exceptionally wide and deep concentration upon desirable facets of personality, aspiration and skill. We do not know which factors are crucial in themselves or which combinations of them are most favourable to success. Nor do we know whether any given combination of factors will be equally effective for all jobs and situations (this seems extremely doubtful). Therefore in selection we try to match a man with a job description and a man profile. Here we are trying to discover the bases of self-motivation in salesmen that will be instrumental in procuring both personal and team selling success. May not the solution to this currently intractable problem lie in attitude research and relationship to selling success?

RELATIONSHIP BETWEEN JOB ATTITUDES AND SELLING SUCCESS

A positive identification of an attitude of mind in a salesman at any given time in any given circumstance is difficult enough. To correlate a clutch of such attitudes of mind to a degree of successful achievement in any field of sales effort might upon the face of things be seen as flying in the face of providence.

The author has for the last two decades been closely involved in the selection, management, education, control and development of many hundreds of salesmen selling a wide diversity of product to a wide disparity of industrial, technical, speciality and commercial outlets. Sales forces provide a special headache for field managers because field managers have to spend a great deal of their working time on matters affecting the training and education of their men. Naturally they feel despondent when some men fail and have to be dismissed in the short term, whilst others seem to have a frantic struggle to keep one step ahead of the executioner by keeping sales just around the minimum sum acceptable to top management. It is the relatively small number of salesmen who cause their field managements no trouble that are the key to a company's sales success. For they consistently outperform the remainder with the joint motivation of financial reward and managerial acceptance that they are members of a professional élite. Incidentally they need virtually no training.

It seemed for a start to be a logical outcome to look at the members of successful selling élites to try to isolate the drives that ensure selling success in such men. This quiet investigation into this problem area cannot be dignified by the title of planned research. It represents an unobtrusive examination of men and their results, an endeavour to compare them with men who were not so successful on other areas. Actual figures like standard questionnaires seemed to offer little if any joy. Salesmen came in all shapes and sizes, of all ages and of all grades of professionalism and intellectual development. All salesmen possess a varying number of the desirable qualities mentioned in the blueprint of a salesman, mostly in different combinations, doing jobs of varying difficulty in different markets.

Discussions have taken place by the thousand with field managers, buyers and salesmen of all types and grades in an attempt to *isolate* individual causes for successful activity. Leading questions have been avoided. The job has been to get salesmen, buyers and field managers talking about the persuasion and interpretation areas of negotiation. And the components of customer satisfactions plus the way in which they were achieved.

From these thousands of separate conversations and listening sessions, the glimmering of pattern is beginning to emerge, which seems to represent the general activities of our better salesmen. It is concerned with the salesmen's active, positive, projection of mental attitudes to prospective buying minds and in turn the reaction of buyers to such selling approaches. A number of individual attitudes have been detected. They are mentioned in the subsequent text. No attempt is made to offer a theory. It is far too early. The most that can be done on responsible and rational grounds is to advance a tentative approach to the importance of the positive mental attitude projection from salesman to buyer, to hazard some tentative ideas about their correlated effects, and to do so in a very provisional manner.

A Tentative Hypothesis of the Role of Attitude in Selling Success

In the world of human relationships, we are extremely sensitive to other men's attitudes. If we agree with them we feel a sense of affinity. When we fear them, or dislike them we can see a yawning gulf of dissociation between our minds. We want none of them, and the possibility of co-operation ceases to exist. We may be so incensed that we switch from a defensive role to an aggressive one and try to take them down a peg, to cut them down to size. Or in business to make sure that our colleagues and others know of the strength of our feeling, and the justice of our disapproving, hostile attitude. Thus it is easily demonstrated that attitudes that exist between salesmen and buyers are conducive either to successful co-operation or to utter and complete failure. Where there is a neutrality of attitude, only a passive relationship can be said to exist.

The second step after identifying fourteen such specific selling attitudes was to try to fit them into a general portfolio of selling approaches. This would be more effective if field management could find a practical way of using them to strengthen salesmen's buying impact. To do this, it would be necessary to identify a hierarchy of attitudes that could produce buying favour. Then the really difficult part would be to discover whether certain combinations were more effective than others in motivating buyers to buy.

FOURTEEN DISTINCTIVE ATTITUDES THAT ENCOURAGE SELLING SUCCESS

1 *Attitude to life*
2 *Attitude to people*
3 *Attitude to job*
4 *Attitude to company and management*
5 *Attitude to selling*
6 *Attitude to ideas and concepts*
7 *Attitude to communication*
8 *Attitude to problem solving and decision-making*
9 *Attitude to security and career*
10 *Attitude to remuneration, rewards and promotion*
11 *Attitude to independence of operation and judgement*
12 *Attitude to self-improvement and development for managerial responsibilities*
13 *Attitude to peer group and team work within company*
14 *Attitude to leadership to self-management and to accountability for activities*

Some Tentative Conclusions

It is invariably tempting to try to draw premature conclusions from a mass of accumulated evidence: particularly so in an area such as selling, where any new discoveries could prove highly rewarding to both practitioners and to their employers. Prematures whether in promulgating research findings or in gunnery are preferably to be avoided. However there are some pointers of a very general kind that can be mentioned at this comparatively early stage, but bearing in mind that the investigations have not been made with a carefully selected research sample.

1 Above averagely successful salesmen and members of selling élites seem to have certain attitudes and approaches definitive to life, people, the selling job and themselves. They seem to be worthy of note and further investigation.

2 The first common attitude and approach is that of being positive thinkers in situations, problems, threats and opportunities. Some, particularly members of the élite, demonstrated creative imaginative approaches and attitude to life, people, job and problems. These were well above those to be expected of the normal run of representation and negotiation.

3 The second common attitude and approach is that of an overwhelming wish and determination to achieve high standards and goals in both life and work. In many of the élite there was a marked drive to excel, to win, and to outstrip all opposition. Not in a power-drunk sense but in a determination to punch their mental weight to the absolute optimum of their potential at every opportunity. These traits appear to confirm the theses of Herzberg and McClelland.

4 *The third common attitude and approach is concerned with a wish to be self-managing, self-planning, self-controlling, self-energising, self-starting, self-developing.* The underlying theme is not one of revolt against authority or resentment against accepting guidance or direction. It is the ego-drive of the competent aspiring professional. He believes that he is fully capable of managing his own cabbage patch or manor, with a minimum of help (and only when requested) from company management. This calls for unobtrusive managerial oversight, almost one of observant neglect. This is in a line with recent American academic thought about the future of sales management. This identifies with the desirability of salesmen at the grass roots of the market to be a projection of company marketing management in

the field and thus to make sales management a more important member of company management teams.

5 The fourth common attitude and approach is to professional status and prestige. Among the above average performers professionalism and customer acceptance as experts are strong motivators. In the case of the élite many saw their role as ambassadorial, consultative, company managerial projection, the specially chosen professional negotiator (with full discretionary powers and powers of decision) for a territory. Again this is in direct line with informed American thinking. In some instances, élite members see themselves as interpreters of company policy, the centres of their company's distribution communication and negotiation networks in the field.

6 The fifth common attitude and approach is to the vital matters of career escalation and the ladder of promotion within the company selling organisation. The majority of the salesmen and field sales managers interviewed are far from being altruists. They have codes of principles and exhibit high moral professional behaviour in their conduct of selling negotiations but they are essentially career oriented and promotion minded. Fame (high professional reputation) may be the spur but cash and status constitute the reward. The Career Escalator is a clearly bifurcated one. Once a salesman becomes a high achiever and producer of sales volume and profit growth he wants like any other worker in the vineyard to be closely associated and identified with the extra values of his labour to the company. He wants to see this value component expressed either in promotion to a title, to special work with visible additional responsibility, or to a junior supervisory post. He wants both visible status rewards and visible monetary rewards in his pay packet. Here are two high motivating areas for field management to consider.

7 The above average and the élites share common ground in their reactions to company management and leadership. Their views are loud and clear. They want management and leadership that are visible and which they can respect. This is more important than liking their bosses, although that undeniably is a bonus. They want to be associated in the public eye with a company that is successful, whose policies are respected, whose progress is steady and comprehensive, whose field management is participative and consultative, and where salesmen get a fair crack of the whip in being consulted upon all matters of common concern affecting their working environment and their careers. Lickert[8] is thus once more confirmed in his thesis.

8 The whole question of training and education of sales forces is thus raised by these tentative conclusions. Above average and élite salesmen want as little training as possible regardless of what company managements may feel about them especially their crying needs for developmental training. The most important tentative conclusion is that we may well have to re-think quite a lot of our most cherished training philosophies. At the moment the bulk of training offered is in selling techniques. These are necessary and vital. What we may well have to re-think is our attitude to man training and educational development. Attitudes of mind and habit are the set pieces by which we face any situation that raises its head within our environment—whether a routine demand or an unexpected challenge.

Defensive thinking is unthinkable for the salesman who wishes to be successful. Negative thought and action get us nowhere fast. But positive imaginative thought processes do not come easily to every man. Positive action is not every man jack's natural inheritance, whilst much routine training may seem to be a chore that will pay off in the course of time and therefore must be endured. Education (or re-education in thinking) in the creation of positive and meaningful thinking and action might seem to some to be an imponderable or an unnecessary and unwelcome challenge to busy and average selling performers. Going back to school to many people is still equated with a publicly regressive step that in some mysterious way could reduce a person's status and prestige. Salesmen earn their corn by their skill in persuading prospective purchasers to be guided into placing a continuity of business with them—no more no less. Training in tools and techniques is thus an accepted if long term benefit by sales staff from field management. However education which is aimed specifically at inducing salesmen to a change or modification of attitude is a very personal challenge to the *amour propre* of each man. Field sales managers cannot change either men or their ways. They can only find ways of inducing men to work the oracle of change in themselves.

This is not a book on sales training. There is no intention of trying to tell a field sales manager how to do his job. The sole purpose of this insistence upon new ideas and approaches being needed in the making of a modern salesman is to get each field manager to check upon his approaches and attitudes, to confirm that his current methods go far enough to ensure that his men will wish to effect attitude changes that will ensure higher productivity, profit and growth.

The foregoing conclusions are advanced tentatively about the growing importance of salesmen's attitudes to make it clear that there is a meld of emotional and mental content required in any attempts that are made to motivate them. There is also an amalgam of monetary and non-monetary rewards. They will be required to be offered in the right blend if motivation of each salesman is to proceed as desired with any hope of success.

Discussions which the author had with some of the more progressively-minded salesmen make it clear that they are little moved by pure reasoning, however clear and convincing it might appear to field sales managers. Training and education matters are not organisational problems that can be formulated and handled in nice and tidy bureaucratic compartments alone. They are very human problems. They require handling in very human fashion. And they need to be given very human solutions. To do this effectively, a field manager needs to use not only managerial techniques or tools, but human data and human mental and emotional tools.

What a field manager is trying to do in such circumstances is to achieve progress, by helping other people to want to progress, and to find ways and means of activating them to do so. However, the art of progress is to preserve and to conserve rational order among the change created. The converse is equally valid. He will have to preserve and to conserve the changes that have been achieved amid the traditional order created by his own organisation. Further, he will have to take one step at a time and consolidate it before going on to the next. Again, the progress in attitude change may vary in pace, and often stand still, even regress. Here a watchful eye and infinite patience are needed so that no salesman will lose heart or become bored with the process. Also, he must realise that each salesman's pattern and need for learning about change may be quite different from those required by other men at that time.

To finalise these tentative conclusions, discussions made it abundantly clear that formalised training is acceptable in the acquiring of a skill. Education in attitude changes needs to be tailored to the individual measure of each salesman at each stage on the way or it will fail. Off-the-peg training methodology has no place in this particular aspect of man development.

We could with advantage quote Ordway Tead[9] : 'The extent to which Management philosophies, policies, and practices take into account the inherent values, dignity, and aspirations of Human Beings has now become the greatest single factor in competitive survival.'

Thus it must be emphasised that the form of managerial motivation that may drive one salesman to succeed can leave another man quite cold. It is the same with the shape of monetary reward. One man will work extremely well on a salary plus increment basis adjusted to results and the man's increasing worth to the company. Others want to see the stick and carrot in action, where they are given visible rewards as they are earned in terms of quota or other achievements. This means gearing commissions and bonuses, to the extra turnover resulting from extra effort which brings the sales volume ahead of the minimum acceptable quota levels. Thus a man gets his salary regardless of results (unless he is fired). The bonus or commission are direct additional rewards for extra successful efforts that have a visible material and financial value to the company. (For instance, once a break-even point has been passed on a man's territory for a given period, the accumulating profit with all fixed cost paid can enable a company to be more generous with its payments for extra volume, on a marginal cost basis.)

Discussions made it clear that salesmen with continuously high volume sales such as those in the consumer goods field liked the meld of good basic salary with high commission and bonus against excess quota figures obtained whilst salesmen of high unit cost plant making the occasional sale preferred a high basic salary with increments to coincide with increased value to the company plus an annual bonus that is related to any annual increase in sales and/or profits made by the company. Here again there is no intention by the author to try to tell sales managements which are the best ways of remuneration linked to the ideal incentives to act as perpetual motivators of selling effort. Each company must use the methods which they find best provided only that they make regular and periodical checks upon the viability of their methods as proven optimum motivators of selling effectiveness.

However it was felt that there is an important place for special rewards for special efforts made during specific time periods to enhance sales, such as when a sales push is needed at seasonal times, to expand production at a time of normal slack, to give a new product an enthusiastic launch in the market by heavy and wide stocking coverage, or to boost the sales of a product that is threatening to come to an early demise. Such tactical campaigns were regarded as battles which everyone could win, merely by

230 The Making of a Modern Salesman

beating the special quotas laid down for the exercise. There seemed to be little if any preference whether the cash reward comes as a series of fixed sums of money tied to specific additional or new sales, or whether it is paid as a commission percentage for sales in excess of a stated target.

COMPETITIONS

The foregoing led naturally to a discussion of competitions as a whole. Sales managers may be surprised to learn how little enthusiasm there really seemed to be for competitions of the normal kind, with a few winners of worthwhile prizes and no reward for the great majority of also rans. There seemed to be a rooted suspicion that the dice were pre-loaded in favour of a small number of salespeople, such men were prepared to go to any unreasonable length to get their names on cups and to pocket substantial prizes in cash, overseas holidays or in kind.

There was distinct enthusiasm for competitions run against individual salesmen's individual quotas, where commissions or bonuses were paid on the amount by which sales exceeded the set norms. In this field there was full support for prizes to be awarded in addition to those men who had exceeded quotas by the largest percentages.

There was a clear majority view in favour of competitions being as varied as possible in nature (i.e. by product), varied by seasonal periods (March, June and October/November being specially favoured) timed to produce the cash benefits just prior to family holiday periods (Easter, Summer and Christmas) with the proviso that the ideal still was the basis of self-competition and self-rewards for as many men as possible.

Another finding that may disappoint many sales managers in the consumer goods and speciality fields is that the enthusiasm for team competitions with weekly team positions and the brouhaha of telegrams and canned pep letters from headquarters, is nowhere so marked as is generally thought to be the case.

Salesmen questioned were not really too keen upon the exposure of their limitations when things were going badly for reasons which they did not feel could be attributed either to poor performance or to neglect. Nor, contrary to many sales managerial views were they all that delighted when their names fortuitously came at the top of the heap. They were cute enough and shrewd enough to fear that their true value to the company in qualitative terms could easily be overlooked in managerial ivory towers. And precedence given to the few who were for one reason or another at the top of the quantitative sales list with almost indecent regularity of personal exposure.

NOTES

1. Herzberg, F. *Work and The Nature of Man*, Staples Press, London, 1968.

2. Lickert, R. 'New Patterns in Sales Management', The Sixth Annual Conference on Marketing Management, University of Michigan, 1962.

3. Sadler, P. J. 'Leadership Style, Confidence in Management and Job Satisfaction. Papers at Ashridge Management College.

4. Maslow, A. H. *Motivation and Personality*, Harper, New York, 1954.

5. McClelland, D. C. 'Towards a Theory of Motive Acquisition', *American Psychologist* **20**, 1965.

6. McMurray, R. and Arnold, J. S. *Building a Dynamic Sales Organisation*, McGraw-Hill, New York, 1968.

7. Mayer D. and Greenberg, H. M. 'What Makes a Good Salesman', *Harvard Business Review*, July/August, 1964.

8. Lickert, R. 'New Patterns in Sales Management', Sixth Annual Conference on Marketing Management, University of Michigan, 1962.

9. Tead, Ordway. *The Art of Administration*, McGraw-Hill, New York, 1963.

CHAPTER NINE

The Field Sales Manager's Role in Educating, Counselling, Training, and Developing The Sales Force

Here we arrive at the nub of the field managerial role in the making of the salesmen under his aegis. There can be no more important long term concept of manpower development than as a company investment being steadily converted into a valuable company asset.

It seems still to be customary for sales directors to fragment this vital area into a nice tidy split of independent vacuums— H.Q. training, field training and developmental training for potential managers. Nothing could be calculated better to prevent a cohesive and integrated process coming into being. For each man should be visualised as an individual who needs to have his mind stretched, guided, and trained for both it and the man to develop into a rounded, fully optimised whole.

It is quite impossible to split this managerial responsibility into the four separate divisions of educating, counselling, training and developing. The reason is that all these activities overlap both in their application and the individual need. The reader may want a further clarification. It could be visualised in the marginal differences in application. *Education* in company philosophy, policies, planning, methodologies is an essential. It is sporadic in its application, because after the initial induction course at H.Q. only the changes need to be notified—a kind of further education in Company Activity. However, education (the acquiring of knowledge and information) continues without a halt in the salesman's need to be up-to-date with changes in his environment, market segments, industries and trades which he serves, particular customers and their buyers, competitive innovation and threat. Further, there is a growing need for salesmen to be acquainted with the wider market and its potentialities for development and change—global conditions as they affect economics, populations, technological discovery. And of course forward-thinking about the individual salesman's potential for ultimate managerial posts.

Counselling is a continuous activity. It is the continuous need of a salesman for guidance in the development of his skills, his job achievement, his job and social attitudes, his career. The salesman wants standards by which he can compare his speed of growth, and guide lines to keep himself on his chosen course.

It is easy to see that training, development and education are all connected intimately with the salesman-field managerial relationship in which continuous counselling is the medium of intercourse. This need for counsel and guidance is endemic. It goes on throughout a salesman's career, even when he reaches top management level, and ultimately the board itself.

Let us look therefore at this comprehensive coverage of the counselling capacity as the key field managerial role in the making through continuous development of each salesman to the optimum of his potential capacity.

COUNSELLING AND APPRAISAL OF SALESMEN

Salesmen ask for counsel and advice upon a myriad of differing subjects. It might superficially seem easy to deal with each enquiry as it arises, strictly on its individual merits. This begs the whole subject and aim of counsel and its attendant guidance upon conduct. For it is guidance upon action and conduct of some kind that the salesman invariably seems to want. And you cannot and dare not treat each enquiry within a separate vacuum. True it has its individual existence and nature. But, enquiries have both vertical and lateral associations. To deal with an enquiry in a vacuum is to deny that the salesman is a unique human being making his living by dealing with a large number of other unique human beings—in this instance buyers. A medical practitioner looks carefully at a symptom. He then tries to diagnose the cause, which may lie deep in either a patient's metabolism, his mind, or his emotions. Or it may be a functional imbalance or a truly organic disease. He then will try to prognose what treatment will do best to arrest the trouble, and ultimately cure it, if that be possible.

That is a true and daily analogy for the field manager trying to deal with a salesman's disquiet or problem. He too must relate symptom to cause, and try to prognose the best course of guidance to eliminate the problem, or at least get on top of it. For only in this way will counsel and guidance have any real and lasting value.

This implies another analogy. The medical practitioner will first look at his records to see if they can afford any guide to the present problem, especially as they may lead to an accurate appraisal of the man as a whole individual, as well as a person who is currently seeking relief through guidance and treatment. The field manager should be equally circumspect in carefully consulting his previous experiences with the man and his appraisal of the man on both qualitative and quantitative grounds. Here the field manager will examine and appraise the man's attitudes, his motivations, his ambitions, his aspirations to achieve. These will provide a reliable, an essential background to the guidance the man is seeking, and the advice the field manager will try to give in the form of wise counsel. In this context a field manager should keep his own private records of each man under his control. They will in appraisal terms go far deeper into the man's character, temperament and personality than the normal company appraisal forms dealt with in the following chapter.

PERSONAL LEADERSHIP

Once away from school, college or university a man's learning comes from his reading, his observation, his inclination to study, from enforced study and from personal judgement of affairs and men culled from the pains and pleasures, the loss and benefit associated with actual experience. This applies more to the leaders than to the led. Men are leaders when they have an unlimited appetite for new knowledge, increased experience, study and expanding their personal horizons to the limit of their potential capacity. The ordinary salesman is not so likely to have such an avid hunger and thirst for learning. He will tend to develop it only when a career hiatus makes him or his wife see it as a previously ignored necessity and currently a must.

Why this emphasis upon field managerial leadership? The reason is that enlightened field managers do not attempt to impose their wills and wishes arbitrarily upon their men. They seek to show them the overwhelming reasons in favour of a postulated type of activity or conduct. Such a manager then shows them clearly where their responsibility lies and how best to meet it. He does not try to do their thinking or decision-making for them. He tries as a continuous part of their developmental training and education to help them to think through their own problems and to come to their own decisions, provided only that they do not conflict with known company policies or major planning. The best field managers see their overriding responsibility to be to educate their men to a level where they can become mainly self-managing and self-leading within their territories. Thus leadership thinking and planning have a major role to play in the counselling and guidance, the education and training, and the development of salespeople of all types.

In this context, a field manager realises early in his career that he can himself achieve only through the medium of helping his men to achieve for themselves. First he appraises the strengths and weaknesses of each man. Then he considers precisely what he must do to create a balance between qualities, and to develop each man as a whole individual. In his personal knowledge of each man, he follows a course of counsel and guidance, of education and training, that is calculated to perform the exact remedial and development job needed in each case.

LEADERSHIP HAZARDS

Just as salesmen must find out how best to persuade their buyers to buy from them by the projection of their personalities in the most pleasing and persuasive manner, buttressed by a flow of imaginative ideas about buying and using benefits, so must field managers similarly do a first class selling job on their men. However there are as many hazards in the path of field managers in this leading role as salesmen experience in their contactual selling roles.

1 *Communication failure with individuals*	— No meaningful, purposeful relationship is built up between manager and man. Words have different meanings and implications for manager and man. There is a lack of mutual liking, respect

2 *Playing at favourites*

and understanding. Real co-operation is not achieved.

— As with children in families, there must appear to be common standards of treatment and support for one and all. Failure in this sector can be disastrous.

3 *Inadequate and inconsistent help and dogmatic attitudes*

— This is a failure of managerial outlook and activity. There is no excuse. It is the field manager's job to be all things to each of his men, at the precise time that help is needed, which is in advance of a man's collapse. Men want preventive medicine, not a curative dose when it is too late to save a situation.

4 *Failure to plan to develop whole men*

— Any sensible hierarchy of plans to make a salesman must take a long term view of the man as a whole and balanced person. Less than this is mere training in odd skills and procedures.

5 *Failure to plan for regular appraisal, audit, control and development*

— This is the procedural application of No. 4 above.

6 *Failure to appreciate the individual motivations of each man and his career escalator aspirations*

— This is the logical outcome of Nos. 4 and 5 above. A manager must know with precision what are the main drives actuating each man, and the aspirations he seeks in career ambitions. How else can he counsel, guide, educate, train and develop his men effectively?

There are many more hazards. Yet attention to the foregoing will eliminate the main risks of managerial failure in the manpower developmental zone.

IMPARTING COUNSEL, GUIDANCE, EDUCATION, TRAINING

Obviously, counsel can refer to an individual in private or to groups in public. Both are essential media and the individual can learn a great deal in the cut and thrust of group debate that he would overlook in private tuition.

Thus we must look at the areas which are best covered in regular team meetings and those best dealt with in solitary isolation. It is however necessary to see the whole picture as on-the-job training because it is the training of individuals in job handling aimed to produce Job Success and through it the success and growth of every individual of a sales team.

The reader will have noted the word tuition used in the context of counselling. Tuition is a private affair, in which the manager stands to the salesman as tutor to student. It implies a two-way involvement in information processing and communication, that is essential if optimum benefit is to be gained from the relationship. It is a success for the duet, or it is a failure for each individual.

It is important here to distinguish between selling job levels in different trades, industries and companies and in particular those in which men have two professional hats, a selling hat and a scientific or engineering hat, e.g., sales engineers. Although there are many common skills and many common factors and features in job training the educational, technical and even social levels may be very different indeed. Hence counselling, guidance, and tuition will assume different levels of expertise and intellectual appreciation. It is vital that a field manager should abjure dialectical clap-trap about all men being equal, etc. Those of us in education are well aware that it is far easier to detect the differences rather than the similarities or equalities. Anything else is mere wishful thinking and self-deception. Take the cases of a man selling toilet rolls to small corner shops and a man selling computers. The required minimum levels of education, technical knowledge, organisational and planning know-how, intelligence and intellect are widely different. This is no reflection upon either man. Each should be chosen to be the best available man for the job description. Each is expected to succeed. Each man will be fully entitled to the professional status and community respect that he can win for himself and his company through the excellence and success with which he does his particular job in selling goods and satisfactions profitably. It boils down to the comparative degree of the difficulties inherent in each job and the differing types of commercial, technical and social competence needed to ensure success.

The differences are patently obvious. One job is a steady

systematic calling upon shopkeepers whom the salesman converts into friends. The product is an absolute necessity to a civilised society and is in regular daily demand. Every corner shop is a stockist of this type of product, in a wide range of colours and texture consistencies. The salesman's problem is to get his market share or more in each shop that stocks his type of product against competitors who will use quantity discount schemes to cut prices to the bone. Corner shops whether members of Symbol Groups or not, have to be ready to pare prices to meet special promotions run by neighbouring supermarkets or those in adjacent towns. Hence such a salesman must be expert in expressing profit margins in terms of speed of inventory stock turn and in getting customers to feature his line in window and on counter and buying a bulk parcel at lowest prices to make the deal worthwhile. The salesman's chief selling weapons in this type of selling and buying are a winning, pleasantly forceful personality, who really has learned to win friends and influence buyers in his favour, and, an extremely self-disciplined attitude to hard work and patient effort. Plus a belief that this is an ideal way of life, which he is lucky to follow. A case of choosing his ideal form of occupation and getting paid for it to boot.

Counselling in such cases is mostly ministering to the ebullience of the salesman's spirits if at any time they get low. He has to get a full head of steam generating once again. Guidance and training are mostly concerned with making sure by visiting the salesman's customers with him, that he really is selling well and effectively. Education is mainly concerned with holding an inquest at the kerbside after each call, in which good points are first dealt with and praised. Thereafter matters in which the salesman failed to shine are patiently discussed, remedial measures are agreed, and the salesman undertakes to put things right.

The computer salesman's job is entirely different in character and perspective. It is a challenge to the modern business of size to become ever more data processing minded and to install a modern computer, with a salesman's invaluable help and advice. It is a constant challenge to computer operating companies to go for bigger, better, or at least more sophisticated computers. In principle, every large company should be a prospective customer, whilst smaller companies should be prospective customers for computer service organisations, that take in other people's washing and process it for a suitable fee on their equipment. Maybe they should, but many do not need, and many which do, do not want. To get in to see potential purchasers a computer salesman must aim at a high managerial level which has the authority to consider and to recommend purchase to its board of directors, should it so desire. Here we have situations that normally demand a deep and wide knowledge of accounting systems, organisational design data, organisation and methods engineering and the investment value of computers to the essential company information banks for top management. This requires much *savoir-faire* and its partner *savoir-vivre*, a capacity to move naturally at high managerial and social levels. It needs both high intelligence and a high intellectual imaginative creative approach to sell the idea of the computer's aid to top managerial decision-making processes —in fact a high degree of sophisticated knowledge, thinking and approach to problems.

This is fine when the prospective company knows its computing onions. But few do. And in such cases computer salesmen have to be expert unearthers of realistic problem areas that are bedevilling company efficiency. Further they have to be clever merchants of ideas and benefits about a whole host of potential uses. These together could revolutionise the prospective purchasing company's accounting layout and systems management. A computer salesman is playing for high monetary stakes, in the unit value of computer hardware alone. His investment analysis of company potential using benefits must be sophisticated, authoritative and capable of being sustained against experts in the prospective purchaser's board room. Here a man's temperament, character and personality come under fire. He has to be a balanced individual under duress who can pleasantly yet firmly make his debating points, one at a time, succinctly and convincingly, never flag at unforeseen interruptions or procrastinations and delays, but get the conversation and selling strategy back on course with professional expertise.

Here we have an instance of a salesman wearing many hats in turn: salesman, interpreter, negotiator and technical demonstrator, accountant and office manager, financial comptroller and company secretary, organisation and methods and systems experts, all at expert level and with an integrity that is obvious: co-operative selling par excellence. The field manager deals with an entirely different kettle of fish. Here is a salesman of considerable intellectual capacity who aims high, working at high levels of management, who can never afford to relax for one moment in any sales situation, particularly when selling to buying committees and company boards of directors. In most cases the field managers' jobs are to keep each man on the tips of his toes.

Here a field manager may well give prior attention to getting his man preparation minded, planning minded, demonstration minded, so that he approaches each call as a specially mounted campaign to be fought on his opponent's ground, and which he is dedicated to win, however long it may take to break down opposition, to remove doubts about change and to convince top management of the wisdom of his proposals. Keeping selling morale high is a problem in such circumstances where delay is the most common hazard, and resistance to change and to high capital expenditure its soulmates. Here a field manager is more concerned with his salesman's attitudes. His skills pose fewer problems. It is when grooming and tutoring men to sell sophisticated products at high managerial levels that one sees the need for planned schemes for individual development as the counselling cause *par excellence*. The delight at successful growth may well be common to both types of salesman just described. The individual causation will differ enormously, probably as much as the opposite polarities of the selling jobs themselves.

SALES MEETINGS—A FIELD MANAGER'S ROLE IN THE MAKING OF SALESMEN

A common approach to sales meetings in a majority of British companies is that of an annual conference; here the Chairman in as matey a way as possible consistent with his dignity expounds the company sales policy (if any) for the year ahead. It is of course telling, not selling. The effects are rarely so enthusing as company boards often imagine. Sales meetings of a local character arranged regularly by a field manager are a very different matter. They serve two broad purposes: to inform salesmen of future company policies or of concern about market conditions, and the company's share of the potential. This is an informative meeting, even although it may also be used as a promotional meeting. The second kind of sales meeting is that called deliberately as a counselling, guiding, tutoring, educational and training aid. Such meetings can be absolutely first class if carefully organised, with specific aims, and controlled by audit and validation of success or failure.

A Promotional Sales Meeting's Aims

A sales meeting of this type is aimed at being both an individual and a sales team sale. To achieve this aim it must be meticulously organised to produce this end, without fumbling, frustrations, and without fail.

The principal aims are:

1 To get everyone vitally interested in the meeting itself, in the information benefits that will accrue, in the new ideas that will circulate, in the tips about dealing with situations, propositions, and snags that colleagues and the field manager will expound. *In short a learning motivated situation.*

2 To help everyone to do a better selling job and to defeat inherent market, product usage and competitive problems. *In short a problem-solving and stimulation situation.*

3 To get each man talking informally to his colleagues within a carefully tailored problem or brain-storming session. To get each man in turn to lead the group's discussions or to read a personal paper on some aspect of the general or particular selling situation that has posed general problems and to which he has found an answer. *In short, a manpower development and public speaking motivation situation.*

THE FIELD SALES MANAGER'S ROLE AS BRAIN-STRETCHING CHAIRMAN

Obviously, the manager should keep minutes of each meeting. He should programme each meeting a few day's ahead, and give each man adequate notice of any contribution he will be expected to make. He should give him any helpful advice that he may seek in order to project both himself and his message to better effect.

1 The manager leads in with a carefully prepared introduction. This should ideally sound off-the-cuff, in order to create the right atmosphere for the particular meeting.

2 As an impeccable salesman himself, he will deliberately create audience interest.

3 He will introduce each speaker with a well chosen welcome confined to a few words.

4 He will impose a chairman's duty of keeping each speaker to a previously agreed time. He will not stop reasonable interruptions through the chair to establish a point of clarity. But he will not permit heckling as such for purely derisive or destructive reasons.

5 He will keep questions and questioners on the ball and conserve time.

6 He will sum up the findings of the meeting, and get audience

I

approval that they are acceptable. He will at the end remind the audience of the date and subject of the next meeting, and who will be the principal speaker or speakers.

7 He will arrange from time to time a forum of interesting speakers from outside the team itself. For instance, a leading buyer, a large user, and get them to put over clearly what their demands from salesmen are in terms of a hierarchy of needs and wants.

The Benefits of Sales Meetings with Participatory Leadership in the Saddle

What a thoughtful manager is trying to accomplish is to stretch each man to the full, in both his own interests and those of the team. He is trying to release the hidden potential awaiting discovery in each salesman. He wants to see it bubbling to the surface as the vehicle for creative, imaginative, innovative and constructive ideas about better sales operations and planning.

This does not happen spontaneously except with the few men who are triggered-off in brain-storming sessions. It is usually the result of a stimulus-response syndrome of carefully calculated but invisible planning. This is a blend of motivating each individual as well as motivating the group as a whole.

CHARACTERISTIC INDIVIDUAL MOTIVATORS

Giving appropriate praise for a job well done, at the time, and in front of colleagues when possible.

Asking each man for his considered views upon matters of current and future operational and planning interest and taking them into real account when decision-making.

Keeping each man fully in the team selling picture with up-to-the-minute information.

Discussing each man's particular needs and wants and practical means by which the better ideas can be used, met and satisfied.

Offering something more sophisticated than the crude carrot and stick method of getting salesmen's response to managerial requirements, i.e. the sandwich technique of praise where just, constructive criticism of lacks or faults as a filling, followed by the other piece of praise to complete the normal sandwich snack.

Taking both a managerial and a personal interest in each man's personal interests in his life, work and career ambitions. This is the human cement that bonds man and leader together, a mutual sense of belonging to a group in pursuit of identifiable mutual objectives, a side-by-side relationship of leader and led.

Making oneself available to salesmen at all reasonable times for private discussion on matters that are worrying or piquing the men, whether they be of a business or a private nature. This makes the human cement take an even tighter bond on the mutual relationship.

Ensuring at all times that each man is visibly getting a fair crack of the managerial time and whip. This could be summed up in one term championing each man and his aspirations.

When a man is championed and his work is imaginatively planned to offer the fruits of success in return for honest and inspired effort, in Herzberg's language he will begin to talk in the idiom of satisfactions, of achievements, of potential growth, of career aspirations—the hygienic conditions for manpower development. When his management observes the principles of observant neglect and full participation in discussion and planning the hygienic conditions of the working environment are in harmony with the job satisfactions the man gets from his own work effort and result in overall manpower development *in toto*.

Personal Tutoring, Coaching, Counselling, Guiding and Individual Development

There is a popular misconception that education, training, coaching and counselling are all words to describe the same thing. Apart from group education and training via sales meetings, a manager's main objective in manpower development is the personal persuasion of each man to become intellectually curious about his own development. This is not so easy as one might imagine. Many men have ceased to be intellectually curious since systematic education ceased for them when they left school, college, or university. When there has been a gap of many years it is not so easy to tie up the loose ends and get started all over again. It becomes progressively harder to think about learning the farther one is separated in time from one's last involvement with it.

Let us take a typical salesman, regardless of his I.Q. His desire to submit himself to a tyranny of learning that will upset his normal leisure pursuits and interfere with his social obligations will have to be justified by the clear benefits that he can see accruing from such a dedication to self-development. From hundreds of personal talks with ambitious salesmen it is possible to see something of a common pattern of response to the development stimulus. It goes in very broad terms something like this, in the form of a personal mental quiz:

If I study what will there be in it for me, to recompense me for the time and cash involved?

Am I able to cope with the course of study after the lapse of so many years of neglect? And what will be the effects upon my family and social lives?

If I can, how long will the course take? And how long will it be before I feel the benefits in my pocket? Will the company recognise my effort favourably?

Am I really willing to stay the course and see it through to the end?

Could I not be better employed thinking and planning tactical operations for growth on my territory?

This in turn boils down to a simple basic soliloquy:

Can I?	*Yes, I can!*
Are benefits worthwhile?	*Yes, then I ought!*
Shall I suffer in rat race if I do not study?	*Yes, then I must!*
Will I really benefit from study and in company's appreciation?	*Yes, then I will!*

The difference between a salesman getting down to a course of study or not often depends upon the field manager's subtle sell to the man. Tutoring is a true meeting and exchange of minds, not a mere matter of manager manipulating men. Tutoring involves the recognition of the individual man in stark contrasts of black and white, with a hundred shades of redeeming grey in between. It involves an acute appraisal of the man's inherent capacity and his potential, plus his will to carry through the learning job to its logical end. It involves the transfer of confidence when a man is feeling under the weather, or is discouraged by other causes from being the perennial optimistic realist a salesman must be by outlook if he is to succeed. It involves the art of encouraging a man to see his true potential, latent within his mind, that he has neglected for so long. The tutor's occasional reward is to watch the joy with which a man suddenly has a vision of the path that he can tread—a glimpse of a previously hidden promised land of achievement.

Most tutoring work is carried out on the selling job, in the actual contactual field of operations face to face with prospective customers, and afterwards in the managerial car, the modern version of the traditional kerbside conference.

Tutoring should be seen as a tripartite activity. It should start in the managerial car. It should discuss the best tactics to be adopted to bring the business in by the shortest, most effective route. It will consider the potential snags—the objections, the buying climate and attitudes, etc. It will consider even whether the particular call is one where the managerial presence would be welcome and helpful. Wherever there is any risk of a manager not being welcome, then he should not compromise his salesman's goodwill by creating an unwanted threesome in the buying sanctum. The tripartite activity is brought to a close with an autopsy on each call. This should be done regardless of its result. We want to know why we got an order, just as much as why one was either deferred or refused. We must never cease to learn from experience, the learning environment of all pragmatically minded men.

Adult learning and coaching are quite different from those in the primary school. Men want to see a practical and beneficial result immediately from any piece of coaching wisdom they receive. Thus, it is idle for a coach to prate and prattle about any technique unless he shows the man precisely how he can put the pearl beyond price to work for him, and do so there and then, before the lesson is forgotten.

Similarly, any corrective teaching offered to a man after a call should be capable of being put into operational application forthwith at the next or an early call, otherwise it will lose its point and sharp cutting edge.

Tutors and coaches should try to avoid any dogmatic teaching about the way to do a thing, and the wrong way to go about it. What is important is that the man under tuition should be offered or shown a choice of alternative methods that other successful men have found to be productive. The man under tuition is not a fool, or he would not have been appointed. What a tutor should ideally want the man to do is to devise his own inimitable way of doing a job, based upon sound premises and experience. But in so doing he must prove that the personal way is viable, or try another until he discovers the basic truth of negotiation. This is that each man must discover for himself the ideal way of putting over a particular proposition to other men, to suit and to meet the infinite variety of winning ways to the individual human mind and to the heart which is equally selective in its likes and dislikes.

On-the-job training or tutoring is a continuous activity, aimed at the steady growth of the man to master his environment. This is constantly changing and posing a succession of new and more difficult problems to be solved.

Expert tutoring is a rare and precious thing. Few companies in their unwisdom are as yet concerned about teaching its basic fundamentals. Yet the field manager is in an unrivalled position of strength to do an effective tutoring job, provided only that he has been specially selected and educated to do such a responsible task in manpower development. This neglect may be because the majority of sales managers at company headquarters seem to be obsessed with quantitative results above all else. Nobody denies the vital role of quotas and budgets and their consistent attainment in the company profit and loss position. However, like the iceberg too many members of sales top management merely see the statistical tip as being the be all and end all of existence. It is quite unforgivable to forget and to ignore the fact that quantitative results are produced in the main by qualitative means. A poor salesman will not for long produce good results. A good salesman may perform prodigies of selling valour, even with a poor range of products or a defective product mix.

A tutor is thus continuously conscious that the excellence of each man will have a decisive effect upon the quotas and budgets set. He will of course teach the man to make the most of effective methodology and training in arts and formal skills. Yet, always he will be conscious of the man's portfolio of personal attitudes, and the spectrum of approaches to the creation of customer satisfactions and goodwill. For he will know that the qualitative competence that a man brings to his job is a main determinant of the quantitative results in the long run.

A simple example is where a good man for one reason or another has slipped up in his selling of a particular item in the product mix. The methodological manager will give him a roasting on his misuse of method or sales aids. A wise manager whilst checking upon the methodological approach of his man temporarily below par would spend his major doctoring in aiming to get the man to see that he had slipped below his professional ideals and that it was a matter of prestige and concentration to put matters to right by raising his selling sights and getting his nose well in front of target once again. Tutoring is not merely getting men to become sharper in their selling skills. It is a matter of heightening a man's perceptiveness, his conceptual thinking, his imagination, his creative ideas, to the carrying out of a more professional job. Tutoring is the subtle skill of sowing seeds that create a passion for the pursuit of professional perfection in a man.

Successful sales managers and field managers in the main support the setting of personal projects for each man to achieve in between a field manager's pastoral visits. This presupposes the creation and design of check lists to validate progress. Three such lists are itemised below. The first is self-explanatory for a field manager. The second and third cover the working study programme for a salesman for a four week period for his own satisfaction and that for an annual programme which both salesman and tutor could monitor regularly over the longer term.

Some salesmen who have no field managers to guide them often opt for correspondence courses or seminars offered by outside bodies as a quick but fairly expensive way of keeping themselves up to date upon contemporary skills and changing techniques. Here they should seek guidance either from their own headquarters or from their relevant professional bodies. They should seek courses that are offered by schools that are accredited by the Council for the Accreditation of Correspondence Colleges, a quasi governmental body. Similarly, there are excellent short courses offered by The College of Marketing, Cookham, Berks. There is an abundance of other courses run by technical colleges and consultants which a salesman could with advantage attend where a particular course met his specific requirements. Here again the professional bodies would be ready to advise a man who might be in any quandary of choice.

A CHECK LIST TO UNCOVER A FIELD SALES MANAGER'S
PROBLEM AREAS IN COACHING

Mark which sectors you wish to discuss.

Tick

...... 1 Giving a formal appraisal of salesmen.

...... 2 Making suggestions to Divisional Management.

...... 3 Scheduling time to give each salesman enough attention.

...... 4 Helping a salesman with his family problems.

...... 5 Maintaining communication with Head Office.

...... 6 Finding enough time for self-improvement.

...... 7 Understanding company policy.

...... 8 Doing the job as I understand it and think it should be done.

...... 9 Travelling too much.

...... 10 Developing my salesmen's confidence.

...... 11 Following a course of study.

...... 12 Writing personal notes and letters.

...... 13 Developing better customer relations.

...... 14 Keeping happy.

...... 15 Sharing the problems.

...... 16 Helping salesmen to analyse their territories, and to plan better.

...... 17 Training salesmen methodically

...... 18 Speaking with salesmen constructively about their shortcomings.

...... 19 Being a good model for my salesmen.

Tick

20 Understanding and interpreting our advertising policies. ......

21 Supervising and upgrading the older salesmen under my supervision. ......

22 Training my salesmen in making better presentations. ......

23 Developing a system of checking on my salesmen's work habits. ......

24 Helping salesmen simplify their paper work. ......

25 Making new salesmen feel that they are part of the 'team'. ......

26 Using a report form to give each salesman on each of my visits with him—to let him know how he has progressed since my last visit with him. ......

27 Developing greater morale in the team. ......

28 Helping salesmen to get in to see important accounts. ......

29 Keeping myself positive, progressive and creative. ......

30 Making constructive suggestions to Head Office. ......

31 Setting my goals for heavier responsibility within the Company. ......

32 Following through on the ideas given at training or sales meetings. ......

WORKING STUDY PROGRAMME

Day/Week	Subject
Week 1	
M. —	Planning—Time Mastery
T. —	Preparation—Prospecting
W. —	Presentation—Demonstration
T. —	Communications
F. —	Closing Sales—Persuasion
W/E Review	Human and Buying Relations—Physical Exercise
Week 2	
M. —	Planning—Time Mastery
T. —	Communications
W. —	Closing Sales—Persuasion—Getting Goodwill
T. —	Presentation—Demonstration
F. —	Prospecting—Getting In
W/E Review	Human and Buying Relations—Physical Exercise
Week 3	
M. —	Preparation—Prospecting
T. —	Getting In—Getting Out—Getting Goodwill
W. —	Communication
T. —	Demonstration—Closing Sales—Presentation
F. —	Human and Buying Relations
W/E Review	Planning—Time Mastery—Physical Exercise
Week 4	
M. —	Getting In—Getting Out—Getting Goodwill
T. —	Communication
W. —	Prospecting—Demonstration
T. —	Presentation—Closing Sales—Persuasion
F. —	Human and Buying Relations
W/E Review	Planning—Time Mastery—Physical Exercise
4 Weekly Review	Thorough Review—Preparation of Grid Progress Chart

THE 'GRID' PROGRESS CHART

For Main Subject Areas.   Specimen Set Up for a Speciality
                                       Salesman.

	A	B	C	D	E	F	G	H	I	J	K	L
Dec.												
Nov.												
Oct.												
Sept.												
Aug.												
July												
June												
May												
April												
March												
Feb.												
Jan.												
Main Subject Areas	A	B	C	D	E	F	G	H	I	J	K	L

A = Persuasion   B = Planning   C = Preparation   D = Presentation
E = Operation   F = Validation   G = Communication   H = Human
Relationships   I = Buying Relationships   J = Time Mastery
K = Development   L = Creativity

Score 5 *for Minimum Progress Satisfaction.*
7 *for Above Average Progress Satisfaction.*
9 *for Excellent Progress Satisfaction.*

and MARK *with a* { Light
Conservative *Hand.*
Suspicious.

RECOMMENDED READING LIST

There are now hundreds of books covering various aspects of Selling and Marketing at different intellectual levels of difficulty. It is not easy for a student to find the books that offer an adequate coverage of the subject for a minimum investment in cash. Comments are made where necessary to guide the student in his search.

1 *Professional Salesmanship* by Cyril L. Hudson (recommended by Institute of Marketing for study for Diploma in Marketing) (Text book for all Salesmanship Examinations for Diplomas). Staples paperback (1971). Fully comprehensive, for all levels.

2 *The Techniques of Salesmanship* by Charles C. Knights. Pitman Paperback (1969). Elementary but good.

3 *How to Win Customers* by Heinz Goldmann. Staples (1970). Practical text. A work book. Good.

4 *Sales Engineering* by D. N. Chorafas. Cassell (1967). Computer selling. Good.

5 *Salesmanship* by Crissy and Kaplan. Wiley (1969). U.S. bias. All round cover.

6 *The Field Sales Manager* by A. Newgarden. American Management Association (1960). Practical manual. Good. U.S. bias.

7 *Selling Industrial Products* by Rowe and Alexander. Hutchinson (1968). More general than Chorafas. U.K. bias.

8 *New Handbook of Sales Training* by R. F. Vizza. Prentice-Hall (1967). U.S. oriented anthology. Good for U.K.

9 *How to Measure and Evaluate Salesmen's Performance* by W. A. Tonning. Prentice-Hall (1964). U.S. oriented. Good for U.K.

10 *Introduction to Business Forecasting. Introduction to Budgetary Control. Selling and Distribution Cost Accounting.* Institute of Cost and Works Accountants. I.C.W.A. (1962, 1963, 1961). Ideal, simple description of financial areas for the salesman.

The Marketing-Sales Operation by Cyril L. Hudson (recommended by Institute of Marketing for study for Diploma in Marketing). Staples (1970). Most comprehensive book on marketing and sales in the U.K. For sales managers and salesmen.

Self-Education and Self-Management

These are vital subjects for all, but particularly for field sales managers and for their men. The principle applies equally to each group. It is the content that differs, mainly in degree.

It is clear that a field manager who is perennially keen on self-study and self-management will make an enthusiastic tutor to his men. And enthusiasm is a crucial factor in the continuing success of all self-developmental activities. There are so many distractions posed by family and social life that it takes considerable determination to keep one's eye perpetually upon the study ball.

Self-Education

To do a sound practical educating job upon oneself is quite a task. It calls for a truthful mind and a capacity for self-judgement unalloyed with any vestige of self-deception. This is why questionnaires and self-rating lists so often come unstuck. It is natural to think the very best of oneself. No sensitive person is easily persuaded to prick the bubble of self-esteem. It can upset the carefully treasured picture of self-confidence in which one is naturally the hero of the piece, plumb on centre of the stage.

However, this is precisely what a self-educator has first to do. He must come to terms with his personal limitations, and those of his environment. He must make a calm and carefully diagnosed assessment of his current educational standing. He must then plan just how far he needs to go, in which direction, with which subjects, to bring himself smack on course to tackle the vital problem of his own planned self-development. Emerson is credited with the *cri de coeur* 'Our chief want in Life is someone who will *make* us do what we *CAN*'. How very true this observation is. In the case of the salesman his field manager has this unenviable task. In the case of the field manager it is usually he alone who must apply his own spur. Even in the case of the salesman with an enthusiastic and able field manager applying the pricks, it will be the salesman's own will to win the battle for self-development that will decide the issue.

Study and its application are harsh taskmasters. They are followed by the practical merciless verdict of success or failure in every trial and error situation, which all learning experiences. There is the essential lesson of mental and emotional resilience to learn from each error of omission and commission. There is the vital need of a creative, imaginative approach to each buying and selling situation so that we can express our potential persuasive powers to the full. These are the pragmatic pivots upon which salesmen who are dedicated to self-development learn their very personal ways to success.

Study and career are interlinked and interdependent. Quite apart from the career escalator provided by the salesman's company, he must to be successful in the long term visualise his life as a continuous, planned, progressive process. In this process he expresses his conscious and latent talents to the full in balanced integrated living, aimed to benefit himself, his family, his employer and the community at large.

The field sales manager has a similar task of self-study, and self-development. And we should not forget that it has to be carried on simultaneously with the development work he is doing continuously with his men. It is quite unnecessary to ask a conscientious field manager how he spends his leisure hours. It will put the matter in clearer perspective if we identify the main aims of self-study and learning in the planned pursuit of self-development.

Some Aims and Objectives

1 To ensure job satisfactions
2 To ensure professional and financial progress and security
3 To enhance career prospects and satisfactions
4 To pre-empt progressive promotions
5 To pre-empt professional and social prestige, status and progressive rise in position
6 To prepare for early entry to supervisory and junior managerial posts
7 To prevent any risks arising out of personal deterioration, decline and obsolescence.

In the case of a field manager he is fixing his career sights upon senior managerial posts, even eventually the board room in a smaller company.

A field manager's career and that of salesmen are similar in symbolical language and depiction as that for a product's life cycle. Preparation, launch, maturity, decline, retirement.

The whole emphasis upon self-study and self-development is to ensure a long period of true maturity. This should include promotion to a man's professional peak of effectiveness, employing his full potential qualities and know-how to the optimum, in both the interests of himself and those of his employer.

SETTING STUDY AND DEVELOPMENT GOALS

Choosing the best way or ways of self-study is very important and crucial to its success. There are part-time courses and seminars available as previously mentioned. Correspondence Courses and Own Study Reading are the more easily controlled. But even here in the privacy of one's own home, there are studying snags. Let us look at them.

Home Study Advantages

Student can read widely, flexibly, and have reference texts always available.

Student can control own work-load in terms of content, and in available time to suit business, home, family and social pressures.

Home Study Challenges

Absence of tutorial critiques unless doing a viable correspondence course with resident tutors who are really competent counsellors and guides to development of each man's individual talents.

Absence of peer group members against whom a man can test his own progress, myopia, short-falls, aberrations, ideas, development progress as opposed to progress in mere knowledge.

Absence of cross-fertilisation of ideas, typical of group work and challenge.

When working entirely alone, a student must direct and control his own progress to timed goals. More dangerous still, he must audit the results of his own trials, errors and progress.

Again, when alone, a man must quantify his own problem areas without external help or counsel. More important, he has continuously to boost his own self-discipline and self-confidence.

Setting Goals for Self-Study and Achievement

Wise students whether salesmen or field managers set themselves three kinds of time targets—short, medium and long. Each will be the subject of careful thinking, tough self-evaluation and an even more tough appraisal of the market and career possibilities both in selling and in Management. Here there are two separate sets of criteria: goal achievement and the study programme essential to achieve the set targets in time to the actual cumulative goals.

Goal Achievement

There are six basic steps:
1 To reduce the main goal to a carefully-timed series of subsidiary goals, each with its own time parameter and each to be completed before going on to the next step.
2 To define precisely each step and the detail of each programme.
3 To state exactly the requirement and aptitudes in knowledge, outlook and skill to make a start to each step in turn.
4 To nominate a starting date for the whole programme and stick to it, come what may.
5 To audit and validate the results of each step before feeling competent to go on to the next.
6 To assess progress in knowledge and skills resultant upon the completion of each step. And to use this new knowledge and skill where apposite in the approach to subsequent steps, in order to enhance performance from experience gained.

SETTING UP STUDY PROGRAMMES

The short term study programme usually for two to three years ahead needs to be tightly scheduled, precise, with built-in checks against time scale. And the exact goals should be clearly defined. In the case of a salesman, the programme must be purposeful, meaningful and capable of being regularly checked for progress in its actual applications within the selling job itself. Whilst similar strictures apply to a field managerial development programme, many of the subject areas dealing with higher managerial levels are less capable of pragmatic check.

Basic Contents will include:
1 An exact formula for each study activity and its precise perimeters.
2 The depth and width of each study activity and a priority list for each in the overall programme.
3 The exact time each week to be devoted to each activity where more than one is being studied. And the degree of emphasis to be placed upon each *vis-a-vis* the others.
4 The creation and design of ways of testing the validity of activity study in the cold terms of its application in on-the-job working. In short is the study worthwhile in its cold pragmatic application value?

5 Timed appraisals of progress against time schedules. Is his effort right in content, direction and application value in the field?

Notes

Typical examples of the application of study to cold turkey practice would be:
Scheduled time improvement in demonstrations skills
Scheduled time improvement in closing business arts
Improvement in problem solving
Improvement in quicker and better decision-making
Improvement in report making and writing
Improvement in general arts of presentation of products and propositions.

Other instances of study validation for content, direction and achievement would be:
Is salesman being given greater responsibility for planning own work loads?
Is salesman appearing to be more self-reliant in most activity situations?
Is salesman's remuneration rising?

Examples of a salesman's study effectiveness would be in his attitude to change and to methodology that would aid him in his work:
Adjusting study to meet new activity situations—flexibility to meet and to master change
Apparatus to record progress and change in visible form being created by salesman. Items such as gridded charts and Z charts with moving annual totals to cover last three to five years sales, as a salesman's indicator of trend analyses to be exploited.

The creation by the student of a selling criteria check list to validate better performance due to study content, continuity, width, depth and application in daily activities.

A Selling Check List
The Thirty Three Steps

Did I plan the year's work well in advance? In quota form for each product, each market segment and each key outlet?
Is my territorial work-load right? Can I take more, where, how and when?

Have I got a proper gridded territorial map on my office wall?
Have I annotated it with every customer, his quota and other vital details?

Am I working to a differential call frequency scheme, so that work time is optimum?

Have I worked out a proper balance between maintenance selling to existing clients and developmental selling to new prospective clients?

Have I worked out a basic series of planned presentations and demonstrations for use with the differing types of client-situations?

Do I plan each calling interview basically in advance? Are my records good enough for this important tactic to be mainly successful in daily practice? What percentage of such pre-planned interviews are converted into orders?

Do I follow up and through prospective calls made previously by cold-canvass?

Do I save time by getting a high percentage of appointments with both existing and prospective clients?

Do I carry out a regular audit upon my personal appearance? Is it both attractive and forceful?

Do I smile my way into creating an excellence of personal relationships, and a minimum of rebuffs?

Am I really effective in getting interviews quickly and profitably started?

Am I infectiously enthusiastic and persuasive in charming my way into clients' minds, and their social and professional acceptance?

Am I a really first-class questioner, listener, talker to the point? Do I combine brevity with attractive persuasiveness?

Am I a first-class discoverer of client problem areas, a clear identifier that they exist and are important to the client?

Is my prognosis of solutions as good as my diagnosis of their identity? Is my product and proposition presentation effective enough? Does it seek to dispose of objections by emphasis upon buying and using benefits?

Are the visual aids excellent enough to whip up buying desire in my favour?

Do I handle objections and stalls sympathetically yet firmly and logically whilst ministering subtly to the clients' emotional need for empathetic help to make a best buy decision?

Are my order-clinching techniques really and consistently effective? Do I sum up the buying and using benefits expertly? Do I watch with an eagle-eye the signs of buying desire to do a deal? Do I subtly help him to make the order-placing decision? If necessary ask for the order directly on a summation of buying benefits and overall value analysis?

Do I create customer satisfactions as a deliberate tactic, followed by an active creation of goodwill?

Do I automatically arrange for the point of re-entry for the next call and the subject for discussion?

Do I automatically follow through the order to headquarters, and progress chase it through the organisation to ensure delivery on time and details correct?

Do I master-mind my productive time so that I get the most from each day's work-loading face to face with people who can influence the placing of orders, or who can place them?

Do I daily and weekly audit my progress against quota and budget in every sector of activity? Do I regularly audit my job and career satisfactions and targets?

Do I see my job and each situation as a personal challenge to change people's minds in favour of my company's products and propositions?

Do I learn from both failure and success through making a regular autopsy of each call?

Do I stretch myself continuously to excel in every aspect of my job, both reporting and contactual? Have I a continuous will to win in all that I do?

Do I maintain a constant state of personal fitness which shows itself in my being self-starting, self-energising, self-educating, and self-managing?

Do I follow a progressive course of self-education, checking its validity regularly?

Am I an impressive and effective communicator, on a two-way feedback basis?

Do I believe that my personal success will be the direct result of my skills in creating and merchandising ideas and benefits for my clientele?

Do I see that my success is ultimately associated with the meaningful and purposeful human and business relationships that I can create with people who can influence business in my favour? How do I rate in this subtle alchemy of creating confidence and generating trust in my professional and personal desire and competence to help people emphatically, continuously and effectively to mutual benefit and profit?

A Personal Check List for Field Managers
The Seventy-two Steps

Human Relations

Do you really know whether each of your salesmen enjoys a happy family life?

Have you bothered to get to know each of your salesmen as a person?

Could you say authoritatively how each of your salesmen views his job?

Do you know the priority of drives of each of your salesmen in his career plans?

Do you know precisely to what extent each of your salesmen views self-study?

Do you know just how far each of your salesmen has progressed in self-study?

Could you say truthfully that you know exactly how to motivate each of your men?

Could you say what the potential of each of your men is? And how much higher they might go with additional spurring and encouragement?

Have you divided your manpower development between those who will be superlative salesmen and those with managerial potential?

Are you satisfied that you have provided norms of performance that are realistic for each man, in terms of stretching his self-imposed limitations?

Have you developed a visible, irrefutable, harmonious relationship with each man?

Are you on a friendly basis with each man which does not end with the closing of your briefcase when leaving him? In short, is there a human link as well as a mere man-made managerial relationship of leader and led?

Are you satisfied that your appraisal of each man is as exact as it possibly can be? Is there a basis of mutual trust, liking and respect between you and each man?

Communications Expertise

Are your personal communications perfectly clear in both content and intent, in meaning and in phrasing?

Do you create effective two-way feedback in all communications relationships?

Is your vocabulary as wide as it should be in every respect?

Can you write a piece of clear succinct reportage so that everyone knows exactly what you mean, and what you expect of them, where, when, why and how?

Do you ever talk down to men? Do you ever condescend? Are you utterly honest in what you say? Is there ever any conflict between heart and head?

How far would you go to help a backward or an over-thrusting man?

Do you confirm everything in writing? Do you ever leave any loose ends about that could create doubt?

Do you keep your ego as far as reasonably possible out of the personal equation?

Are you ever tempted to play favourites?

Have you a warm, outward-looking, friendly attitude to all whom you meet?

Are you automatically empathy-oriented in every communication? Do your sales meetings go with a swing?

Is your platform manner natural and uncontrived? Can you get across to your men with a minimum of time and effort? Are you an apt questioner, excellent listener and quiet analytical talker to whom no problem is too tough to discuss?

Do you believe that tutoring is both a tremendous responsibility but also a trust and a privilege? Can you really get close to your men and have their confidence?

Are you a master of merchandising ideas to your men? Do you sow seeds, then water and fertilise them, so that the reaping may give you and your men a bumper crop?

Control of Men

Can you get immediate and loyal compliance to your wishes without using force?

Will you give each man the chance to disagree pleasantly with you, and if his point of view is a better one than your own will you be willing to accept his suggestion?

Do you demand absolute rigidity in response to requests, instruction and commands?

Do you prefer to manage by objective or by exception or by a meld of both?

Do you insist upon regular reports that are graded for both source and content?

Do you insist upon instant response to letters or telephone calls? Do you feel that christian names terms on the job are desirable or beneficial? Or, do you insist upon 'Mr' on the job, and revert to christian names after work?

Do you keep paperwork down to a minimum in both directions? Do you try to get salesmen's involvement in the fixing of targets, quotas and budgets? How do you keep them on their toes throughout the year without badgering them and creating resistance? Do you constantly keep your men's eyes on their dual goals of revenue, plus maximum profitability of activities?

Do you insist upon the management of productive time as an absolute must in your men's activities?

Do you keep a close scrutiny on expense accounts, car and sample management? And, insist upon high standards of care?

Do you keep an eagle eye on distribution cost analyses and sales control ratios for each salesman's area? And, help him to improve the position when and where it may be necessary?

Sales Training, Tutoring, Counselling, Guidance, Career Education and Development

Have you a watchful eye and ear for a salesman's weaknesses or gaucheries? Do you commence remedial treatment immediately after you discover it on a contactual call? How do you insist so that he does not feel it to be a rebuke or the shadow of failure? How do you treat such a situation so that you can measure improvement within a short time?

When a salesman gives vent to a *cri de coeur* for help, how do you handle it? Do you make a meal of it? Or, do you cut it down to size and treat it as a very normal matter from which all men suffer at times?

How do you manage to tutor and counsel the older man, say in his fifties? Do you insist upon his showing a good example to the young men, as an appeal to his innate pride? How else can you deal with a man who may be still potentially valuable unless he is introduced to new ideas, which you subtly allow him to discover for himself?

Do you use a sales manual as a training basis? How far do you check whether your men use it as they should?

Have you got your men working on courses of self-study? How far do you interpolate your ideas and support, when you feel that guidance and counselling are needed?

How far do you encourage role playing in sales meetings as tutoring aids?

How far do you encourage your men to create their own gridded maps of selling activity and to lay on differential call frequency calling? Do you actually train them in such techniques and how? Do you check regularly your men's expert usage of merchandising or promotional techniques? And the usage of sales literature as a selling tool?

Do you educate your men in the arts of presentation of products and propositions? Do you encourage them to create their own presentations, demonstration style and content?

Do you place a great deal of emphasis upon training for cold-canvass calling? Do you encourage them to get appointments, and get H.Q. help through letter writing to expedite time conservation?

Do you educate your men specially in the art of overcoming objections and in the supreme skill of order clinching?

Do you regularly expose yourself to sales training at H.Q. or self-study?

Do you regularly read management books and magazines to widen your knowledge?

Do you regularly revise your ideas about the amount of time to be spent upon each activity? Less time with some men, more with others? How do you gauge these changing differentials? Do you monitor your time spread between training, etc., and managerial activities regularly?

Do you write personal notes to your men on, say, their birthdays? Or on a spectacular order? Or when they are sick? Or undergoing a course of remedial treatment from you on some aspect of their job activities?

Do you help a man with his family and social problems on request?

Do you make a practice of visiting your men regularly in their homes, and bringing their wives into the business equation?

Do you make special efforts to improve your communication, your management and your leadership and tutoring expertise?

Do you see yourself as a selling and negotiating model upon which your men could with advantage mould themselves?

Do you make conscious efforts to improve team morale?

Are you specially and regularly concerned to ensure that your attitudes become even more positive, progressive, creative and empathetically oriented?

Do you see yourself as a developer of manpower? What steps do you take to ensure that you are keeping abreast of the latest teachings upon the behavioural sciences?

What steps are you taking to train a man to follow you when you are promoted?

What progressive steps are you taking to be ready to pre-empt your next promotion?

How receptive are you to new ideas and techniques?

Do you regularly brainstorm new and better ideas for your men to use, or for the company to improvise and to develop?

Are you utterly devoted and dedicated to your job, as the one you would choose regardless? Do you pursue excellence for its own sake? Do you try to inculcate this aim into all your counselling with your men?

Have you got a happy ship?

Do you make your own enquiries to make sure that your men are getting every item of information that would help them to better results? Do you and they get and use input-output analysis tables to ensure that you are selling to every market segment as well as your competitors, if not better?

Are you satisfied with anything less than the absolute best in selling performance?

Self-Management

The aims in general of the activity referred to loosely as self-management are similar in the main to those listed under self-study. The common aim is self-development that leads progressively to joy of achievement in life, career and job. The very important secondary aim is eventual recognition of being a worthwhile candidate for a company managerial development scheme, and thence onwards and upwards to the top of individual competence as manager or administrator of senior grade.

There are five major constraints upon self-management achievement in search of the senior management break-through. They are :

1 *Self-Knowledge*   The basic material in the early and basic learning process. We have to identify ourselves. We must come to a decision upon our personal equipment at current value and assess with exact truth what our personal potential and company potential really are, evaluating the exact personal and company constraints that could, unless eliminated, impede our planned progress to such goals. We must

have the will to win and to excel in order to make our dreams come true.

2 *Limitations of Self and Environment*

Knowing what we can change to our benefit on our upward climb to our goals is the first essential step in self-management and self mastery. It is also the beginning of personal wisdom, an essential commodity in very short supply. For wisdom cannot be taught. It can only be won by imaginative application of blood, sweat and tears through a deliberately sought catholicity of personal experience, through defeat to victory.

3 *Leaders and Led*

A successful salesman, let alone a field manager, must demonstrate the qualities of perceptive and sensitive leadership wherever he goes and whenever he operates. This is what the persuasive arts are all about. Every buyer wants to be led to the best buy. He may never admit it, but he needs it and appreciates it in the salesmen who serve him. Every field manager wants to lead his salesmen to successful achievements in the selling field so that the company market share is augmented and each man made richer by the result. Moreover each salesman wants and appreciates successful leadership from his field sales manager. *It is a strange commentary that so little of the literature upon the subject starts with the premise that leadership is a quality, an attitude, an aptitude that is born in the mind by a sense of inner intuition or vision. It is never bestowed. It has to be painfully acquired and meticulously maintained by keen watchful self-leadership and management, through impeccable control of self and surroundings.*

4 *Planned Career Forecasting*

This is self-evident, self-descriptive and self-perpetuating. The mental reach must always outstrip the physical grasp. The horizons must always be receding before us. As one range of hills is reached, others to be climbed recede. This means continuous forecasting of career goals in terms of distance ahead and in time available for their winning.

5 *Goal Aspirations and Achievement*

Each goal should be split up into a convenient number of subsidiary goals, each specifically related to a time scale for its achievement. What is important is a direct linkage between a man's aspirations and their realistic chance of achievement. This implies a regular audit of actual performance in terms of goals set.

It is not easy to draw a straight line between self-management and the management of men. The dividing lines become blurred because the former is vital to the latter, and must come first.

The self-mastery achieved in deliberate study has a spin-off in the creation of a number of acquired arts and skills that become invaluable when the salesman student is put in charge of the education and control of other men.

The student's company also gets an unexpected bonus. This spin-off from study is the far greater appreciation in width and depth of the company's problems, and its operational planning and activities. The salesman acquires an appreciation of the supportive role the salesman should give his field manager and other leaders. He acquires a feeling of the interdependence and interlinkage of all company employees in the active creation of customer satisfactions and goodwill. He sees the point of the importance of daily routine chores that would otherwise be boring and pedestrian in the extreme. He gains a truer sense of belonging to a team and group activity, of being a vital link between company and field, a communications centre of the company-cum-customer information and servicing network. He gets a positive sense of personal identity and of corporative identification with the company and all its people and works.

The final accolade of serious constructive creative study is the light that it sheds upon the job and its satisfactions. These in turn become career activities with promotion vistas extending attractively forwards into a bright future.

This applies equally to the field manager student who is looking forward to his promotion to managerial responsibilities of greater importance. The field manager pushes forward his most enlightened and promising men to the first-hand attention of headquarters' sales management, for consideration for further advancement on the promotional conveyor belt. This will be either a specialised selling job of greater status and value, or to the most junior rung on the ladder of supervisory management. The field manager alas has to sell himself forward and upwards unless he has a regional manager above him in the hierarchy who will do that promotional job for him.

At this stage it could help the reader to have a list of the various courses that company sales training centres lay on for the progressive development of their sales manpower, in their desire to optimise company manpower resources. This is an organisational framework within which the making of modern salesmen and sales managers can progressively take place. In view of the very real difficulty in recruiting future members of senior sales management from external sources as and when they might be wanted, a grow-your-own scheme of this kind has its merits. Particularly, as it enables a company to claim that they fill executive vacancies from within the ranks of their own sales staff.

There are at least seven different types of course available in the larger companies. These are:

1 An induction course for new salesmen. Diagram No. 8 offers typical details.

2 An induction course based and centred upon the creation of a company sales manual. This is described in great detail in Chapter Ten.

3 Refresher courses for salesman's development. Page 267 refers.

4 Remedial courses for salesmen who seem to be worth reclaiming. Page 268 refers.

5 Development courses for successful salesmen with managerial potential. Page 270 refers.

6 Development courses for field sales managers earmarked for promotion. Page 271 refers.

7 Development courses for senior sales managers to fill top sales posts. Page 272 refers.

Sales training programmes of this type offer a flow chart of progressive promotion. This is very important to salesmen with career aspirations to actually see that provided only that they work hard and successfully there is an escalator, a conveyor belt of developmental education, upon which they can hitch a ride in their search for optimum self-development within their chosen company.

There are still varying views in top management circles about the value of sales manuals, both as training and developmental tools. Even many who favour their use fight shy of the cost of their compilation and their being kept up to date with essential revisions. Fortunately there is a fast growing view that sales manuals, properly designed and produced, can be an invaluable selling tool and weapon in the salesman's armoury. In fact, the more technical and complex selling, buying and product technology become, the greater the need for and scope of sales manuals as an interpreting, promoting and selling medium in the provision of viable value analysis of a product and service. Besides its promotional use, it provides a forthright guide to the required conduct of the salesman in every communication activity between himself and H.Q. A veritable Enquire Within upon Everything!

The Refresher Re-Training of Salesmen

From time to time successful salesmen need to be retrained in their normal arts and skills, with a view to opening their minds to new vistas of selling expertise and to new horizons of selling strategy. These together are aimed to increase job satisfaction, and to re-kindle the salesman's interest in the promotional escalator that leads to career ambitions becoming realised in terms of timed goals.

Such training will include the following areas :
1 A careful appraisal of the salesman's current arts and skills in terms of the norms laid down for him against carefully fixed time goals.
2 A careful audit of his usage of routines in terms of team norms of performance.
3 An appreciation of the salesman's sales target and budget achievements to date against quotas allocated to him.
4 Sessions upon attitude creation. The vital importance of positive, creative job and career attitudes and aptitudes. Inculcating the continuous desire to excel and to win over competitive or

market constraints. Fostering a desire for continuous learning, and the role of self-education within it.

5 Sessions upon self-development associated with innovatory ideas. The role of personal creativity in the world of ideas, imagination and their adoption or adaptation to new applications of selling and marketing.

6 Sessions upon new products or new market segments the salesmen will be called upon to develop. New usages of existing products. The need to sell the whole product mix wherever possible. New thinking upon the best ways to develop the purchasing power of each key outlet upon whom salesmen call.

7 Sessions upon a re-examination of worth of own product range and uses compared with the markets available to them under the potential revealed by input-output tables.

8 Sessions devoted subtly to the increased usage of selling approaches, presentations, demonstrations, order clinching and objection overcoming skills and satisfying arts by means of an improvement in appreciation and practice.

9 Sessions subtly centred around job and career development. Motivating, measuring, auditing, appraising the changes wrought by the refresher training upon each man in terms of potential for future development in style and level of promotion.

10 Helping salesmen to set new and higher personal targets of achievement as a direct result of the stimulation and new content of the course.

The Remedial Re-Training of Salesmen

When a salesman's results drop dramatically below his set targets and budgets the field sales manager faces an instant challenge to discover the cause. This may be one of several external causes or be of a nature entirely personal to the company or the salesman himself.

A salesman may slip suddenly because of a market constraint that plays havoc with his sales volume. Seasonal fluctuations beyond the salesman's control may cause an unexpected drop in order volume. A new competitive item offering far better value may have been released on the salesman's area, backed by heavy advertising and promotions, and the fall-off in sales is a direct result. A drop in sales can result also from causes within the company itself. Examples are production failures resulting in time-lags in deliveries and consequent drops in territorial sales either because the product is unobtainable in the shops or because the trade are cancelling their orders. The fault may lie in the quality control function resulting in faulty goods getting to the customers and users, and a natural drop in sales following dissatisfaction with the product's performance.

It is when the drop in sales can be attributed directly to a salesman's own failure that field sales management has the un-enviable task of recommending a decision upon the salesman's future to his company H.Q. The decision may well be that the man is unsuitable and should be either prematurely retired if elderly and regarded as unteachable, or sacked if younger and thought to be unredeemable. Drastic decisions of this kind are rarely taken lightly or quickly. A field sales manager will look to find the direct cause of a salesman's lack of excellence. It may be home or family environmental troubles that are being reflected in poor work results, as a direct reaction of worry and anxiety about his personal life. It may be a sudden health trouble demanding instant medical examination, diagnosis, prognosis and recom-mendation for a change in duties or scene. Or a let-up in work altogether. It may be due in an elderly man to an inability to adjust himself to the pace and change in working conditions and the challenge posing too many problems for him to cope with in practical fashion.

The decision facing the field sales manager is one of whether the erring salesman can be quickly pulled back into line by means of a remedial retraining course, or whether to recommend that he should be allowed to go: and to start a costly search for a suc-cessor. We now assume that he will be sent for retraining.

What form does typical remedial retraining take?

1 Identify shortfall areas, and compare with the team norm of minimum acceptable performance.

2 Identify symptoms of shortfall, and those of any other weak-ness. Get the man's agreement with the diagnosis.

3 Start attitude training to develop pride in learning and excellence in performance.

4 Start at square one with each weakness—educate, motivate, get participation.

5 Measure progress daily. Audit and control overall improvement weekly, until ready for management to take final decision upon the worth of proceeding further.

6 Gradually rehabilitate. Try to reinstate the need and desire for job satisfaction, and career aspirations. When ready, recommend date of return to field selling job.

7 Field sales manager then has responsibility for converting man back to a profitable producer by constant motivation, unobtrusive watching, and empathetic leadership.

Developmental Training Course for Successful Salesmen with Managerial Potential

This is the point in field sales management's work where it all becomes so very worthwhile. On the job training has resulted not merely in the making of a salesman. It has been effective in the growth of a salesman with managerial aspirations and potential. This is a very difficult area of decision. Many men exhibit managerial ambitions without the essential human qualities and skills to make the dream a reality. To promote would lose the company a fine salesman and replace him with a poor managerial prospect. It is best in such cases to motivate a man to take the other branch of the company escalator into selling posts of seniority with responsibility for special projects and assignments which do not entail the management of others.

What does a Development Course of this nature involve?

1 It involves at least a ten-point plan.
2 It involves tuition over a period of at least one year, at a number of time intervals carefully spaced to allow for theory, practice, audit and appraisal, followed by further specialised studies, interspersed with continual bouts of self-study.
3 It involves careful assessments of progress at quarterly intervals.
4 It involves a great deal of tailored-to-measure study.

A Typical Developmental Course

Training in time organisation and productive usage as a basis for work measurement.
The *Control* of Salesmen—motivation, leadership, management, control, discipline.
Human Relations—attitude training, standard setting, pursuit of excellence.
Profitability of Operation—cost control, forecasts, budgets, quotas, control ratios.
Planning—expansion by outlet, product, market segment, usage, territorial expansion on differential calling frequency basis and optimum routeing effectiveness.
Reporting—intelligence to and from the field.

Education, Training, Tutoring, Counselling—sales meeting handling—guidance on job.

Sales Promotion—planning optimum coverage and distribution of promotions, teaching optimum usage of sales literature, planning exhibitions, merchandising, special demonstrations, competitions, etc.

Administration—ensuring optimum work-loading, smooth communication between H.Q. and field, forward planning, development of field sales manager's trusteeship overall, in the making of modern salesmen assets from raw material originally allocated to him for development.

Self-Development—in all human and managerial skills and management by objective and by exception.

Development Training Course for Successful Field Sales Managers

Such courses are best handled in two sections, with a gap of years in between. Course A is aimed to bridge the gap between field sales management and a more senior managerial post such as regional manager or assistant H.Q. sales manager.

Part B is a more definitive training aimed at equipping a senior manager for either a H.Q. sales manager, or a sales director's job with a seat on the board.

The thinking behind such a split is that many may be called to senior management in a sales organisation, but very few indeed rate a further promotion to board level. Hence, premature training for a top post may not merely be a waste of time and cash but create acute disappointment for those who thought they were of top grade material but were subsequently side-tracked.

A Typical Development Training Course for Ambitious Field Sales Managers

1 *Planning* for company expansion at senior management level.

2 *Forecasting and Budgeting* allied to product pricing strategies, break-even points and new product introductions.

3 *Trend Analyses* of market, of company sales by product, market segment, use, sales area and key outlet.

4 *Market and Marketing Research* basics of activity and application.

5 *Financial Control of Company* at senior managerial level—use of ratios to control company cost centres, marginal costing techniques, profit and loss accounting.

6 *Sales Management*—management of sales force and their effective deployment, creating work standards and controls, creation of sales manuals, remuneration and reward bases for the sales force, selection of field sales manager, and recruitment and selection of the sales force, creation of sales training schemes, sales conference planning and administration, appreciation of computerised controls in company working.

7 *Marketing*—market analyses, corporate and long-term planning, statistical tools and market model creation, marketing economics, competitive monitoring of policies and planning for innovatory or diversifying trends, governmental tendering, etc. advertising, public relations, and distribution channels and distributor choice.

8 *Management Techniques*—objective, exception, delegation, decentralisation, etc.

9 *Inter-Departmental Linkage*—getting supportive and empathetic action for sales.

10 *Administration*—the smooth planning of organisation, of information services, of communications that makes for optimum control at least cost, with a maximum of efficiency. Introductory knowledge of return upon investment, capital growth, etc., cash flows, factoring, relationships with trade unions, law affecting marketing and sales. The creation of optimum profitability of company operation.

Part B of Developmental Training Course for Senior Management of Board Potential

This training will vary company by company. Much of it will be of an entirely private and confidential nature operated within small groups of men and members of boards. In many ways, it is an exchange of faces and minds, a slow maturing of board opinion upon whether the man under training will make the board grading they impose for a sales director or for the post of general or H.Q. sales manager, or sales controller.

No attempt is made here to give a typical example. These courses vary so much that it would be easy to give a wrong impression in content and scope. However, it is much easier to list some of the more important aspects of course content. For example:

Finance will be studied in much more detail under the following broad headings—

Methods of business financing and discounted cash flow operation.
Investment analysis and appraisal.
Balance sheet appreciation.
Inventory control in conjunction with production and purchasing policies.
Taxation.
Variance analysis.
Corporate planning as basis of long term policy formulation.
Management ratios in balance sheet appreciation and long term planning.
Information and management systems. Information banks and economic forecasting in long term.
Usage of right computer and computerised controls in management planning and accountancy.
Usage of operational research techniques in planning and control.
Network analysis, critical path planning, value analyses, cost, design, value engineering.
Technological forecasting, project selection, research and development tools and techniques.
Decision-making techniques.
Manpower development and trade unions, governmental legislation pending.
Manpower planning for the long term to optimise long term planning of enterprise.
Innovation and diversification techniques applied to marketing and board policies.

The foregoing will give a student some idea of the far ranging scope of training in a modern company concept.

Training within a company ideally is a planned and controlled flow of education and skills. This with fullest board backing, is an escalator that enables promotion-worthy candidates to progress upwards in a steady manner towards the peak of their potential value and usage to the company. Unless training is handled as a whole for whole men it will not provide the springboard that it should and could.

This is what the making of a modern salesman means in purely pragmatic terms.

K

CHAPTER TEN

The Company Sales Manual

PURPOSE

The company sales manual aims to provide each salesman with a standardised book of reference (impeccably designed and compiled, and continuously brought up to date) which contains a clear answer to every question, and offers a guide to conduct in every possible selling or contactual situation. Many salesmen refer to their own company manual as The Family Bible, without any intentional disrespect to the Christian ethic.

The underlying theme is that no salesman should err either in performance or in his judgement of any situation. If in doubt, he merely has to consult Old Faithful. It is a touching theme and a most useful vehicle for selling expertise when rightly and imaginatively used. For certainly, no company contact need ever be left in the slightest doubt about company policy or thinking about any matter of mutual interest or concern. Certainly, a properly trained salesman can avoid any loss of business through otherwise being unaware of the knowledge upon which to make a correct spot decision.

From the company angle, it obviates the continuous cost and effort involved in the daily miscellany of unnecessary two-way messages that flit to and fro in many companies between headquarters and the field of selling activities. Moreover, it prevents the loss of potential business caused by the delay experienced by potential buyers when a salesman cannot offer a solution on the spot but has to refer even trivia back to head office for a junior potentate's pontifical decision.

USE

The sales manual should ideally be with each salesman on every call that he makes. It has a reference use, a promotional use, a selling use, a creation of confidence in the company use, a solution of customer problems use. In addition, it has a home use for each salesman. Within its pages are instructions upon every aspect of organisational operation in which the salesman is involved in a reporting role to H.Q. It covers car usage, maintenance and repair, expenses submissions, order presentations, quotation and enquiry drill, attendance at exhibitions and promotional conduct needed, the training of distributors' salesfolk in elementary product knowledge handling of complaints and reporting of information; in fact every possible contingency is thought by its designers to be covered.

MAKE-UP

Ideally, a sales manual is of quarto or A4 size according to the nature of the product mix. It should be loose-leaved, easy to insert new material and to withdraw old. It should within its loose leaf construction have covered sections at the rear which can be kept private from customers' eyes, whilst the bulk of the manual is so constructed that each page can depict product, accompanying blueprint, specification, features, buying and using benefits, photographs of product in use, all in glorious technicolour, or in excellent sepia or black and white, according to the designer's wish to present the product in the best possible promotional light. Accompanying each product should be a famous-user list which can do wonders with otherwise doubting Thomases of the purchasing world.

Ideally, the sales manual should be presented in absolutely pristine condition, without a note in it, to the salesman upon his first day with the company on his induction course at company H.Q. It is his job to insert matter as it is provided at each training session, with as much blank paper as he needs to make his own notes upon the training session and the material provided as he goes. Men learn not by sitting alongside Nellie, however attractive she may be, but by listening, thinking, talking, questioning, relating, correlating, making notes and then trying either to put it on perfect record, by putting the message into practice forthwith, or at the earliest possible moment.

During the course of several days, the sales manual begins to take shape, at the speed with which the newcomer is hoisting in and digesting the immense amount of new knowledge being thrust upon him from so many differing departmental directions. His notes are a vital part of his primary learning stint with the company. They are the first impressions that are so vital to a new relationship, and so germane to the way in which it develops. It is in fact, an ideal way of indoctrinating new men in the necessity for order and method in the assimilation of new material, in its mental storage as well as in its best place in the sales manual itself. This is vital if a newcomer is not to become bemused, should he be, the new information will not be retrieved upon the stimulus for its recall. Memory is a most essential selling tool.

The most excellent benefit from memory is to know where the information is available in the sales manual, and not to have to guess or to take a chance.

Prospective purchasers are a natural prey to a well designed and colourful sales manual used as a promotional weapon. People love to gaze, to brood, to observe. It saves idle chatter. It serves to concentrate attention upon the product that he is going to consider for purchase. It serves as a check upon the salesman's spiel. Together they can form the platform for a successful sale.

CONTENTS OF A SALES MANUAL

(Note—Each section to have separate plastic cover which can be removed at will)

Here are the basic contents for a sound promotional informational sales manual:

1 *A simple but factual introduction* preferably signed (if not written) by the Chairman about company policies, company corporate image and prestige, company research and development (as a community service) and enough of long range planning to make the salesmen feel their fortunate identification with a company that matters in and to the whole community and nation.

2 *A simple, brief, potted history of the company.* Its birth, development, important periods of change that have produced an entrepreneurial entity. This is of interest to customers and users, and provides a sound and proud background for the sales staff

to enthuse about and with which to identify. Managers often overlook the contribution of a stable historical tradition to company morale, that most elusive and invaluable commodity in generating sales success.

3 *A comprehensive company organisational chart.* There are thousands of British salesmen who as yet cannot piece together in their minds a true picture of company organisation as it affects their everyday lives, their competence and success. All that they seem to possess is a fragmented jigsaw puzzle that they have acquired by their occasional visits to company H.Q. and the rare interdepartmental memoranda that they see. This should be closely associated in every salesman's mind with the patterns of supportive servicing and communications which each salesman should get, in his search for business in pursuit of his company's sales objectives. If a salesman cannot see how his company's inter-departmental communications work, how in Heaven's name can he be expected to operate smoothly and effectively within the organisation? And, more to the point, service each department's needs via his reports through H.Q. sales office.

The organisation chart should be so large and clear that the names of each departmental head and section clerks with whom the salesmen may have to deal, are clearly given. An organisa-tional chart is not a matter of painting a pretty picture. It is doing a company sum. If it cannot be effectively used, then it is better not to provide one in the first place.

4 *A brief, succinct, but fully informative history of the industries and trades* which the salesman will be called upon to supply with his product mix and services. History lays down typical patterns of organisation: habits and patterns of buying, types of distribu-tion, the forms of value analyses and economic quantity ordering that have been built up over the years. These together have a profound effect upon creating selling practices that are most acceptable to them. For instance, industrial processing charac-teristics have not grown up overnight. A new salesman must under-stand comprehensively the total industrial and trade background against which and into which he will be expected to sell successfully. How else can he do a professional, competent job?

5 *A complete and competent description of each item in the company product mix.* This is the material backbone of the total sales activity. Here in the case of a technical or industrial product

mix, we shall need also to have the blueprints and specifications and performance criteria germane to the buying and using need. We can list these requirements as:

(a) Product features, characteristics, performance criteria, using benefits, buying investment benefits. Everything nicely and clearly blueprinted so that both salesman and prospective buyers can see the product's form at-a-glance. Where systems selling is the order of the day then the individual products forming the system will have to be bunched together, so that intending purchasers can see the inherent attractions of the proposed package deal.

(b) A complete and competent description of each competitive item on the market. It is both stupid and myopic to ignore competition wherever it lurks. It is always a potential danger, a risk to be realistically underwritten and its dangers avoided. A modern buyer is not just making a choice between one company's product and another. He is making a cogent, critical, analytical diagnosis of value between the merits of each competitive product offered to him. His decision will fall upon that product which offers the best, total superiority, in comparative, competitive value over all others. Thus a salesman must be given conscientious critiques of each competitive item, its strengths and weaknesses compared with the salesman's product. This should be followed by ideas upon the best ways of circumventing competitive opposition, and presenting the salesman's propositions in the best light, to offer a better deal in product suitability and value including, the free wide-ranging services that the salesman presents along with his proposition.

(c) Each product in the company mix should have a sales story attached to it. This story is an amalgam of past experience of the promotional ideas that proved to be successful, plus new ideas being fed in from current selling experience in the market. Preferably, the ideas offered should be in the form of suggestions and not official protocol demanding a specific planned presentation as the company line that has to be followed regardless. Ideas are best offered to salesmen as pointers to the order book, which have been proved in practice by successful salesmen over a period of time. The managerial aim should always be to encourage each salesman to use his own fertility of idea and his creative imagination: to find ever better approaches to the buyer that will open order books more certainly and more readily.

(d) Input-output analysis tables should where relevant be used to show salesmen the wide range of market segments open to the company's individual products and special uses. In this way, salesmen can be triggered-off to see their responsibility to promote each item in the product mix to its visible and realistic optimum.

6 *A comprehensive price list.*

7 *A comprehensive list of reporting routines.* This will cover every item of a salesman's day. It will show precisely what has to be done, in which particular way, and the person to whom the information must be relayed. It will lay down a clear routine for enquiries, suggestions and complaints. It will make clear exactly how each part of the day's work must be processed. There must be no loophole for variance in the daily routines whatsoever, or mistakes and confusion will quickly supervene.

8 *A special section on selling and servicing the purchaser* (actual and potential). Properly and imaginatively constructed this is the bridge and the engine-room of the selling ship. This is the common basis for all on-the-job training and for the salesman's rise to stardom. There is no salesman who would not benefit from having a guide to the very best practice within his briefcase, ready for instant and constant reference and application. Ideally, it should contain the most important items of a salesman's professional practice.

(*a*) *The psychology of selling and buying*—inseparable twins. Simple suggestions and ideas that will help a salesman to build bridges of understanding between himself and a wide spectrum of buyers, each with differing viewpoints, problems, wants, and needs, and each with different ideas about protocol, likes and dislikes which must be taken into account before empathetic communication can commence.

Simple ideas about the subtle art of persuading purchasers to exchange ideas as well as faces with salesmen. Managers too often overlook the very real difficulties present in an initial contact between people. The problems inherent in trying to read facial expressions, the hazards in trying to penetrate beneath the surface of an unknown's mannerisms and statements, the realisation that we are chasing hidden people behind facial masks. Yet salesmen have to solve these contactual problems before satisfactory relations can be created and consolidated. Until mutual respect is achieved, not much will be built in the way of human relations.

(*b*) *The hazards of personal communications*—the corollary of (*a*) above. The building of bridges of understanding just mentioned is dependent upon a series of successful two-way communications between salesman and buyer. Simple ideas should be offered to make salesmen more effective communicators of meaningful and purposeful thoughts and messages about mutual co-operation. The syndrome of question and answer, of listening in depth, of interpretation of meaning, of feedback. All these should be made clear textually and backed by simple factual diagrams of usage. A man's voice is an important communications tool. It should be clear and pleasant, attractive and compelling. It should make people eager to listen to its messages. Clear and effective communication demands salesmen who can talk interestingly, well and to the point. And do so with a wide range of buyers with entirely different cultural, social, professional, technical and personal backgrounds and interests. This vital communications area deserves more attention than it often gets. Managers should appreciate that buyers tend sub-consciously to equate salesmen's standing and value with their ability to discuss matters of concern intelligently, cogently and to display intellectual capacity in their approach to the buying company's problem areas. Field sales managers have a particular responsibility to offer guidance and help where such are obviously needed, in order to get salesmen interested in their own improvement. Hence the value of sales meetings for such a purpose. Shakespeare had a point: 'Mend your speech a little, lest it mar your fortune'. Beginners beware!

(c) *Prospecting and cold canvass calling.* Full guidance in considerable detail should be offered in getting salesmen development minded, in which a confident systematic approach to cold canvass calling is the hub. The ways of taking the cold out of the canvass by appointment scheduling either by telephone or by letters written from company H.Q. should be listed. Further, the life assurance salesman's technique of always having a substantial suspect list which through careful investigation he converts into a prospect list should be outlined in detail. The vocational hazards of the commissionaire, the receptionist, and the private secretary should be underlined, and their solutions stated.

(d) *Territorial planning, grading of customers, and differential frequency calling.* The main methods of effective personal planning for territorial development and work-loading should be given *in extenso*. It is vital that salesmen should be encouraged and where necessary prodded to make visible gridded map records of their territories. And, to record every vital piece of developmental data on such maps with coloured pins or other devices. In this way form-at-a-glance operational intelligence attitudes can be inculcated from the start. Further, a Z trend chart should be in the possession of each salesman for his territory. It should include all the main areas where the pulse rate of expansion needs continuously to be monitored. There are the basic initial steps in getting a salesman management-minded through the daily use of self-management techniques and tools.

(e) *The management of productive time*—a corollary of (d) above. The relation of productive time usage to selling costs is the first ratio that a salesman must learn and acquire, even if blood, sweat and tears are involved. He will be no more effective than his effective time planning and usage permit. The principle of work-study and time measurement should be simply yet clearly enunciated. Not merely in the most effective planning outlined in (d) above, but in the actual conduct of the operational selling job itself. Self-discipline and exact priority planning are not the normal equipment of every salesman in terms of either genetical blueprint or from early environmental training. They have to be acquired the hard way. They have to be learned. The manual can trigger the man off. The field sales manager must always be on hand to monitor and to stimulate and guide his men to ever better time performance.

(f) *Sales promotion translated into additional sales volume and profitability of action.* Sales promotion can indeed cover an extremely wide field of differing activities. It is the salesman's invaluable role with which we are concerned here. This role again differs according to the nature of the product sold and the sales distributive channels used.

Sales promotion in a salesman's portfolio of activity varies from merchandising for a consumer goods manufacturer at every worthwhile food outlet to the enlightened usage of sales literature and audio-visual equipment in an industrial purchaser's buying office, and to the employment of a technical or industrial salesman on an exhibition stand either here or overseas.

Merchandising is the art of getting the goods out of a retailer's warehouse into the housewife's basket, onwards to the quickest consumption possible, and its speedy replacement with yet another packet or tin. It is the art of visualising the salient spots in a store window and within the shop where the traffic flow of housewives will be most intense and comprehensive. It is the subtle skill of knowing how best to attract the housewife's eye and hand to the product in question in the easiest handling spot whether on a fixture, within a special bin, or other piece of show furniture. It is the intuitional judgement of knowing the type of price ticket or other showcard that will virtually pre-empt

the impulse purchase, and make the sale a natural. In this connection, there is also the art of reminder ticketing or showcard
flair aimed at reminding the purchaser of the very staple item she
wanted and might easily forget.

Finally, in this connection of merchandising is the selling *in*
to the store of special bulk offers at special discounts. These
offers make the speed of stockturn in terms of the special discount
a profitability item that only a moron could afford to ignore or
to reject. Such special offers are a sales promotion manager's
stock-in-trade, for backed by national advertising plus co-
operative local advertising or special local bill distribution, or
couponing a lively entrepreneurial supermarket operator is faced
with a promotional proposition that he must not overlook or turn
down lightly. This is an area in which special training may well
have to be given to salesmen in the methodology and administration and outlook of top management in supermarket operation.
This would be a meld of H.Q. and field sales managerial training
activities.

Sales Literature as a promotional weapon in a salesman's
armoury can be used very effectively in a host of potential selling
situations provided only that a salesman is taught how to handle
the literature, himself, and the client as a complete trinity, in
an interesting compelling manner, without drama or histrionics.

Literature has a co-operative content denied to other types of
selling activity. It is the easiest way to the order book, when it is
relevant and apt, and when it is handled with expert skill. In
the normal cut and thrust of verbal debate, it takes two men to
participate, one to talk and the other to listen, question, and
answer. There is participation only of a sort. The remainder often
becomes the modern replica of a gladitorial contest. When handling a piece of literature with sensitive skill, the salesman is
actually and visibly sharing something of common interest to
both men. Ideally, the salesman edges tactfully and tactically with
quiet confidence to the buyer's side of the desk, so that with his
hand still on the piece of literature he can point out the news or
the picture he wishes to share with his client. Psychologically, the
whole bias of buyer to salesman shifts from a wary outlook to one
of trust. For, are they not now considering something to the
buyer's benefit, rather than the salesman's normal spiel in support
of a contention or proposition?

Audio-Visual Material is used in a similar fashion. The salesman is still in control of the medium, but he uses it from the
buyer's angle in true empathetic fashion.

Exhibitions have their distinct promotional uses, particularly in the field of technical and industrial selling, where the product is often bulky, highly intricate, sensitive, and needs to be seen either operating, or where at least the major selling points can be demonstrated with a verbal running commentary. Ideally, such products can be supported with films or audio-visual equipment. In this way, a salesman denied an easy opportunity to sell costly items from sales literature can overcome the impediment with a carefully planned and timed exhibition in locations ideal to prospective clients' comfort and convenience. Systems selling especially reacts well to exhibitions. Demonstrations are dealt with under a subsequent paragraph.

(*g*) *Planning the pre-approach presentation to each call* is the distinctive difference between the professional and the amateur salesman at work. This implies the possession of an impeccable personal customer record system. Again this personifies the difference between the men and the boys. No professional salesman would make a blind call even on a suspect let alone a customer. He must know what the best approach will be and which product should be the best order-book opener. Memory is too often a lying jade. Only a carefully compiled customer record will give the most reliable information upon which realistic and successful planning can ensue.

The manual should teach a basic truth. Each customer is a special customer, whose problems, needs and wants change continually. Thus if the optimum development of a sales territory is a salesman's objective, it will inevitably be composed of the sum of the individual customers' orders. Each customer must thus be handled in such an individual way that he will place the optimum business with the salesman. This can only be the result of careful, inspired, pre-approach planning of presentations.

(*h*) *Planning the approach and the presentation to the decision-makers.* Effective methods of getting in to see potential purchasers will be outlined as well as effective ways of getting appointments to call. It is the ability to produce presentations of various types that will appeal to every kind of potential purchaser that has to be fostered and to be taught. In this connection, the growth of buying committees with their content of anonymous buyers must be dealt with in great detail. For, although in a retail store a salesman can quickly locate where the powers of decision lie (owner or manager or again the wife or chief assistant) this is far from easy in a complex industrial managerial set-up. Decisions are not necessarily made by top management whether in the guise of purchasing directors or no. Top management may merely affix its rubber stamp to decisions made elsewhere, disguised as professional advice from another director or manager in cases where special expertise is the governing instrument to the deed.

In this context of important purchases of considerable cash value, there are certain buying techniques and tools that merit the special training of salesmen to exploit to their full advantage. This is the new approach of value analysis, which is the special-ised and detailed appraisal of each manufacturer's or supplier's offer, in terms of overall suitability and value, couched in comparative and competitive terms of market availability. And there is its half-brother: value cost and design engineering. From the angle of H.Q. or field management training in such skills they involve the following criteria:

Value analysis demands superiority in—suitability, cash and content value, competitive and comparative value, optimum dependability upon guaranteed delivery times, specifications, prices, terms and freedom from trouble in overall considerations. Cost, design, and value engineering; economic ordering quantities; systems technology applied to inventories—each have their devotees in the sophisticated buying world. Salesmen who have to sell to such folk need to be carefully trained by H.Q. and field sales managers in the specific methodologies.

For instance, cost, design, and value engineering is directed at optimising the cash resources and their deployment within the purchasing company's business, both in the factory and in the markets to which it sells its completed wares.

Economic ordering quantity routines are aimed at getting the lowest inventory at least cost, with the least risk of being caught out of stock.

Systems technology applied to inventories is to create a similar position to economic ordering benefits, but produced quite automatically and controlled in similar fashion.

A comprehensive knowledge of purchasing procedures and patterns of behaviour is an essential pre-requisite for a salesman who aspires to success by the shortest route, for they will condition the form of his presentations to each individual upon whom he calls to sell.

A presentation has four main parts:

(a) *An opening salvo*   The gaining of attention, and its sub-sequent interest.

(b) *Some ranging shots*   The identifying of purchasing problem areas.

(c) *Firing a broadside*   The main attack upon problem solution, using sales literature and carefully constructed arguments disguised as creative discussion, and aimed to overcome any inhibitions to the order being placed. Here the better solutions for ordering are put forward, and the best selected and recommended.

(d) *The final salvo*   The best solution of the problem is demonstrated where possible, and buying conviction in the choice is created and cemented. The buying and using benefits are re-considered, one by one, and validated to prospective buyer's complete content. At this stage, the order should be ready to drop. It should be clinched there and then. Customer satisfactions with purchase should be sown and goodwill quickly reaped. Point of re-entry for next call should be introduced. This is the price of the continuity of the salesman's intent to develop each buyer's business to the optimum possible.

It is in such a way that creative salesmen actively create business, through the active creation of attitudes of change in buying behaviour.

Dealing with Buying Objections and Stalls

Objections are inevitable and natural in everyone who is expected to buy anything, however essential or desirable the product or service may be. Salesmen must learn the facts of buying life early, grow accustomed to them, and actually learn to like them if they wish to thrive upon a continuity of progressive success in their planned careers. Most stock objections to the purchase of a product or a service are well known. These should be answered completely in the selling mind. Then they should be incorporated in the actual weaving of the pattern of the individual story aimed at the particular buyer. In this way, the majority of the potential objections can be dealt with in the presentation itself and dismissed from the subsequent negotiations. This leaves the salesman to deal with any special objections dreamed up on the spot to further the particular buyer's innate procrastination, or to consider an entirely new objection that has to be cracked before selling can really get under full steam. H.Q. and the field sales manager will enumerate a list of typical objections and their formulae for overcoming them. What a salesman must learn for himself is that objections are formed in the mind. This is the medium in which they have to be rationally overcome by sheer logic. However, because men are a curious and changing admixture of mind and emotion, there are emotive objections also to be overcome in a number of cases. These are usually more difficult to detect, to diagnose, and to circumvent. Here one is dealing with a lack of confidence in the buyer himself or in the product, or in the salesman and his proposition. Each cause must be carefully diagnosed, exposed with its cure to the buying mind with due delicacy, and the buying agreement sought to the fact that it has been overcome. Then on to the next. Buying minds deal with one objection at a time. They erect subsequent hurdles as the previous ones are jumped. Only when the last hurdle has been clearly and demonstrably jumped will such a buyer be ready and willing to be led to consider the opening of his order book.

Clinching the Order

For some quite unknown reason this is the area where the majority of selling casualties occur. Salesmen fall down having surmounted the last objection hurdle with distinction. Psychologically it is most likely that they fear the ignominy of a refusal, and therefore avoid it by not exposing themselves to the risk of being given an order. Strange and disquieting. But salesmen have two demonstrable occupational fears : the first of failure in their career; the second of failure of acceptance both professionally and socially by buyers. These are the twin hostages to fortune which every field sales manager has to deal with in far too many modern salesmen. Clinching orders is a logical natural procedure. It is created patiently in a rational build-up of selling arguments, the removal of objections, and the realisation of the psychological moment when the buyer is ready and willing to say 'yes'. It may be quite early in the discussion, when the traditional objections have been overcome in the presentation. It may be midway. It may be at the very last fence. A salesman will diagnose the touch point by constantly interpolating leading questions, and from the answers deciding just how far the buyer has to go before he will say 'yes', if asked either directly or indirectly.

Demonstrations

Not all salesmen have products that need to be 'demmed' to be sold. 'Demming' is an acquired art and skill. It is also an exercise in the diagnosis of buying readiness to say 'yes'. *Demonstration, unless carefully prepared and immaculately carried out, is a vocational time bomb that will explode at the most important moment in the salesman's face to the detriment of clinching an order.* Training by a field manager is an absolute must. *And no salesman should be let loose upon an unsuspecting client until he has become reliably expert in two kinds of demonstration—self-projection and the projection of product benefits and features, with consummate expertise, at all times and in all circumstances.*

Handling Enquiries and Complaints

This is a matter for expert tuition by field sales managers. The corporate image of the company is at risk in every case. An enquirer wants a cast iron reply that will please, edify and benefit him. A complainant wants satisfaction retrospectively, regardless of the fairness or justice of his diatribe against the firm or its products, services, or personnel. This is a public relations job *par excellence* for the salesman. It needs to be handled expertly, even more so where the answer to a complaint may have to be a 'dusty' one or to the enquiry may be a 'deferred' one.

Intelligence

The salesman *per se* should be the eyes and the ears of his company in the markets he serves. Every item of worthwhile knowledge should be carefully appraised, graded, and sent off as soon as possible to the field sales manager or the H.Q. sales manager as protocol demands. Market opportunities and threats, competitive innovations or threats. All are grist to the company information bank mill, for it to grind down to the minutiae which will interest company top management.

Competition

No salesman worthy of his salt knocks competition directly. Competition is not a subject that should occupy his mind, unless or until it has to be considered in a particular proposition. In a presentation or demonstration or proposition in which competitors are directly involved then discussion of their products will not be sought by a sensible salesman. However, where the competitive product or proposition is brought up by the buyer, then there is no alternative but to take a positive stand. This is on the following lines: 'We prefer to talk about our own product and proposition. We believe that it is the competitors' job to talk about theirs. We believe that our proposition has the edge or we should not be here discussing our comparative competitive value analysis as the best available,' etc.

A TEN-POINT PLAN FOR SALES MANUAL MAKE-UP

In the author's view a well prepared sales manual is a wonderful sales promotional weapon. It illuminates ten key selling areas in an official responsible and authoritative way.

1 Company policies, plans and corporate image.
2 Company procedures and organisational chart for operational activities.
3 Company promotions.
4 Product knowledge, features and buyer and user benefits.
5 Company oriented education and training.
6 Managerial oriented education and training.
7 Marketing oriented education and training.
8 Time oriented education and training.
9 Sales, knowledge and skills education and training.
10 Motivation and attitude education and training.

Is there any other vehicle of an educational and training character that could provide such a comprehensive compendium of counselling and guidance material in one single publication, whilst, at the same time offering a means which lends itself to both the Self-Education and Self-Motivation of the salesman to create Attitudes of Mind that will lead to positive and meaning-ful operation and in turn to the fullest development of the salesman himself within a career background orientation?

CHAPTER ELEVEN

Sales Control Ratios and Performance Appraisal of Salesmen

A field sales manager must have viable standards of measurement in order to do a sound appraisal job on each man within his control. Sales control ratios offer such a basis when each man's performance is compared with a minimum norm, and also with the standards of performance turned in by fellow team members, and with the national average.

Sales Control Ratios

Sales control ratios are essentially navigational instruments by which a field sales manager can see at a glance whether each of his men is on course. Sales targets are achieved by the success with which each salesman handles each prospective customer at each contactual call. This is the logical area in which quantitative and qualitative measurements should be taken. It is where the sales cost centres exist and can be mainly controlled by obtaining optimum sales volume at least operating cost. So we can state quite dogmatically that a field sales manager uses sales control ratios not merely to measure performance against carefully selected norms but to evaluate it in terms of sales targets set and budgets allocated to each man.

COMMON BASIC SALES CONTROL RATIOS

1 Total number of contactual calls made to orders booked in a given time period.

2 Total of contactual calls made per day compared with standard company norm.

3 Average value of orders gained compared with team and national averages.

4 Average number of new accounts opened compared with team and national averages.

5 Conversion ratio of enquiries received into quotations for a given time period.

6 Conversion ratio of quotations into orders compared with team and national averages.

7 Cost per contactual call compared with team and national averages.

8 Cost per enquiry converted into quotation compared with team and national averages.

9 Cost per enquiry converted into order compared with team and national averages.

10 Cost per order gained compared with team and national averages.

11 Cost of cold canvass calling per new customer gained.

12 Actual sales value against sales quota set and budget allocated for given time period.

13 Quota percentage gained against team and national averages.

There are well over 100 different sales control ratios in universal use. It is up to each company to opt for those which prove to be most beneficial in stimulating its sales force to optimum selling activities and profitability in operation.

The continuous monitoring and evaluation of each salesman's performance is clearly germane to the continuing profit and growth rate of any company.

These measurements so far discussed are purely quantitative. This is the visible tip of the iceberg. What is much more difficult to see and to measure is the bulk of the iceberg. In this context the qualitative aspects of man which, whether marketing purists like it or not, are the hidden factors that control the mainsprings of human behaviour, and indirectly the overall results of selling performance. The author has conducted intensive field research into these so-called hidden areas in a salesman's make-up that together can condition the creation of outstandingly successful selling results. He identified twenty separate power areas which he has termed the power game. They are qualitative phenomena that materially condition the overall quantitative results in productivity and profitability of selling operations.

THE POWER GAME

1 Power to become self-starting
2 Power to be self-energising
3 Power to become self-organising and self-managing
4 Power to plan work effectively
5 Power to handle self, products, and propositions effectively
6 Power to handle all types of personal services effectively
7 Power to handle people at every level and of every type wisely and well
8 Power to establish mastery over productive time usage
9 Power to create friendly relationships that lead to customer satisfactions and goodwill
10 Power to operate profitably and at full boost
11 Power to communicate expertly, fluently, interestingly, powerfully
12 Power to create imaginative ideas
13 Power to question expertly, penetratingly, pleasantly, and well
14 Power to listen sensitively to words and meaning, to content and to intent
15 Power to become an artist with language, presentations, and demonstrations
16 Power to speak to the point on a wide range of subjects, expertly, to all types of audience
17 Power of empathetic understanding of people, problems, needs, and wants.
18 Power to create high standards of negotiating that others envy and seek to emulate
19 Power to persuade and to influence people favourably and to win their confidence, their trust, their admiration, and their enthusiastic co-operation
20 Power to create and to project a favourable company corporate image, through the care with which the clients on the territory are handled, as a trusteeship for both company and each individual customer.

Appraising the Performance and Growth of Salesmen

Most company directors take great care with the regular

appraisal of their financial investments. They plan for growth of their capital value and similarly for the growth in value of their businesses as going concerns. They know that their survival is geared to the progressive profitable growth of every asset. They know that they must manage their invested resources by a continuous process of exception. So that any variance from the planned norm will be thrown up for immediate remedial attention.

Unfortunately as a nation we have not yet given comparable care to the appraisal of our manpower resources (on a regular or even a definitive basis) that we automatically seem to give to our investment appraisals. Yet, the effective growth in skills and experience of such manpower resources can reflect itself immediately in the healthy look of company balance sheets. And, it is the sales forces of this country which create the end-products of our planning for profitability and growth. Appraisal of manpower as a management tool and technique seems to be still in its infancy in Great Britain.

Just as money values seem to have been the prior concern of our investment appraisers, so are cash returns the predominant concern of our management accounting brethren who appraise selling performances against quotas and budgets. This is fair enough so far as it goes. We are inevitably involved in manpower productivity which shows in its contribution to each pound sterling of sales volume and profit earned. The danger lies in seeing sales manpower performance purely as a material asset that creates output in terms of profit or loss. We tend to see each salesman as a piece of organisation structure meant to pay its way or be fired when it does not keep up to scratch. In more sophisticated language we judge salesmen as cost centres that are either worth retaining or getting rid of, according to their value as contributors to the company profit and loss account.

MANPOWER PERFORMANCE APPRAISAL

This is becoming more and more the era of the expert in every field of operation. It is field management that is closest to the salesman's daily activity, the area in which he succeeds or fails, face-to-face with the company's prospective purchasers. This is the rational area in which appraisal should be made, in the on-the-job activity.

We have agreed that the basis of manpower appraisal is the

quantitative one of being a remunerative and profitable working asset. Yet we know that it is the particular level of professional expertise to which a salesman has attained that can greatly determine his financial asset value to the company. Here the qualitative aspect looms heavily into view and cannot be denied a hearing. But, there is an additional dimension in this equation that creates a trinity of effective values. This is the customer. So the field manager has to evalue three separate and distinct considerations : The financial returns of the salesman; his qualitative development in selling expertise, skills, and the usage of modern methodology; and his capacity to create customer satisfactions, which will in the long run determine the salesman's performance in the financial sector. These three considerations are interlinked, interwoven, and interdependent. No one area can with safety be ignored or written down, if a reliable appraisal of a salesman's current and future value to the company is to be made regularly and accurately.

Where then are the difficulties in accurate manpower appraisal of the sales force? The man's quantitative financial results are clear for the field manager to see and his qualitative values are equally obvious to the trained observer, although not so easy to measure. A salesman has good and bad days, and thus a spot check may give an erroneous result. *The real problem lies with the salesman's standing with his customers. All other considerations being equal, this is the decisive area. It ultimately will do much to condition the salesman's financial position as company asset or liability.* Customers rarely go out of their way to praise salesmen who call upon them. On the other hand they will grumble quickly enough if things go wrong. Thus, it is the field manager who has to observe and try to assess the existing relationships quality between a salesman and his customers as a whole. And it may take a period of years before a field manager meets every important customer on a salesman's individual area. Hence his judgement could be to that extent based upon a non-representative sample, which he will have to weight to offset any undesirable variances.

Here is a performance appraisal sheet. The author devised it as the result of experience with a wide range of differing sales forces, selling to a wide range of differing types of buyer, a great disparity of products and services. No special claim is made for its particular excellence. It has proved itself to be a useful managerial tool. It appraises a wide spectrum of considerations. Upon them it would seem to be fair and just to assess the growth or recession in value to the company of each of its sales manpower assets. It is wider in its scope than many. Yet, to judge a man's potential career value, his happiness and welfare or his company's interests on a narrow or narrower portfolio of activities would surely not be sufficiently sound as a basis for a professional decision on manpower investment.

THE 'HUDSON' PERSONAL PERFORMANCE APPRAISAL MATRIX

SALESMAN Jones   PERIOD 1971/2   MANAGER Smith

Marking Scheme and Values
  Under 5 unacceptable. 5 poor. 6 fair. 7 average. 8 good. 9 v. good.
  10 excellent.

SECTION A

	Grade	*Quarters*			
		1st	*2nd*	*3rd*	*4th*	*1st*

Quantitative Appraisal
No. of Calls per Day
Percentage of Orders to Calls
Percentage of Quota to Date
Percentage of Quota achieved by Team
Percentage of Quota achieved by Country

SECTION B 1
Qualitative Appraisal
Knowledge of Company Products
   Ditto   Competitive Products
   Ditto   Industries contacted
   Ditto   Trades contacted
   Ditto   Customers' businesses
   Ditto   Customers' potential
          Own growth potential

SECTION B 2
Qualitative Appraisal
Planning and Organisation Methods
Itineraries and Routeing
Objectives
Work Load

Time Scheduling
Special Surveys
Individual customer quotas
Individual customer development
Recording Information
Reporting Information
Collecting Information
Preparing for each Call
Approach for each Call
Presentations
Demonstrations
Objections Handling
Closing Propositions
Getting Right Order
Merchandising/Promoting
Selling Full Range
Selling Satisfaction/Goodwill
Point of re-entry next call

SECTION B 3
Qualitative Appraisal
Work Skills and Habits
Communication Skills—Listening/Questioning/Talking to effect
Empathy
Interpretation of Briefs
Negotiating Skills
Setting up Deals—Selling Benefits and Ideas about Usage and
    Promotions
Persuasion
Human Relations
Social Arts and Skills
Problem Solving—Diagnostic and Prognostic Skills/Value Analysis
    Skills
Trouble Shooting of Complaints
Dealing with Suggestions
Prospecting
Getting past the Hazards—Commissionaire, Receptionist, Private
    Secretary

SECTION B 4
Qualitative Appraisal
Attitudes and Qualities

To Job—Prestige, Status, Work Loading, People, Promotion,
   Progress, Study, Life
To Planned Escalator of Study and Progress towards Promotion
To Remuneration and Rewards
To Quotas and Budgets
To Company and Customers
To Education and Training through Tutoring
To Self-Development by steady close study in spare time
To Reporting and Research on Territory
To personal health and appearance
To manuals and instructions
To correspondence
To car and equipment

SECTION C 1
Qualitative Appraisal
Proofs of Customer Acceptance
Customers praise in letters
Customers praise by telephone
Customers praise in conversation
Customers show respect during interviews
Customers show liking during interviews
Customers consult salesman for guidance and advice
Customers are uninhibited with salesman
Customers give information readily to salesman
Customers recommend salesman to other buyers
Customers leave complaints for salesman to handle

NOTES ON SCORING   Score by a quarter of a mark where necessary.
Each grade scores ten marks, thus $\frac{1}{4}$ mark
equals $2\frac{1}{2}\%$.
Grade without accompanying percentage mark
is useless.
This is why 60% (grade 6) is seen only to be
Fair.
This is why 69% (grade 6) is nearly Average.
The élite should score 90% plus.

SUMMARY SHEET   Field Sales Manager marks report with the overall percentage figure secured, and endorse-
ments such as plus and minus trends in various
items are made. Where remedial treatment is
needed the programme for it is given. Sales-

man is always told what action is needed from him to improve his score and competence. Salesman and Field Sales Manager sign report appraisals and the matrix is sent to H.Q. for Sales Manager's delectation or concern.

CONCLUSION   *This matrix plus managerial tutoring can make Manpower Development by the tripartite co-operation of Man, Methods, and Management a viable entity.*

Epilogue

We should now try to help ambitious field sales managers and salesmen by offering them a simple way in which to progress their success in their chosen career. Success is born and activated in the individual mind. The mind itself determines the line and the shape that individual success shall assume. It is made more difficult in the selling arena, because selling is a human engineering activity. Here human tolerances must be as carefully respected and as well known as Machine Tolerances. In Graham Howe's inimitable words 'We must always be able and willing to measure and allow for the *"refractive"* error of our own eyes and prejudices'. Buyers have innate fears that salesmen must replace with faith in them, their companies, products, services, and propositions. Buyers also have doubts salesmen must oust by the conviction that they bring to the consideration of buying problems, needs, and wants. Interpreting and solving problems, and negotiating deals, call for a wholeness of outlook, a balanced mind, wise judgement, and utter integrity. Selling in its essence is a sharing of the buying load, by the co-operation it offers in the search for the buyer's best value and most suitable buy.

Twelve Simple Ways to Success in a Sales Career

1 *Demonstrate* utter integrity in every situation with every contact.
2 *Exhibit* a balanced and harmonious wisdom of judgement of men and affairs.
3 *Develop* the will to win, and to plan and achieve success.

4 *Be empathetic* to and with every person whom we meet. Allow for and bridge any gulf in human tolerance or bias.

5 *Excel* in communication, interpretation, and negotiation in a pleasant persuasive way.

6 *Excel* in self-management, and management of men, media, means, and methods.

7 *Develop* an infinite capacity for hard patient work, planned to achieve objectives.

8 *Be creative* in ideas and their applications that will benefit customers and users.

9 *Be ruthless* with self-criticism and self-audit to achieve highest work standards.

10 *Be Courageous, Resilient, Resourceful* in competitive conditions, determined to excel and to win. *Keep* at peak fitness to be able to punch full weight.

11 *Become* a perpetual student, determined to extend the horizons of knowledge relevant to better performance and to career aspirations.

12 *Set Timed Goals* to accomplish by set dates. Monitor progress with an almost divine dissatisfaction. Stretch the mind to its absolute limits to ensure that its reach always exceeds the immediate grasp. Continue to learn and to profit from experience gained.

ACCOUNTABILITY AND RESPONSIBILITY

Accountability for the effective 'Making of Modern Salesmen' lies squarely upon the shoulders of every field sales manager and salesman. The responsibility for the effective creation of modern salesmen lies with the company as a corporate whole. It starts with the board room where policies and plans are made which will come to fruition in the market place only through the excellence and determination of the sales force. Salesmen are no better than company policy, planning and operational support will permit. Thus selling success is dependent upon the whole and total support given the sales force by every member of the company staff in every function and department of the business. Finally, selling success depends upon the excellence and determination of each field manager and salesman to win and to go on winning *ad infinitum*.

Index